D0467418

THE NINETY DAYS

THE NINETY DAYS

THOMAS N. CARMICHAEL

With maps by Arthur Hawkins

KONECKY&KONECKY

Konecky & Konecky
72 Ayers Point Rd.
Old Saybrook, CT 06475

ISBN: 1-56852-380-7

Designed by Arthur Hawkins

Printed in the USA

To my wife and son,
who put up with a lot,
who asked for very little,
and who persevered to
the end of its creation,
this book is dedicated.

focus five:
BARENTS SEA

focus four:
STALINGRAD

EUROPE

ATLANTIC OCEAN

focus three:
TORCH

focus two:
EL ALAMEIN

AFRICA

IND

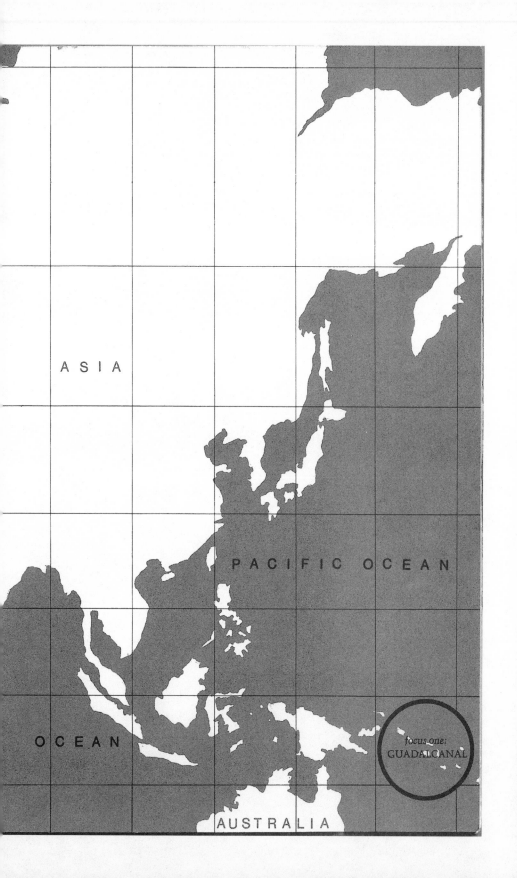

ASIA

PACIFIC OCEAN

OCEAN

focus one:
GUADALCANAL

AUSTRALIA

contents

maps

PROLOGUE...
A PAGE OF GLORY

Hermann Graebe was a construction engineer. In October, 1942, he was supervising some building next to an unused airfield at Dubno in western Poland. Hitler's armies were hundreds of miles to the east far inside Russia and Graebe was not too busy. After several police vans full of prisoners had arrived on the field, Graebe sauntered over to see what was going on.

This is his own account of what he saw:

An old woman with snow-white hair was holding this one-year-old child in her arms and singing and tickling it. The child was cooing with delight. The parents were looking on with tears in their eyes. The father was holding the hand of a boy about ten-years-old and speaking to him softly; the boy was fighting his tears. The father pointed toward the sky, stroked the boy's head and seemed to explain something to him. At that moment the SS man at the pit shouted something to his comrade. The latter counted off about twenty persons and instructed them to go behind the earth mound. The family I have described was among them. I well remember the girl, slim and with black hair, who, as she passed me, pointed to herself and said: "Twenty-three-years-old."

I then walked round the mound and found myself confronted by a tremendous grave. People were closely wedged together and lying on top of each other, so that only their heads were visible. Nearly all had blood running over their shoulders from their heads. Some of the people shot were still moving. Some lifted their arms and moved their heads to show they were still alive. The pit was already two-thirds full. I estimated that it held a thousand people. I looked for the man who did the shooting. He was an SS man who sat at the edge of the narrow end of the pit, his feet dangling into it. He had a Tommy gun on his knees and was smoking a cigarette. The people—they were completely naked—went down some steps which were cut in the clay wall of the pit and clambered over the heads of those who were lying there to the place where the SS man directed them. They lay down in front of the dead and wounded. Some caressed the living and spoke to them in a low voice. Then I heard a series of shots. I looked into the pit and saw that their bodies still twitched or that their heads lay motionless on top of other bodies before them. Blood ran from their necks.[1]

Extermination is not an easy business. Even the experts of Hitler's SS needed bucking up from time to time, and that was something their chief, SS Reichsfuehrer Heinrich Himmler, was good at. In a hotel lounge in Posen, Germany, he later told a hundred of his top men, "Most of you know what it means when a hundred corpses are lying side by side, or five hundred or a thousand. To have stuck it out and at the same time—apart from exceptions caused by human weakness—to have remained decent fellows that is what has made us hard. This is a page of glory in our history." [2]

On that October day in 1942 when Hermann Graebe witnessed those "decent fellows" in action near the unused Dubno airfield the forces of the Rome-Berlin-Tokyo Axis had reached their highwater mark. But within ninety days an ebb tide of retribution had set in. This is the story of those ninety days.

[1] This quotation is from Hermann Graebe's testimony before the International Military Tribunal at Nuremberg. Cf. Gerald Reitlinger, *The Final Solution*, p. 205.
[2] Crankshaw, *Gestapo*, p. 18.

THE STAGE IS SET

At dawn on September 1, 1939, Adolf Hitler started his war on Poland—and started it with a gross miscalculation. Only a week before he had concluded a pact with Stalin's Russia, forming an alliance of strength that he thought would keep the British and the French from intervening. It didn't. Sensing, albeit vaguely, that the gigantic evil that was Hitler must be fought, Britain and France had honored their pledges to Poland and had declared war. Totally unprepared, they were forced to sit by and watch Hitler's army overrun Poland in four weeks. On October 4th the British and French ambassadors in Rome were called in to the Italian Foreign Office. Through the Italians, neutral but allied to Hitler, they were informed that Hitler was willing to offer a peace. It was, however, to be a hard peace imposed by the victor and, as such, was not acceptable to them. The war would go on.

Three years later, by October 4, 1942, Hitler's Polish war was a war of vast proportions, a second world war. Germany, with Mussolini's militarily impotent Italy now an ally as well as a liability, had conquered Europe from the Pyrenees to the North Cape of Norway and had gouged her way deep into European Russia. Hitler's ally Japan had conquered Southeast Asia. Ranged against these Axis powers were Great Britain, Russia and the United States. Armies numbering in the tens of millions, planes and warships in the thousands were arrayed over continents and oceans. On that October 4, the decisive ninety days of the war began. In each of the five major battle areas of the war the vast surge of military power was now being sharply focused. The armies and the navies were now to meet in five head-on clashes. At the end of those ninety days, by January 1, 1943, it would be a very different war. Indeed, it would be a very different world.

FOCUS ONE—GUADALCANAL

In the Pacific, the largest of oceans, the war was focused to the south, on the blue, tropical waters of the little known Solomon Sea and on two islands which bordered it. Australians and Americans on one side, Japanese on the other, faced each other on the huge mountainous island of New Guinea to the west and on the small, steamy, pestilential island of Guadalcanal to the east. Within this area the focus of war came down to a few hundred feet of bumpy, bulldozed airstrip on Guadalcanal called Henderson Field.

FOCUS TWO—EL ALAMEIN

Along the African shore of the eastern Mediterranean, across a 600-mile stretch of rocky wasteland called the Western Desert, the German-Italian Panzer army of the already legendary Erwin Rommel had fought the British for two years. Now, after winning his greatest victory, Rommel stood only sixty miles from the Nile and the great British base at Alexandria beyond which lay the oil of the Middle East which Hitler needed so desperately. Near a railroad whistlestop, actually only a fuel shed, called El Alamein, the two armies now prepared for the greatest of all the desert battles.

FOCUS THREE—OPERATION TORCH

While the desert armies prepared for battle, huge British and American convoys were sailing toward the other end of the Mediterranean. Their destination was French North Africa. This operation, called Torch, was to be the focus of the American war effort against Germany in 1942. But it was an operation entered into by the United States high command only with great reluctance, grim forebodings, and a feeling that it had been had by the British. The scar of distrust left by the bitter Anglo-American debate preceding the operation was so deep that not even the famous Eisenhower grin could erase it.

FOCUS FOUR—STALINGRAD

Since Hitler believed the solution to all his problems lay in the defeat of Russia, he concentrated the major Axis effort there in 1942. That summer the German offensive came in the southern sector of the 2,300-mile front which stretched from the Arctic to the Black Sea. Great battles were fought in the flat, bleak steppe country of the Don and Volga rivers and in the high mountains of the Caucasus. But the focus was upon a few blocks in the gutted city of Stalingrad. There, some of the finest troops in the German Army were poised for the one last push that they hoped would carry them to victory. Some of Stalin's toughest divisions held those few blocks, not because of their tactical value but because they were the bait in the biggest military mousetrap the world had ever seen.

FOCUS FIVE—THE BARENTS SEA

Essential to all Allied strategy were the sea lanes that crossed the Atlantic. Hitler's U-boats fought a stubborn battle to sever them, for if the men and machines of war could be brought from the New World to the Old, Hitler would inevitably be beaten. Although the battle raged across thousands of square miles of ocean, on the eighty-ninth of the ninety days it focused on the cruelest of all the seas, the Barents, between the North Cape of Norway and the Arctic ice cap. There, the German admirals were looking forward to the worst convoy massacre of the war as the odds were overwhelmingly in their favor—or so they thought.

Thus, on October 4, 1942, the world stage was set for the ninety-day drama that would literally determine the course of civilization. The purpose of this book is to show how the tide dramatically and inexorably turned against the Axis during that period. But first we must go back a few years and see how the great powers reached this point of departure.

How had Hitler's Polish war become a world war? The answer can be found in the summer of 1940. After seizing Norway and Denmark in April, the German Army had attacked in the west on May 10. Hitler's spearhead of 2,400 tanks roared through Holland, Belgium and France against armies prepared for the static trench warfare of 1914–18, not for the fast-moving blitzkrieg of the Panzer divisions. Mussolini's Italy joined in, jackal-like, to share in the spoils while Britain's small army was forced from the continent at Dunkirk. France surrendered. A part of southern France, its capital at Vichy, was permitted a satellite status to Hitler. The rest was occupied by the Germans.

Any chance of a negotiated peace with Britain had vanished on the opening day of Hitler's attack in the west, for on that day, May 10, 1940, Winston Churchill had become the British prime minister. Churchill's policy was not negotiation, it was "fighting hard and winning victories." [1] Churchill found a somewhat reluctant ally in a United States appalled by the fall of France. But Roosevelt's America had an Army smaller than Belgium's and a Navy grown old and gray in two decades of peacetime neglect.

Although it was greatly feared, an attack on Britain had formed no part of Hitler's original plans. He had neither a Navy nor an Air Force trained or equipped for such a venture. He could have hit at the peripheral points of British power— Gibraltar, Malta, Suez—but in that victory-filled summer of 1940 these seemed of little importance. Western Europe was now his. If he could smash Russia, then he would have all Europe. With this enormous power base there was nothing he could not achieve. Thus, the stage was set for the great attack on Russia in 1941.

During the last months of 1940 through the early spring of 1941, Hitler was forced to send a handful of troops to Africa, just enough to keep the Italians from complete collapse. He

[1] Winston Churchill, *The Second World War*, Vol. IV, *The Hinge of Fate* (New York: Bantam Books, 1962), p. 504.

invaded the Balkans, easily taking Greece and Yugoslavia, and so tidying up the southern flank of his forthcoming Russian attack.

So confident had the Fuehrer become that he decided Russia could be beaten in a single campaign, three months. To achieve this he did not even feel it necessary to put Germany on a full wartime mobilization. Nor did he consider it necessary to coordinate plans with his new Japanese ally.

In Tokyo, the Japanese war lords, long bogged down in a senseless campaign in China, saw in the defeat of Britain and France a heaven-sent opportunity to mothball their China venture and strike south toward the Indies, one of the richest concentrations of natural wealth in the world. There were two stumbling blocks. One was the United States, who had remained intransigent in her opposition to Japan's attack on China and was slowly tightening the economic screws on Japan. The other, and to the Japanese more important, was the concentration of first-class divisions which the Soviet Union kept in Siberia. There could hardly be an attack to the south, reasoned the Japanese strategists, with this threat in the north. It was little wonder, then, that, though totally surprised at Hitler's invasion of Russia, the Japanese were delighted by his initial victories.

Hitler's Russian campaign opened on June 22, 1941. In the next four months his armies won a series of victories on a scale hitherto unknown. The Red Army, inept and handicapped by the appallingly bad generalship of Stalin and his associates, lost 2,000,000 men in prisoners and a further 1,000,000 in killed and wounded. But in the fall came the rains and the mud. The impetus of the German advance died down. Stalin, at long last, called in a professional, General Georgi Zhukov, and ordered the crack Siberian divisions to Moscow. The combination of Zhukov and the Siberians saved Moscow and denied Hitler his victory in a single campaign.

The Japanese, though, had seen their chance as the first reports of German victories came in. In July the decision was made to head south. Stalin, through his excellent espionage apparatus in Tokyo, knew of the Japanese decision within days of its being made, and it was with that knowledge that he had felt safe in bringing the Siberians to Moscow. The Japanese, though, had not seen any reason to tell Hitler—tit for tat.

As December, 1941, came to neutral Washington, D.C., it was obvious to President Roosevelt and his admirals and generals that a Japanese drive into Southeast Asia was imminent. That much American intelligence knew. What was not known was where or when the blow would fall. There was little action Roosevelt could take. Not only was the United States still militarily weak, but it was bitterly divided on the subject of the war. One group called for more aid to Britain and Russia, although Roosevelt was already giving "all aid short of war," and then some. A more vocal group, centered around the Republican opposition in Congress, was calling for American isolation from what they called "Europe's old quarrels." Only that September this group had come within a single vote of preventing extension of the draft, a move which would have crippled the barely started buildup of United States military power. Most Americans wished the whole mess would go away. They simply wanted no part of it.

December 7, 1941, changed all that. That morning 361 planes flying from six Japanese aircraft carriers ripped apart the American Pacific fleet lying at anchor at Pearl Harbor. Seven battleships, three destroyers and most of the military aircraft in the Hawaiian Islands were put out of action. Over 2,000 Americans were killed. The Japanese Navy had managed to unite America. It was its first, but by no means its last, mistake.

Now it is necessary to look at each theater of war in more detail, for in the first nine months of 1942 the statesmen, with their generals and admirals, would make the decisions, both brilliant and stupid, which would bring the war to its five climactic points in the last ninety days of that year.

FOCUS ONE: GUADALCANAL

Two hours after it had begun, the Japanese raid on Pearl Harbor was over and those two hours were all Pearl Harbor would see of the Japanese for the entire war. There was no follow-up. With the United States fleet crushed and only a handful of undamaged planes left, Hawaii was wide open to invasion but no invasion came. Instead of being thrown back to the Golden Gate and San Diego, the United States was left with a base from which the inevitable counteroffensive against Japan could be mounted.

Any American counteroffensive was considerably discounted in Japanese war strategy. The Army, which now controlled the government through its front man, General Hideki Tojo, who was prime minister, firmly believed in a German victory in Russia and, in due course, the surrender of Churchill's Britain. War with the United States was not a pleasant prospect to either the senior generals or admirals but they felt that the economic squeeze the United States was putting on them left no other alternative. Particularly critical was the oil embargo, and oil was one of the riches of Southeast Asia which now seemed easily obtainable. Their strategy dictated a quick conquest of Southeast Asia. Any trans-Pacific United States drive later would be worn down among the myriad islands of the central Pacific and in some vague, unspecified way a negotiated peace would be arranged with the Americans.

The conservative group of admirals who headed the Japanese naval general staff in Tokyo, although slow to act, essentially went along with this thinking. Not so the seagoing commander of Japan's combined fleet, Admiral Isoroku Yamamoto, the most prestigious of all the Japanese admirals. Yamamoto knew the United States. He had learned a great deal as a post-graduate student at Harvard, including how to play a very good game of poker. He had served as naval attaché in Washington during the twenties, absorbing much of the United States Navy's growing fascination with the aircraft carrier. Back in Japan he took command of the Naval Air School, Japan's Pensacola, and showed himself a hard-driving, no-nonsense professional in a navy where easy-going affability was considered the hallmark of a commanding admiral.

To sit and wait for the United States fleet to attack did not appeal to Yamamoto. He wanted to go for that fleet on the war's opening day and he proposed to do this with his big aircraft carriers. It needed all Yamamoto's efforts to put across

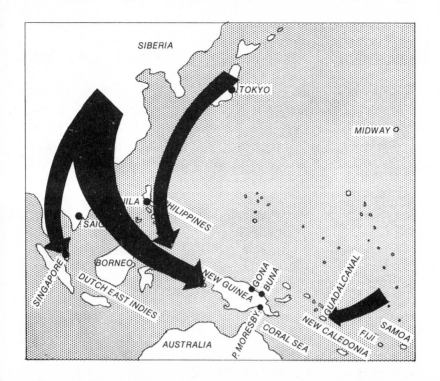

THE COLLISION AT GUADALCANAL   The Japanese, having conquered Southeast Asia and the mid-Pacific Islands west of Midway
in early 1942, decided to attack southward toward Fiji and Samoa
in order to cut off Australia from the United States. By mid-summer
they had started construction of a forward air base on Guadalcanal
when the United States hit back. American Marines landed on
Guadalcanal on August 7, 1942, and captured the nearly finished
air strip there. The Japanese moved up ships and troops to counterattack. The decisive battle of the Pacific war had started.

the idea of such a raid on Pearl Harbor. The old admirals of
the general staff were aghast at the risks involved. Thirty-five
days before the attack was to take place Yamamoto, playing
very smart poker, made the ultimate raise. If there was to be
no attack on Pearl Harbor, he would resign. The admirals could
not replace him with war only a month away. They reluctantly
agreed to the Pearl Harbor plan.

Even though his plan was accepted, Yamamoto was far
from optimistic. "In the first six months to a year of war with
the United States and England I will run wild. I will show you
an uninterrupted succession of victories," he told the govern-

ment, "but if the war is prolonged for two or three years I have no confidence in ultimate victory." [2]

In the months following Pearl Harbor the Japanese did run wild with victory following victory. Nine hours after the Hawaiian attack, Japanese planes hit the Philippines where the careless United States commander, Douglas MacArthur, was caught with his planes on the ground. His new bombers, the four-engined B-17's, were smashed. Two days later Japanese troops landed and MacArthur's American and Filipino troops could fight only to delay the day of surrender.

On the same day that Japanese troops landed in the Philippines the British Royal Navy suffered its own disaster north of Singapore on the other side of the South China Sea. Against the advice of his admirals, Winston Churchill had sent the brand new battleship *Prince of Wales* and the old battle cruiser *Repulse* out to Singapore. It was a piece of romantic recklessness. Without air cover they were as defenseless as a pair of tugboats, and Japanese planes operating out of Saigon sank them both with ease.

As though someone had pulled out a giant stopper, the whole Allied position in Southeast Asia went down the drain. From the border of India to the Solomon Sea, Japan ruled what she grandiloquently titled the "Greater East Asia Co-prosperity Sphere." If Admiral Yamamoto wasn't happy, it seemed as though everyone else was. Indeed, the once conservative admirals in Tokyo were now looking for new worlds to conquer. That would take some negotiating with the Army, for in Japan the Army and Navy were two separate worlds and any joint operation had to be negotiated as though between foreign, and not always friendly, governments.

The Navy's first proposal was nothing less than the invasion of Australia. The Army was staggered. Bogged down in China and a bit apprehensive about those Russian divisions in Siberia now that Hitler's bid for a quick victory before Moscow had failed, the Japanese Army adamantly refused to take part in any operation involving large numbers of troops. Something which would involve only a few regiments would be all right though. So the naval staff came up with an alternative. If

[2] Potter, *Yamamoto*, p. 43.

Australia was not to be invaded, then it should be cut off from the United States.

To do this they proposed a two-step operation. The first step would be the taking of the eastern tip of New Guinea and the lower Solomon Islands. From eastern New Guinea, and especially from the airstrips at Port Moresby on its southern coast, they could mount aerial attacks on Australia and pin down what few Australian and American troops there were with threats of an invasion. In the lower Solomons they could build air bases for a further advance southward. They had their eye on the small island of Tulagi which was ideal as a base for seaplanes and an anchorage for smaller fleet units. Across a twenty-mile stretch of water from Tulagi lay the bigger island of Guadalcanal for which, at the moment, the Japanese Navy had no plans.

Once Tulagi and Port Moresby were secured, step two of the operation would begin. This was the capture of New Caledonia, the Fijis and Samoa. These were the stepping-stones on the United States supply route to Australia and with their capture Australia would be isolated.

Once again it was Fleet Commander Yamamoto who objected. The planners were forgetting the United States aircraft carriers, he argued. Before any such operation was mounted the carriers, which had not been at Pearl Harbor on December 7th, should be brought into action and destroyed. To do this he proposed an invasion of Midway Island, 1,000 miles west of Hawaii. Yamamoto reasoned, and correctly, that the United States would be forced to commit everything it had to prevent the capture of such a strategic outpost.

In Tokyo Yamamoto's plan got little more than a polite hearing. The naval staff wanted none of the risks involved in an all-out fleet engagement. They were still after easy pickings and the South Seas was the place for those. All they were waiting for was the return of their six fleet carriers which were then carrying out a very successful but strategically pointless raid in the Indian Ocean. But on April 18th, before the big carriers got back to Japanese waters, American bombers appeared over Tokyo.

This small raid by sixteen twin-engine bombers caused

only slight damage, but it changed the whole course of the Pacific war. The Japanese were not only completely surprised but, even worse, humiliated. Yamamoto himself donned his full-dress uniform and went to the Imperial Palace to deliver a formal apology to the Emperor.

Where had the American bombers come from? No one in Japan knew, but 2,000 miles away to the east stood Midway. Suddenly Yamamoto's plan to take this tiny island became very popular. Now the full power of the Japanese fleet would be used and the Army would assign a crack regiment to storm the beaches. The date was set for early June, six or seven weeks hence.

With a complete lack of traditional Oriental patience the Japanese admirals decided to use that six or seven weeks to pick up Port Moresby and Tulagi. The two newest and best of the six carriers would be sent south to support the operation. There would be plenty of time, they reasoned, to bring them back in time for the decisive Midway battle. Their reasoning could not have been worse.

They had not reckoned with the United States Navy, now far from the half-asleep outfit it had been in December. Admiral Ernest King had taken over the top command in Washington and the unsmiling, rock-hard King had swept away a generation of peacetime cobwebs in an instant. Chester Nimitz, whose blue eyes and Texan courtliness belied his aggressive intent, had been brought in as Pacific fleet commander by King. It was Nimitz's carriers that had launched that all-important raid on Tokyo. And Nimitz's carriers would be ready for any Japanese attempt to take Port Moresby.

Japan's attack on Moresby and Tulagi came off in early May. Tulagi was taken easily enough, but United States carrier planes stopped the Moresby invasion force in its tracks. Then, on May 8th, came the climax as the big carriers tangled in the Coral Sea, south of the Solomons. It was two Japanese carriers against two American. When the fight was over, it looked as though Japan had won. Both Japanese carriers were afloat, but the *U.S.S. Lexington* had been sunk and the *Yorktown* had been badly damaged. But neither Japanese carrier was in any shape for the June operation against Midway. One was a floating wreck and the other had lost most of her planes and pilots. Instead of six Japanese carriers for Midway, there would only be four. Even worse from the Japanese point of view, the *Yorktown* limped back to Pearl Harbor and what would have been a three-months repair job in peacetime was finished in forty-eight hours. The *Yorktown* was ready for Midway.

On June 4, 1942, Yamamoto's six-month stretch of running wild came to an abrupt halt off Midway Island. It was four Japanese carriers against three American this time. The first American strike caught the Japanese carriers landing and taking off planes and, although the inadequate United States torpedo planes were massacred, the dive-bombers polished off three Japanese carriers. The fourth, though, got off a strike which mortally wounded the *Yorktown*. Almost simultaneously the dive-bombers found that last Japanese carrier and she went down, too.

With his four big carriers lost, Yamamoto returned to Japanese waters with his depleted fleet. The results of the battle were kept from the Japanese people and, with fair success, from the Japanese Army as well. The Fiji-Samoa advance was "temporarily" suspended. The most damaging blow the Japanese sustained at Midway, though, was not the loss of the four carriers. It was the one dealt to the ego of Admiral Isoroku Yamamoto. Some small part of the fleet commander's nerve was now gone. Never again would he commit his whole fleet to action. The showdown of the Pacific war was about to come and Yamamoto was now a bit cautious, a bit timid, which is fatal both to an admiral and to a poker player.

As Yamamoto's confidence waned, that of the American admirals and generals waxed. Now was the time for a counterstroke against the Japanese. It had to be a limited one, for agreed United States-British war policy was to defeat Germany first as she was considered the most dangerous of the two enemies. In the United States Navy, where some saw the war against Japan almost as a personal vendetta, this basic decision was supported although at times with something less than a full heart.

The Germany-first strategy did have one great opponent —Douglas MacArthur. He had been brought out of the Philippines before they fell and had been installed in Australia as supreme Allied commander for the Southwest Pacific. He was the giant among American commanders. A World War I hero, later chief of staff of the Army and now acclaimed by the United States public as the hero of the Philippines, he seemed cast in the Homeric mold of the generals of a more romantic era. He was a soldier of not inconsiderable military talents and a not inconsiderable ego. To MacArthur, the decisive theater of war was his theater, the Pacific, and he felt that every effort should be directed toward an offensive against the Japanese, with all American and British resources gathered under his command. To him plans for an invasion of the European continent were foolish and unrealistic. Aid the Russians to fight Germany and then concentrate everything else under his command and, from Australia, launch a massive offensive against the Japanese. If the United States high command in Washington were to oppose these views, then it was obvious there was some sort of conspiracy against him. Such strategic nonsense was not only opposed in Washington, it was ignored.

Running the Army in Washington was Army chief of staff, General George Marshall, the antithesis of the flamboyant MacArthur. The quiet, self-effacing Marshall had emerged from World War I with a brilliant record as a staff officer and administrator but with no public image at all. When he took over the United States Army on the day Hitler invaded Poland, he was more or less unknown outside its confines. His main job, put in simple terms, was to increase the Army and Air Force forty-fold and direct the strategy by which first Germany and then Japan were to be defeated. It was a job of almost superhuman proportions. Handling a man like MacArthur was only part of it.

MacArthur's immediate plan of action was for a drive from New Guinea against the great Japanese base at Rabaul. He wanted a naval task force, including two carriers and an amphibious division, assigned to him for the venture. He sent his plan to Marshall and followed it up with a typical MacArthur warning that the Navy was determined to "reduce the

Army to a subsidiary role" in the Pacific. This, MacArthur saw as a probable part of a plot he had discovered years before for "the complete absorption of the national defense function by the Navy."[3] Marshall, not as plot-conscious as MacArthur, wrote back tactfully that Japan, not the United States Navy, was the main enemy.

Admiral King, rather than planning the abolition of the Army as MacArthur suspected, wanted an advance on Rabaul, too, but with the first step a United States attack in the Tulagi area. There would be no giving over of aircraft carriers to Mac-Arthur under any circumstances. Marshall, deeply committed to building up an attack in Europe and afraid of getting too deeply involved in the Pacific, argued with the Admiral. King, determined to hit the Japanese, threatened to go it alone if necessary. But King was actually a more willing compromiser than his harsh attitude suggested. He and Marshall got together and, at King's suggestion, agreed on a compromise plan. The attack on Tulagi and the Lower Solomons would be under naval command, later stages of the advance on Rabaul would come under MacArthur.

In early July, King had confirmation of a startling piece of news. In addition to their small seaplane base at Tulagi, the Japanese Navy had started work on an airstrip on neighboring Guadalcanal. Word went out from King that the whole attack was now on a crash basis. If there was to be an airfield on Guadalcanal, King was determined that it be an American one.

The Navy's commander for the operation, Vice Admiral Robert Ghormley, was a capable administrator, a man of diplomatic talents but a bit of a pessimist. Both he and MacArthur advised postponement of the attack as it was far too much of a shoestring operation to suit either of them. But with that Japanese airstrip progressing daily there could be no waiting. King ordered full speed ahead.

On August 7th, the 1st Marine Division, 19,000 strong, landed on Tulagi and Guadalcanal. It was not a smooth amphibious job, but the few Japanese around were caught totally by surprise and very quickly Tulagi and the uncompleted air-

[3] Pogue, *George C. Marshall,* p. 380.

strip on Guadalcanal were in Marine hands. Behind a screen of Australian and American cruisers the Marines' transports started unloading.

The Japanese recovered from their surprise very quickly. As the Marines were hitting the beach, the Japanese commander at Rabaul, Vice Admiral Mikawa, was putting together a cruiser force for a counterattack. It came less than forty-eight hours after the landing. Mikawa caught the Allies napping and in twelve minutes he sank one Australian and three United States cruisers. The United States transports, only half unloaded, hauled away and the Marines were left stranded. The American offensive had suddenly turned into a defensive.

Only one bulldozer had been brought ashore but, luckily for the Marines, the Japanese construction crews had fled the airstrip without destroying their equipment. Using this, the Marines got the strip into operation by August 20th. It was named Henderson Field after a Marine hero of the Midway battle.

Before dawn the next morning Henderson Field was attacked. Japanese intelligence had estimated the Marines at only 2,000 and so only 900 Japanese troops were sent in to the first attack. Without even bothering to scout the American positions, they came on in a series of ridiculous bayonet charges. They were slaughtered. Japanese intelligence upped their estimates.

At sea, though, the Japanese were having some success. In an indecisive carrier battle fought on the 24th, the big U.S.S. Enterprise was hit and knocked out of action for two months. A week later a Japanese submarine got a torpedo into the carrier Saratoga, and she was out for three months.

Nor were the Japanese sitting on their hands on the other side of the Solomon Sea on New Guinea. In July they had established an airstrip near the tiny north-coast village of Buna, 100 miles from Port Moresby and separated from it by the towering 13,000-foot peaks of the Owen Stanley Mountains. MacArthur, demonstrating to the full his talent for accomplishing a good deal with very little, had built a series of bases in northeastern Australia as well as a very respectable advance base at Port Moresby. He had added an airstrip at Milne

Bay to prevent any Japanese end run around the eastern tip of the island. The Japanese had no intention of letting him build up any further.

At dawn on August 26th, the Japanese commander did exactly what MacArthur's intelligence chief had predicted he would not do. He started an all-out offensive directly over the mountains. At the same time a Japanese force landed at Milne Bay to capture the airstrip there. The Japanese thought there might be two Australian companies at Milne Bay. There were two full Australian brigades, and the Japanese attack was thrown back into the sea. But in the Owen Stanley Mountains, the main Japanese advance moved with startling speed. Under Major General Tomitaro Horii, the best of the Japanese generals in the South Seas, the Japanese troops skillfully threw the outnumbered Australians out of one position after another. Horii got over the mountains and to within thirty miles of Port Moresby but there he stopped.

Orders had come down the chain of command from Tokyo that all operations would be suspended except for those designed to recapture Henderson Field on Guadalcanal. Planes from the field might dominate the waters around Guadalcanal by day, but at night Japanese destroyers full of Army troops would run down through the chain of islands which ran from Rabaul to Guadalcanal; this passageway was known as the Slot.

By mid-September these "Tokyo Expresses," as they were dubbed, had built up Japanese strength to 6,000 troops. Once again they were thrown into action against the Marine perimeter, and once again they were the victims of a total lack of tactical skill. The main attack came along a bare, hogback ridge in the center of the Marine position. When the battle was over, it would be aptly named Bloody Ridge. There were 600 Japanese corpses sprawled on it and the Marine positions were intact.

Once again the Japanese compensated with a success at sea. A United States convoy brought in another Marine regiment to the island but one ship of its support force, the carrier *Wasp*, was sunk by a Japanese submarine.

In Rabaul Lieutenant General Harukichi Hyakutake, who

was in charge of Army operations on both New Guinea and Guadalcanal and who was considered a comer among Japan's younger generals, finally decided to take charge. He ordered General Horii on New Guinea to pull back over the Owen Stanleys and take up a purely defensive position around Buna and Gona. As for Guadalcanal, he would proceed there himself in October to take personal command of operations. With him would go the 2nd Sendai Division with another division, the 38th, under orders to follow. Yamamoto's fleet would be in support. The entire October operation, the focus of all Japanese effort in the Pacific, was directed at one thing—the capture of Henderson Field.

FOCUS TWO: EL ALAMEIN

As the German Panzer divisions rolled across France in the summer of 1940, Mussolini rushed into the war at Hitler's side. It was not his intention to do any serious fighting. All he was after was a share of the spoils. He got a small slice of land in the south of France but that was hardly enough. Next door to Italy's colony in Libya was Egypt and the Suez Canal. There was something worth going after.

That fall, an Italian army of a quarter of a million men advanced across the Egyptian border opposed by a British force of about 25,000 men. The Italians advanced forty miles without serious opposition and halted to regroup. Even with odds of 10 to 1 in their favor, the Italian generals were inclined to timidity. The British commander, Richard O'Connor, was just the opposite.

On December 9, 1940, O'Connor struck in what was planned as a five-day raid. The raid, which netted 38,000 Italian prisoners, was so successful that O'Connor turned it into a full-scale offensive. In a classic campaign of less than two months, O'Connor showed his genius for desert warfare. He advanced 500 miles to El Agheila, half-way across Libya, capturing almost the entire Italian Army, generals and all, on the way. Four hundred miles farther on lay Tripoli, Italy's one big Libyan port. With its capture the British could gain control of the entire southern shore of the Mediterranean, a strategic

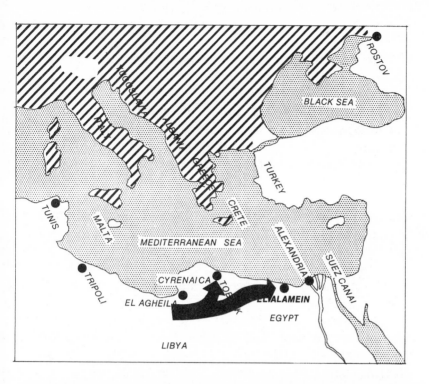

THE BATTLE FOR THE MIDDLE EAST   The German 1942 offensive against the British in Africa began on May 26th and, within four weeks, Rommel's German-Italian army had destroyed the British tank forces and had captured Tobruk. Rommel, ignoring the British base at Malta which lay astride his Italy-to-Tripoli supply line, drove deep into Egypt, looking forward to a link-up with Hitler's Russian offensive which was sweeping around the Black Sea. Rommel was stopped by the British 8th Army at El Alamein where a new British commander, General Bernard Montgomery, began to plan an offensive of his own.

prize of incalculable value. In Tripoli, the remaining Italian generals had already conceded the victory to O'Connor and many were packing their bags for a fast trip back to Italy.

The Italian generals were spared the trip. At El Agheila, O'Connor got his orders to stand fast. Winston Churchill had become absorbed with the idea of building up a major front against the Axis in the Balkans. Mussolini, using Italian-occupied Albania as a base, had invaded Greece, unsuccessfully, and Churchill now wanted to go to the aid of the Greeks, hoping for support from the Yugoslavs and the Turks. He stripped

O'Connor's desert army for the men and tanks to make up his Greek expedition, leaving only a small covering force at El Agheila. It was a disastrous decision.

All chance of a quick capture of Tripoli was thrown away. For while British forces landed in Greece, Hitler was sending German troops to Africa to aid his rather helpless ally, Mussolini. With the German troops came another commander with a real genius for desert warfare, Erwin Rommel. He had shown himself to be one of the best Panzer division commanders in France but, at the same time, had shown a tendency toward personal publicity which his superiors on the general staff did not like at all. Africa, a sideshow to the German high command, seemed like a good spot to let Rommel cool his heels. Besides, his doctor had once recommended a rest cure in the dry air of Egypt.

In March, 1941, Rommel attacked, although his orders from Berlin expressly forbade such a move. The weak British forces collapsed. O'Connor, on leave back in Egypt, rushed to the front but was captured by a German patrol. Rommel drove his Panzers clear to the Egyptian frontier, often riding with the lead tanks like a cavalry general of a century earlier. All that was left of O'Connor's conquests was the small town and harbor of Tobruk. There, about fifty miles inside Libya, an Australian division hung on in spite of everything Rommel could throw at them.

Thus, Churchill's decision to send an expeditionary force into Greece had thrown away all O'Connor's work as well as forfeiting the chance of taking Tripoli. Worse still, the troops he sent to Greece met with predictable disaster. Two weeks after Rommel had attacked in Africa, the full weight of the German Army hit in the Balkans. The Germans made short work of the poorly equipped Greeks and Yugoslavs while the Turks remained neutral. The British, after losing 12,000 men, got on their ships and sailed away—having accomplished nothing. Thus, in April, the British were thrown out of both Libya and Greece.

But in May, Hitler made a blunder to equal that already made by Churchill. Rommel had won an astounding victory in Africa. To take advantage of it, to drive on into Egypt, he would have to have a secure supply line across the central Mediterranean—from the ports of southern Italy to Tripoli. But across this supply route lay the small British-held island of Malta. Hitler had at his disposal a crack paratroop division and Malta was only weakly held. It was his for the taking. But he decided not to take it. Instead, he sent his paratroopers against Crete as he was afraid that one day the British would mount air raids from Crete against the oil fields in Rumania which supplied the German Army. Crete was taken but Malta stood. Hitler had taken the wrong island.

Rommel himself soon came to understand the vital importance of Malta. In the following month, June, 1941, Hitler attacked Russia and there was precious little left over to send Rommel. Of what little was sent, only a third arrived. Malta's submarines, planes and ships took care of the rest.

The British supply route lay around the southern tip of Africa and ended at Suez. It was a long route but a safe one. Along it flowed mountains of supplies, for all of Winston Churchill's incredible energy went into building up the British desert forces, now named the 8th Army. In November, 1941, three weeks before Pearl Harbor, the British attacked. Churchill called for a victory to rank with Waterloo but what he got was a very bloody version of Bunker Hill. The British, at great cost, finally relieved Tobruk and established, by February, 1942, a line about thirty miles beyond it.

Although they had won a victory, the British had discovered what a magnificent instrument of war a well-handled Panzer division could be. It was no mere collection of tanks but a beautifully coordinated tank-infantry-artillery team. The British armor was often committed in piecemeal fashion, not properly coordinated with either infantry or artillery, and addicted to making charges as though tanks were simply mechanical horses, and with disastrous results. The British victory was, like Bunker Hill, one of raw courage wasted by stagnant generalship.

For 1942 Hitler's war plan was quite different from that of 1941. This time, although the main effort was again to be made in Russia, the Mediterranean theater was not to be neglected. The German U-boat forces in the Mediterranean were heavily reinforced and the British Navy suffered accordingly. More planes came south and air attacks on Malta were intensified. And as Malta suffered, so Rommel's supply lines prospered. More and more supplies reached his army and soon plans were made for a May offensive. Rommel was to attack and drive the British back over the Egyptian border. Then all available German and Italian forces were to assault and capture Malta. Finally, with full control of the central Mediterranean in Axis hands, Rommel would drive forward into Egypt, across the Suez and on toward the great oil fields of the Middle East.

Rommel's attack started on May 26, 1942, and reached its climax in the tank battles of the 11th and 12th of June. In those two days the British lost over 250 tanks and Rommel's Panzers were masters of the battlefield. The infantry of the 8th Army pulled back to the Egyptian frontier but, at Churchill's insistence, left behind a South African division to hold Tobruk as the Australians had done the year before. The town was not in a proper state of defense, for the generals had not contemplated holding it in case of retreat. Before much could be done about it, Rommel came roaring in for the kill.

Winston Churchill, who had implored Heaven and raised Hell to get a victory in the Western Desert, was then in Washington for a series of conferences with President Roosevelt, discussing among other things, "tube alloys," a code name given to the possible development of an explosive derived from atomic fission. On the morning of the 21st he breakfasted late, as was his custom, and then went into the President's office. Shortly a telegram was handed to Roosevelt who read it and, without a word, passed it on to Churchill. It said, "Tobruk has surrendered with twenty-five thousand men taken prisoners."

Tobruk was gone. Tobruk, whose long defense the year before had made it a symbol of Britain's long, single-handed fight against Hitler, had fallen in a matter of hours. Churchill knew for a moment the blackness of defeat and despair. But only for a moment. He no longer fought alone, for Roosevelt asked, "What can we do to help?" Churchill, instinctively thinking in terms of counterattack, replied, "Give us as many

Sherman tanks as you can spare." [4] The Sherman tank, vastly superior to anything the British then had in the desert, was only just coming into production and was worth its weight in gold. Roosevelt put the matter up to General Marshall who, with a speed that might have made Rommel blink, got 300 Shermans and 100 big self-propelled guns assembled, loaded and on their way within four weeks.

The fall of Tobruk had its effect on the Axis plans, too. Suddenly it seemed as though Rommel's supply problems were solved. At Tobruk he had captured not only prisoners but 2,000 trucks, 1,400 tons of fuel and 5,000 tons of food. With this windfall, why bother about capturing Malta, which was supposed to be the next step? Rommel wanted to seize his chance and bundle the defeated British clean out of Egypt. He put it up to Hitler. The Fuehrer, who had an aversion to overwater operations, readily agreed. So did Mussolini, who, caught up in the enthusiasm of the moment, flew across the Mediterranean in a heavily-guarded Red Cross plane. His favorite white horse was shipped across, too, for the triumphal entry into Cairo.

In Cairo, meanwhile, the British commander-in-chief, Middle East, Sir Claude Auchinleck, packed his bags—but not to make room for Mussolini and his horse. He had fired the 8th Army commander and was going out into the desert to take personal charge of the wreckage that was flowing back toward the Nile Delta. "The Auk," as he was called, was a big Scot, a tough fighter and possessed of more tactical skill than any British desert general since O'Connor.

Out in the desert, the Auk watched the retreating army stream by. Units were jumbled together. There was confusion, but not panic. To his practiced eye this was not a beaten army. The 8th Army still had its tail up. The Auk decided to fight it out and made his whole policy clear in two sentences. "The British pride themselves on being good losers. I'm a damn bad loser." [5]

On the military railroad running along the coast near a

---

[4] Churchill, *The Hinge of Fate*, p. 332.
[5] Barnett, *The Desert Generals*, p. 184.

whistle-stop called El Alamein, there was one last defensive position covering the great British base at Alexandria, sixty miles away. Here, the Qattara Depression, an impassable salt marsh, came to within forty miles of the Mediterranean. Thus, there could be none of those wide sweeping movements by the Panzers which were Rommel's specialty. The British could turn and make a head-on fight of it which is what the Auk wanted. Sorting out his units, bringing up reinforcements, the British Commander waited for Rommel to make his move.

On the first day of July, Rommel came on. He was stopped short of a breakthrough. He came on again the next day, achieved some success but still could not break into the clear. On the third day, the Auk put in a neatly timed counterattack. His New Zealand division tore the Italian Ariete Armored Division apart and Rommel had to call a halt. On the fourth day the Panzer General wrote his wife, "Unfortunately things are not going as I should like them to. . . . I'm rather tired and fagged out." [6] After its fearful defeats in June, the 8th Army had turned and fought with magnificent courage. They had, to the Germans' surprise, not acted like a beaten army at all. The Auk, whose tactical skill was fully appreciated by Rommel, had slammed shut the door to Egypt—the first Battle of El Alamein was Auchinleck's victory.

Along the Alamein line the desert war reached a stalemate, and a severely disappointed Mussolini flew back to Rome. Both sides started their buildup for the next battle. From the United States and Britain, huge convoys made their way slowly around the southern tip of Africa and then headed north for Suez. It was a long voyage but a relatively safe one. Rommel's supplies had only to cross the narrows of the central Mediterranean but, with Malta still in British hands, it was a very dangerous passage.

The situation on the island in August was not a good one. Food for Malta's people and fuel for her bombers and torpedo planes were running short. A convoy had to be passed through from Gibraltar at any cost. On August 10th, fourteen British and American merchantships sailed eastward from the Rock. Escorting them were two battleships, three aircraft carriers,

[6] Hart, ed., *The Rommel Papers*, p. 249.

seven cruisers and two dozen destroyers. But waiting for them along the way were 1,000 German and Italian planes, twenty-one submarines, twenty-three motor torpedo boats and a task force of the Italian Navy, six cruisers and a dozen destroyers.

In a three-day fight of epic proportions, nine of the Allied merchant ships were sunk, as well as an aircraft carrier, two cruisers and a destroyer. But five merchant ships, some barely afloat, got through. That was enough. Malta was in business and her planes and submarines went to work with a vengeance. Only a third of what was shipped to Rommel was now getting through. In desperation Rommel decided to make one last try for a breakthrough at the end of August.

This time, though, it would not be Rommel versus Auchin-leck. Winston Churchill had decided that the whole Middle East war effort needed new commanders. To replace the Auk as commander-in-chief, Middle East, he appointed General Sir Harold Alexander who, from his immaculate moustache to his immaculate boots, was the very epitome of the British Guards officer. Behind the swagger, tempered by an inbred charm and grace of manner, was a first-rate military mind. Alexander had presided over the last stages of the Dunkirk retreat in 1940 and the Burma retreat of 1941, not only with the sangfroid expected of a Guardsman but with a great amount of skill. But he was not sent to the Middle East to preside over another retreat. Churchill's directive to him made that clear. "Your prime and main duty will be to take or destroy at the earliest opportunity the German-Italian Army commanded by Field Marshal Rommel together with all its supplies and establishments in Egypt and Libya." [7]

Alexander, however, would not take over the 8th Army as well. Under him was to be one of the old desert veterans, General Gott, as 8th Army commander. Gott, though, was killed in a plane crash, and a new man was brought out from England. He was Lieutenant General Bernard Law Montgomery, whose last combat command had been that of a division at Dunkirk.

The 8th Army, rather like an exclusive London club, regarded new members with considerable skepticism and ex-

[7] North, ed., *The Alexander Memoirs*, p. 10.

pected them to lean heavily on the advice of old members during a long breaking-in period. The new Army Commander,
therefore, came as something of a shock. With the complete
backing of Alexander, he let it be known that there would be
no more interminable, argumentative conferences of commanders. He would do the commanding and would do it with
a dictatorial bluntness that would have done credit to a Hollywood Prussian. Montgomery was not the usual type of British
general. He was not from a fashionable regiment, his social
graces were few and he was even an indifferent horseman.
He was given to exaggeration rather than understatement and
was known to court publicity rather than shun it, as was
deemed more proper. He was almost monkishly devoted to his
profession and he had a firm faith in hard fighting and hard
fighters. He was both ruthless and ambitious or, as Churchill
put it with a wink, "Monty's on the make." [8]

Methodically, Montgomery prepared to receive the attack
everyone believed Rommel would make at the end of August.
This time the 8th Army would fight no great swirling tank
battles in the desert dust. Montgomery planned a tightly controlled, defensive battle and that's just what he got. Rommel's
German and Italian tanks attacked and were repulsed. There
was no pursuit by the British armor but it was a very tidy victory for Montgomery. Rommel was both impressed and depressed by the efficiency of the Royal Air Force who plastered
his tanks and their truck supply columns unmercifully. He had
lost 3,000 men and fifty tanks, which he could ill afford, and
had gained nothing.

Everyone knew that now it was Montgomery's turn to
attack. Churchill, characteristically, tried to rush things and
argued for a September date. Montgomery was not to be rushed
and he had the suave Alexander above him to take the brunt
of the Churchillian prodding. Premature attacks had always
been a feature of British desert warfare. Montgomery and
Alexander would attack only when fully ready.

While the desert remained quiet, Rommel, late in September, flew back to Europe for a cure. Both his liver and his
blood pressure had been troubling him. He stopped off at Rome

[8] North, p. 16.

to see Mussolini who thought him both a morally and physically shaken man. Then he went on to see Hitler to plead for more supplies if the Alamein position was to be held against the coming British attack.

The Fuehrer greeted him with promises of huge new Tiger tanks and multi-barreled rocket launchers which Rommel knew could never arrive in time. Rommel explained his fear of an 8th Army backed up by the great productive capacity of United States industry but was put off by Goering's remark that "the Americans only know how to make razor blades." [9] It was in no mood to help his blood pressure that Rommel flew off to the mountains outside Vienna to take his rest cure.

FOCUS THREE: OPERATION TORCH

The basic decision to defeat Germany first had been taken jointly by the British and the Americans even before Pearl Harbor. Roosevelt and Churchill considered Germany as the more dangerous enemy and their judgment was confirmed as intelligence reports came in to Washington and London of certain German projects which pointed toward the possibility of an atomic bomb in Hitler's hands. There were only a handful of men in the West who had even heard of the possibility of such a weapon. No one knew whether one could be built or not. But even a thousand-to-one chance that Hitler could build one made a beat-Germany-first strategy absolutely imperative.

But how to defeat Germany? Just where should the vast forces assembling in the United States be used? Some thought of United States reinforcements for Britain's 8th Army in the desert, others of an expedition to northern Norway, which was a favorite idea of Churchill's. Both British and American strategists placed a great deal of faith in the effectiveness of the heavy, four-engined bomber. The more fanciful of them saw Germany brought to her knees by a joint United States-British bombardment. The more realistic saw such a bombardment as a help, but looked upon the clash of armies on land as the deciding factor. The British foresaw the land power of the

---

[9] Hart, ed., *The Rommel Papers*, p. 295.

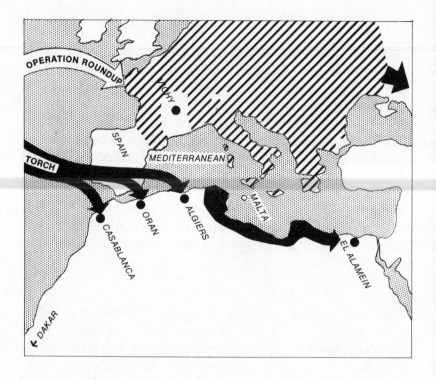

ROUNDUP OR TORCH? While Hitler's forces attacked eastward in Africa and southern Russia, the British and Americans argued, often bitterly, about where they should attack. American Generals Marshall and Eisenhower argued for Operation Roundup, an invasion of France in early 1943. Churchill and the British, fearing that neither they nor the Americans were ready to take on the powerful German armies in France, argued for Operation Torch, the invasion of weakly defended French North Africa. Marshall and Eisenhower were overruled by President Roosevelt and Torch became the Western Allies' main effort for 1942.

Allies, transported by sea power, closing a ring around Hitler. As he grew weaker they would be poised for a blow to knock him out. To the Americans, this was all too vague. They wanted something blunt, head-on, with no time and strength wasted on pinpricks around the periphery of Europe.

The United States chief of staff, General Marshall, was a firm believer in this direct approach—the concentration of maximum force at one decisive point. Under Marshall's chief planner, General Dwight D. Eisenhower, the Army's overall strategy for beating Hitler had been worked out by the early spring of 1942. American commitments to the Pacific, China, India and the Mediterranean were to be cut to the bone. Every bit of strength the United States could muster would be poured into England. In May, 1943, a massive cross-channel attack would be launched against the French coast with forty-eight divisions, thirty of them American. Then would come a drive to and across the Rhine and into Germany's industrial heart, the Ruhr. There was a corollary to this plan which called for a small-scale landing on the Cherbourg peninsula in the fall of 1942. This would be undertaken only if the Germans showed signs of cracking, or if the Russians were in a truly desperate plight which, at that time, seemed likely to most Allied planners.

To Marshall it was necessary to get complete agreement to this overall plan, and quickly. United States industry must be geared to a definite objective so that production priorities could be logically laid out. It was the firm conviction of both Marshall and Eisenhower that unless a master plan were adopted, American power would be frittered away in a whole series of small operations which would end up nowhere.

The first man for Marshall to convince was President Roosevelt and this Marshall accomplished. It was not easy, as the President was a bit leery of a frontal assault on the Germans and still inclined to look favorably on an older plan for some sort of action in French North Africa with the long-range objective of opening the Mediterranean to Allied shipping. But by April the persuasive Marshall had gained Roosevelt's grudging assent to his invasion plans, and he headed for London to sell them to the British.

On the surface the London meetings seemed to go well. Churchill said that Marshall's proposals were accepted in principle and, letting his rhetoric get the best of him, proclaimed that the United States and Britain would go forward "in a noble brotherhood of arms." [10] Actually, Churchill had very serious reservations to the American plan but, at that point, thought it best to minimize them. To him the all-important thing was

[10] Pogue, p. 318.

Allied unity, and he did not see this as the time to argue with the Americans, fresh to the war and eager to fight.

It was the attitude of Sir Alan Brooke, chief of the Imperial General Staff, that convinced Marshall that British reservations to his plan ran deeper than Churchill had let on. Brooke appeared abrupt and rather condescending to the Americans. They knew he had a fine combat record in the first war and that he had commanded a corps at Dunkirk with real talent. Marshall thought that Brooke was a good combat soldier but lacked real brains.

Brooke more or less returned the compliment, writing in his diary that he found Marshall "a pleasant and easy man to get on with, rather over-filled with his own importance. But I should not put him down as a great man." [11] It was hardly likely that Brooke would think otherwise of a man who proposed grandiose offensive plans at a moment when the Germans were sinking Allied shipping at a horrifying rate, when Britain's Middle Eastern position was in crisis and when Japanese carriers were cruising the Indian Ocean as if they owned it. Hitler had yet to launch his 1942 offensive in Russia, and this might well be the worst Allied disaster of all.

The basic divergence between Marshall's and Brooke's thinking on a cross-channel attack was not on whether it was correct strategy but as to whether it was feasible. Each man's thinking was conditioned by his own and his country's experience in World War I. The United States had entered the war late. The United States Army did not launch a major offensive against the Germans until after the war was four years old. In the Meuse-Argonne attack, where Marshall had made his reputation as a staff officer, the raw amateurs of the American Army had won a fine victory. But it had been won against a German army which was on its last legs, bled white in four years of slaughter.

Alan Brooke had fought in the Battle of the Somme, two years before the Meuse-Argonne. There it was the British divisions who were the raw amateurs, but they had been fighting a German army far from exhausted. With enormous courage

[11] Bryant, *The Turn of the Tide,* p. 285.

but little tactical skill, they had gained a few, worthless miles of land at the cost of half a million casualties, five times the cost of the Meuse-Argonne. The British had no desire to repeat such a slaughter of innocents. A friend of Churchill's warned Marshall that, in pressing his plans for a 1943 invasion, he was fighting "the ghosts of the Somme." [12]

It was Eisenhower who found out just how strong those "ghosts of the Somme" really were. In June, Marshall relieved him of his staff post in Washington and sent him to London as prospective commander of the cross-channel attack. Eisenhower quickly found, and reported back to Marshall, a hardening British attitude that 1943 was too early for an invasion. The United States military began to suspect that what the British were up to was scuttling any cross-channel attack at any time. They suspected that the British wanted American involvement in the Mediterranean and in Eastern Europe for "political" reasons. They naively regarded war as a purely military affair, not as a political one.

In Washington, Marshall felt that the British were now going back on that "brotherhood of arms" pledge Churchill had made back in April. He proposed to Admiral King that they seek a showdown with Roosevelt, threatening that if the British backed out of a 1943 invasion, the United States should then forget about Europe and concentrate on Japan. As Marshall later admitted, this was pure bluff. Roosevelt wasn't fooled for a minute.

The President, who sometimes referred to himself as "a pig-headed Dutchman," made his position quite clear to Marshall and King.[13] There would be unity with the British. There would also be a major commitment of United States ground forces to fighting Germans in 1942. He packed them off to London in July and, to make his point perfectly clear, he signed his instructions to them, "Franklin D. Roosevelt, Commander-in-Chief."

If the American Army was to fight Germans in 1942,

[12] Morison, *Strategy and Compromise*, p. 27.
[13] Greenfield, *American Strategy in World War II*, p. 77.

there were only two places it could be done—North Africa or the Cherbourg peninsula of France. Marshall argued for Cherbourg. With severe shortages of shipping and of landing craft, the landing could only be a small one. Alan Brooke saw it as suicide. Churchill agreed with him. As the attack would have to be made mostly by British troops, they had a veto and they exercised it. There would be no Cherbourg invasion in 1942.

Marshall and King had no alternative but to give in and agree that the big American-British effort for the year would be an invasion of French North Africa. It was labeled Operation Torch and the target date was set for October 30th. The Operation's future commander, Dwight Eisenhower, was so staggered at the news of the switch from France to Africa that he said the day of decision might go down as "the blackest day in history." [14] It was actually the day which started him on his way to the Presidency of the United States.

It is no easy thing for a commander to have his pet project dropped and an entirely different one substituted for it. Nor is it an easy task to weld the forces of two nations into anything resembling a unified military organization. With complete lack of selfishness, Eisenhower forgot his pique and determined to make Operation Torch a success, just as though it had been his idea all along. He, unlike MacArthur in the East, forged an Allied staff within which there was inter-Allied coordination such as the world had never seen before. It was a remarkable personal achievement, especially for a man from the Middle Western United States where Albion had always been looked upon as more than perfidious.

Almost at once a great debate ensued, mostly via transatlantic cable, as to just when the African invasion should begin and who should invade what. The United States Navy, deeply involved in the Pacific, found it hard to make a firm commitment on just what ships it could make available to Operation Torch. This kept everything in suspense. Marshall's headquarters was having severe second thoughts on the whole thing. The Washington staff officers, who had wanted to tackle the coast of France in the spring of 1943, were now

[14] Butcher, *My Three Years with Eisenhower*, p. 29.

telling Eisenhower that his African invasion had only a fifty-fifty chance of success.

One of the main worries in Washington was the security of the great British land and air base at Gibraltar. The staff officers were concerned that, once any Allied troop convoys had sailed past Gibraltar into the western Mediterranean, the Spaniards, with an assist from Hitler's Luftwaffe, would knock out Gibraltar. Then all the Allied troops inside the Mediterranean would be trapped, as no follow-up supply convoys could reach them. The United States argued for an assault on Casablanca on the Atlantic coast of French North Africa. Its capture would give the Allies an overland supply route which would bypass Gibraltar.

The British were not as worried about Spain as were the Americans. They knew that Generalissimo Francisco Franco had, before the war, become dictator of Spain with a decisive assist from Hitler and Mussolini. They also knew that in 1940, when Hitler had tried to collect on that debt by getting Spanish assistance for an attack on Gibraltar, Franco had turned him down flat. The British reasoned that if Franco hadn't wanted to join Hitler in 1940 when all had seemed so rosy for the Germans he would hardly want to in 1942. The British believed that the entire strength of the expedition should be thrown inside the Mediterranean. The British admirals proposed that landings be made near, or even at, Bizerte and Tunis. With Tunis taken, the Allies could succor Malta and completely cut off Rommel's army from Europe. The risks were great, admittedly, but the Royal Navy had been taking far greater ones in these waters for the past two years.

The debate finally reached Roosevelt and Churchill. The British Prime Minister did most of the giving-in. No landing would be made closer to Tunis than Algiers, 550 miles away. Oran, even further back, would be attacked as well, but that would be all inside the Mediterranean. Casablanca, on the Atlantic coast, would be the third target of the invaders. The distance from Casablanca to Tunis was more than 1,200 miles. United States caution had won out.

No one knew what the reaction of the French would be. It was thought that the French, remembering Lafayette, Pershing and such, might welcome the Americans with open arms. Thus the first assault waves were to be all-American. Still, uncertain of French reaction, Marshall advised that planning proceed on the basis of all-out French resistance.

The British Navy was to escort the Oran- and Algiers-bound convoys into the western Mediterranean and was quite confident of doing the job. The Italian Navy was not considered a threat, and Algiers was at almost extreme range for the Luftwaffe.

The United States Navy was to deliver the attacking American divisions to Casablanca directly from the States. A transoceanic amphibious operation was really something to boggle the planners. And boggle they did when they began to learn of the awesome surf that broke upon the Atlantic beaches.

D-Day for Torch was finally set for November 8th. It was hoped that, at the other end of the Mediterranean, Rommel would have been beaten by Montgomery and that such a victory would soften the attitudes of both the Spanish and the French. But victory in the Mediterranean had been a very elusive thing in the past. Operation Torch, with all its imponderables, looked to many as something of a long shot.

FOCUS FOUR: STALINGRAD

As the Western democracies laid their plans and fought their battles, another war, of far greater proportions, was being fought deep inside Russia. Here two of the most powerful men in the history of the world were locked in a fight to the death. Each, coincidently, practiced the arts of terror under the guise of socialism—National Socialism for Adolf Hitler and Marxian Socialism for Joseph Stalin. In reality they were simply practitioners of personal power, and each was determined upon the elimination of the other.

By the beginning of 1942 the original strategies of Hitler and Stalin were in shreds. Hitler had attacked Russia in 1941 counting on a quick and complete victory. He had failed with the towers of the Kremlin almost in sight. During the winter the German Army had been badly mauled by Russian counter-

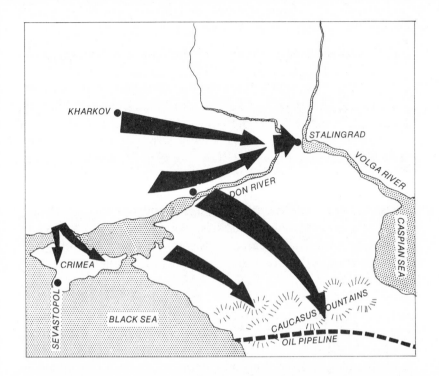

OBJECTIVE: CAUCASIAN OIL   Hitler's 1942 plan for the conquest of southern Russia called for an offensive in four successive steps. First, the Crimea was to be taken. Second, German forces would sweep through the great bend of the Don trapping the Russian armies there. Third, the Germans would cross the Don and reach the Volga at Stalingrad. Then would come the last step, the attack south to the Caucasus Mountains and the oil that lay beyond them. Hitler, overconfident and impatient, tried for both Stalingrad and the Caucasus at the same time—and his offensive bogged down.

attacks. However, no vital positions had been lost. But, in 1942, Hitler would have to attempt the conquest of Russia all over again.

Stalin's original hope had been for a long war in the West between Hitler and the French and British. After both sides had exhausted themselves as they had in the First World War, the Red Army would step in to dominate an exhausted Europe. However, the instant collapse of the British and French in 1940 had caught Stalin off guard. Moreover, the German invasion of Russia in 1941 had almost toppled him from power, but he had survived it. Now, with the United States and Britain as allies, Stalin could look forward to the defeat of Hitler. But could he look forward to a postwar domination of Europe?

To achieve that war aim, Stalin needed all the military aid he could get. This he demanded of the British and Americans, accompanied by scarcely veiled threats that he might seek a separate peace with Hitler. To keep Russia in the war, Britain and the United States gave all they could and then some. British generals argued in vain that the aircraft going to Russia in the early months of 1942 could have saved Singapore. While the United States Navy was fighting its critical battles around Guadalcanal, its warships were helping get convoys through to Russia. American and British aid flowed into Russia.

The Red Air Force was to get 22,000 planes. The Red Army got 12,000 tanks. Its soldiers moved in 375,000 American trucks and marched in 15,000,000 pairs of American boots. The Russians talked on 2,000 British telephones over a million miles of American telephone wire and ate over a billion dollars worth of American food. The Western Allies received no accounting of how this staggering mass of supplies was used, received no information of what the Russian industrial situation actually was and, when they inquired of future Russian war plans, were treated more like German spies than allies. There were, from the Russians, only more demands.

Stalin's second need was for the blooding of the Anglo-American armies. It would hardly suit his purpose to defeat the Germans only to find Europe in the hands of powerful, fresh American and British troops. The cry, therefore, went up from Moscow for a "Second Front Now." Every pressure that the Russians could bring to bear was put into the effort to get the Western Allies to commit themselves, prematurely, to the fight. The Americans and British explained with great patience that large-scale amphibious operations were things of great complexity and put down to naiveté Stalin's refusal to listen. Joseph Stalin, though, was hardly naive—especially about the power of the German Army. He kept up his pressure, but in vain. He, like George Marshall, was fighting a hopeless fight against "the ghosts of the Somme."

As the Russian winter victories of 1941 had brought confidence to Stalin, so they had to Hitler as well. To the Fuehrer,
the blame for the failure to win complete victory before winter
rested with his generals. He fired them wholesale. Thirty-five
corps and divisional commanders were dismissed. The Army's
commander-in-chief, Walther von Brauchitsch, who had led
the German Army through Poland, France, the Balkans and
up to the suburbs of Moscow, was thrown out and catalogued
by Hitler as a "vain and cowardly wretch." [15] Hitler, knowing
of no one better for the job, appointed himself as Army commander-in-chief.

Throughout that terrible winter Hitler's one order had
been to hold fast. The German Army was forced to give ground
but it did not break and with the coming of the spring mud,
Hitler could, and did, congratulate himself for having done
what even Napoleon could not—for having survived a Russian
winter. He spoke of his "unbounded confidence, confidence in
myself, so that nothing, whatever it may be, can throw me out
of the saddle, so that nothing can shake me." [16]

The winter, though, had left its mark on the Fuehrer. He
was now a graying man of fifty-three, occasionally given to
dizzy spells, as he began to mature his plans for 1942 in the
grotesque gloom of his headquarters in the dark forest of Görlitz in East Prussia. What had once been a collection of wooden
chalets was now, due to the threat of air raids, a group of
concrete bunkers. That of the Fuehrer was the gloomiest of
the lot. All its windows faced north, as Hitler did not like the
sun. Its concrete walls were bare and its furnishings sparse.
To his chief of operations, General Alfred Jodl, the whole
place was "a cross between a cloister and a concentration
camp." [17] To Hitler, it was the Wolfschanze, the "Wolf's Lair."

Hitler invariably rose late and breakfasted alone. Then
he would go to the daily Fuehrer conference where he would
listen to extremely detailed reports from all fronts. Then he
would issue his orders. After the conference it was time for

[15] Bullock, *Hitler, A Study in Tyranny,* p. 668.
[16] Bullock, p. 668.
[17] Warlimont, *Inside Hitler's Headquarters,* p. 87.

visitors, Hitler's favorites being the gutter politicians who had
risen to power with him. With them he was more at ease than
with the stiff-necked generals with their aristocratic manners
and their monocles.

Dinner was always late, sometimes not until midnight.
Always on the table were the pills of Dr. Theodor Morell, Hitler's personal physician. Morell was a quack, a gross, dirty man,
who catered to the Fuehrer's hypochondria with a variety of
medicines including one particularly vicious item called Dr.
Koester's Antigas Pills, concocted of strychnine and bella-
donna. The forest of Görlitz seemed less the lair of a wolf than
that of some mad barbarian chieftain from the Dark Ages.

Hitler's own military staff was headed by Field Marshal
Wilhelm Keitel who would have made a fine valet. He was
totally subservient, almost too perfect as a yes-man, and was
conspicuous for his lack of military talent. Chief Clerk would
have been a better title than Field Marshal. Under Keitel was
General Alfred Jodl as chief of operations. Jodl did not lack
military talent or knowledge, but there was a streak of sub-
servience in him, too, and at the Wolfschanze this was more
important than military talent.

The Army, over which Hitler now reigned as commander-
in-chief, was actually headed on the Eastern Front by the chief
of the General Staff, precise, scholarly, pince-nezed Franz Halder. He was a professional staff officer, a Bavarian Catholic
who had no sympathy for the Nazis. It was Halder who would
have to argue with Hitler if the campaign was to make sense.

The plan for 1942 which emerged from this strange
mixture of men was a combination of dreams and reality. Hitler himself set the objective of the campaign, the oil fields of
the Caucasus. The Wehrmacht needed oil badly, and Hitler
believed that without oil the Russian war machine would collapse. The oil was better than 700 miles away. To get to it was
not going to be easy for a German army which had already suffered a million casualties, a quarter of them killed.

Hitler intended to reach his objective in four consecutive
steps. First, his southern flank would be cleared with the
elimination of the Russian forces in the Crimea and the capture of the Red fleet base at Sevastopol. Second, Army Group

South would clear out the vast lands in the great bend of the Don River, trapping and annihilating the Russian armies as they did so. Third, an attack would be launched across the Don in order to reach the Volga near Stalingrad. From the Volga, back along the northern Don, the Germans would then set up a long defensive line, a blocking position against the Russians to the north. Once this blocking position was set up, step four would begin—the drive down between the Black Sea and the Caspian, the drive which would carry the German Army over the Caucasus Mountains and into the oil fields beyond.

For 1943, there were the lands beyond the Caucasus. A drive to the south would sweep into the Middle East and the far greater oil fields of Arabia. To the east lay the ancient route of Alexander the Great to India and the possibility of a meeting with the Japanese under the old walls of Delhi. There was no lack of dreams in the Wolfschanze.

There was, though, a lack of troops. It was the German infantry and Panzer armies who would have to smash the Russians in the opening phases of the campaign. The problem was that blocking position running back from Stalingrad and along the Don. Someone would have to hold it while the Germans switched their power south to the Caucasus. Hitler's solution was to use the troops of his satellites. He ordered up forty divisions from Hungary and Rumania and even decided to use Italian divisions, something he had previously sworn he would never do.

In January Hitler's number two man, Reichsmarschall Hermann Goering, arrived in Rome, wearing what Mussolini's foreign minister, Count Ciano, described as "a great sable coat, something between what motorists wore in 1906 and what a high-grade prostitute wears to the opera." [18] The Italian generals bowed before the gross Marshal and in due course nine Italian divisions went to Russia. Like the Rumanians and Hungarians, they had no enthusiasm for doing Hitler's fighting nor were they even adequately equipped to do so had they wanted to.

Hitler's campaign opened in early May with the planned

[18] Gibson, *The Ciano Diary*, p. 443.

attack in the Crimea. Here the German Army commander was General Erich von Mannstein, considered by most of his peers to be the best operational brain in the German Army. Already in the war he had performed as chief of staff to an army group, as commander of an infantry corps and then of a Panzer corps—and each time with brilliance. Against von Mannstein, even though they outnumbered him, the Russians never had a chance. By the beginning of July he had beaten the big Red forces in the eastern tip of the Crimea, the Kerch peninsula, capturing 100,000 of them. Then he had swung back to the west and had taken the immensely powerful fortress of Sevastopol.

While von Mannstein was fighting his Crimean campaign, Stalin tried his hand at an attack at the opposite end of the Southern Front near Kharkov. Stalin put the operation under the only one of his old associates left in high command, Marshal Semyon Timoshenko. Using two full armies and 600 tanks, Timoshenko tore a gap in the German lines south of Kharkov and poured his men through it.

To the north of the Red breakthrough was the German 6th Army commanded by General Friedrich Paulus, and it was taking some heavy punishment. Paulus, getting nervous, wanted immediate counter action to the Red breakthrough. His old friend and tutor, Franz Halder, back at General Staff headquarters, knew better. He let Timoshenko roll into the gap for six days while he built up the Panzer forces to the south of it. Then Halder gave the word.

An entire Panzer army swung into action. Timoshenko got a sharp lesson in just what tank fighting was all about. In less than a week, Timoshenko was pulling back a bare remnant of his force. A quarter of a million Russian troops and most of their tanks were cut off and rounded up. The way into the great bend of the Don was wide open.

Now the German armies surged forward as they had the year before and, as July wore on, they seemed unstoppable. "The Russians are finished," Hitler told Halder and the Chief of Staff had to admit that it looked that way.[19] Hitler now split

[19] Baldwin, *Battles Won and Lost*, p. 158.

his southern armies into two groups. The overall commander in southern Russia, von Bock, was fired. He was a little too difficult for the Fuehrer to get along with. Now Army Group B, under the more pliant General Maximilian von Weichs, would move toward the Volga and Stalingrad while Army Group A would move south toward the Caucasus. Commanding Army Group A was Field Marshal von List, an expert on rough-country fighting, whose blitz through the Balkan mountains the year before had been a near-perfect operation.

The scent of victory had made Hitler both impatient and over-confident. The overall plan called for a drive over the Don and on to the Volga to be followed up by establishing a blocking position before the main advance on the Caucasus. This was the job of von Weich's Army Group B and, for it, he had Paulus' 6th Army and the 4th Panzer Army of General Hermann Hoth. There seemed little doubt that they could force their way right through to Stalingrad against what was now weak Russian opposition. But this, Hitler was not about to let them do. He could smell oil.

So the Fuehrer ordered Hoth's Panzer army to halt its advance toward the Volga and join forces with von List's Army Group and head south for the Caucasian oil. Halder, the staff professional, pointed out that von List already had a full Panzer army under von Kleist, the victor of Kharkov. The roads, railways and bridges over the southern Don would allow the movement of one Panzer army, not two. Hitler disregarded Halder's arguments, and two full Panzer armies headed for the crossings of the lower Don. The result was a monumental traffic jam.

Paulus' 6th Army kept pushing toward Stalingrad but without the power of Hoth's Panzers, their progress was agonizingly slow. Russian resistance was beginning to build up. Finally Hoth's troops were disentangled from the confusion on the Don and turned back on Stalingrad. But by then it was fast becoming obvious at German headquarters that Stalingrad, which could have been taken easily in July, was going to be a different matter in August. Russian reinforcements had begun to arrive on the Stalingrad front.

Meanwhile, von List's Army Group A, spearheaded by von

Kleist's Panzers, swept on toward the Caucasus but supply priority was now being given to the Stalingrad push. Slowly von List's advance began to peter out. On August 21st a German sergeant drove a Nazi battle flag into the snow on top of the highest peak in the Caucasus. But that was as far as von List's men could go. His twenty divisions were stretched over a 500-mile front and so bad was his supply situation that camels were being used to bring up gasoline to stranded tanks. The oil fields were out of reach and von List's Army Group A was way out on a limb.

Seven hundred and fifty miles to the north von Weichs' Army Group B had a bridgehead over the Don only forty miles from Stalingrad itself. Paulus' 6th Army was ordered to make a dash for the city. On August 22nd Major General Hans Hube, the hard-nosed, one-armed commander of the 16th Panzer Division, toasted his chief of staff, "Tomorrow night in Stalingrad!" [20] With the Luftwaffe blasting gaps ahead of him, Hube, next day, drove his division over that last forty miles. At nightfall they were on the Volga just to the north of the industrial suburbs of the great city.

Behind Hube's division, the rest of Paulus' army was coming up and from the south Hoth's 4th Panzer Army was advancing. It looked as though Stalingrad was in a vise. The Luftwaffe rained fire bombs on the city. The wooden huts of the workers burned and left nothing but little forests of stone chimneys. But the big steel and concrete factories running along the edge of the Volga stood. From them the troops of the 62nd Siberian Army counterattacked and rocked Hube back on his heels. From now on the 16th Panzer Division would measure its advances in yards instead of miles.

A steady flow of Russian reinforcements was now arriving at the Southern Front. As Paulus and Hoth fed in more troops, so did the Russians. The German advance continued, but very slowly. Here they captured a building, there a cellar or a single room. Always the cost was high but Paulus drove his men on. In this kind of fighting the great advantage of the Germans, their mastery of the art of mobile warfare, was lost.

[20] Paul Carell, *Hitler Moves East, 1941–1943* (New York: Bantam Books, 1966), p. 590.

Only the guts of the German infantry kept the attack moving. In the rubble-filled city streets, there was little the Panzers could do. It was now up to the infantry divisions of Friedrich Paulus.

As autumn came on, the realization dawned in Hitler's headquarters that victory over Russia in 1942 was not to be had. Hitler, as commander-in-chief, now had to decide what to do. He could assume a defensive posture. Von List's Army Group A could be pulled back from the Caucasus to the lower Don and Paulus' men pulled back from Stalingrad into the Don bend. Reserves would thus be created to deal with any Russian winter offensive. Such would have been the General Staff solution to the problem, but it was not Hitler's.

The Fuehrer had gone to war with his slogan, "Guns instead of butter." But it had only been a slogan. Not until the end of 1941, when his great drive on Moscow had been halted, had Hitler finally decided to make it a reality. He had ordered Albert Speer, his personal architect, to take over German war production. Speer had turned out to be a genius, but even a genius needs time. Even so, by the spring of 1943 there would be new armies of tanks and more planes than ever before. Back in April Hitler had witnessed a demonstration of the prototype of a new tank, a 55-ton monster called the "Tiger." With weapons like this coming up, Hitler was not thinking in terms of defense but of further attack.

In the spring of 1943 his new Panzer armies would drive past the Caucasus and into the Middle East. The victory that had eluded him in 1942 would then be his. So there should be no withdrawals to prepared positions in the rear. If there were, it would only make the 1943 offensive more difficult. The drives at Stalingrad and in the Caucasus would both be continued and no position, once taken, would be given up.

To direct operations, Hitler had moved his headquarters from the old Wolfschanze in East Prussia to a new headquarters at Vinnitsa in southern Russia. To his new headquarters he summoned Field Marshal von List. Hitler directed that the offensive in the Caucasus get cranked up. He listed objectives he wanted taken, he gave full instructions but he didn't give his Field Marshal any more troops with which to carry out the plans. Von List returned to the mountains and Hitler waited for things to get moving. They didn't.

Hitler sent his faithful chief of operations, General Alfred Jodl, to von List to spur him on. Jodl, who had often protested his faith in the Fuehrer's will and in his intuition, seemed like a good man for the job. But Jodl was a trained soldier and he quickly recognized the obvious. Von List had failed because he had followed Hitler's instructions to the letter. He flew back to Vinnitsa and told this to the Fuehrer. Hitler instantly flew into a violent tantrum. He fired von List and took over the Caucasus command himself. Naturally that didn't get things moving either.

The Fuehrer sulked in his sunless blockhouse. A chill settled over the whole headquarters area. Generals were treated with frigidity and contempt. The Fuehrer would not condescend to shake hands with Jodl for weeks. Now, at all briefing conferences, secretaries especially cleared by the Gestapo were there to take notes on everything that was said.

Jodl had learned his lesson. As he explained it to one of his own staff officers, it was completely wrong to point out to a dictator where he had gone wrong. This would only shake the dictator's self-confidence, "the main pillar upon which his personality and his actions are based." [21] Having thus learned the basics of the art of servility, Jodl hung on to his job—by a thread.

One who didn't, though, was the chief of the General Staff, Franz Halder. The professional skill of the meticulous Bavarian was not in question. The more Halder pointed out to Hitler the dangers of being out on two limbs, Stalingrad and the Caucasus, the more infuriated the Fuehrer became. The cold facts of military administration, of logistics, did not intrigue Hitler. "What matters now," he told Halder when dismissing him, "is not military skill, but the ardor of the National Socialist creed." [22]

To replace Halder, Hitler brought in a very junior Lieutenant General from France, Kurt Zeitzler. The short, stocky

[21] Warlimont, p. 257.
[22] Halder, *Hitler as Warlord,* p. 58.

Zeitzler, always bubbling with optimism and energy, had impressed the Fuehrer. As he was not only quite junior but also quite new to the Eastern Front, it seemed fair to suppose that he would argue far less than had Halder.

Just to make sure that Zeitzler would know where he stood, Hitler greeted him on his arrival with a monologue lasting several hours. The new Chief of the General Staff got the point. Later he told his assembled officers, "I require the following from every staff officer: he must believe in the Fuehrer and in his methods of command. He must, on every occasion, radiate this confidence to his subordinates and to those around him." [23] It certainly looked as though Hitler had found just the right man for the job.

Joseph Stalin was doing some personnel shuffling as well. The complete defeat of his old friend Timoshenko at the start of the campaign had convinced Stalin that a professional touch was needed in the south. The man for the job was, obviously, Georgi Zhukov, the man who had saved Moscow the year before. A first-class soldier in the Tsar's Novgorod Dragoons, Zhukov had joined the Soviets in 1918. That fall he had fought in some vicious battles against the Don Cossacks around Tsaritsyn where Stalin was commissar. Later Stalin would rename Tsaritsyn, Stalingrad.

After the battles of the Russian Civil War, Zhukov had acquired some professional polish at German Army schools in Berlin where he earned a reputation as a hard drinker and an even harder worker. He proved he had learned his lessons well when, in the week before Hitler invaded Poland in 1939, he fought a brilliant battle against the Japanese in Mongolia. Zhukov's victory was swallowed up in the enormity of events in Europe and was written off by most people as just another border clash.

In 1941, at Moscow, Zhukov had had to extemporize his counterattacks. He had played the part of the military opportunist, for when he had arrived the Russian military situation was critical. Now, in southern Russia, there was time to plan,

[23] Warlimont, p. 260.

time to concentrate against the German weak points, time to organize more than mere counterattacks. What Zhukov now had in mind was a full-scale counteroffensive.

The key was Stalingrad. The Germans had to be kept busy there while Zhukov's plans and preparations matured. With the full force of Paulus' 6th Army being thrown against the city, it was not going to be easy. By mid-September the Russian 62nd Army was all but exhausted and its commander, General Lopatin, a tired, depressed and beaten man. On the night of September 12th a ferry crossed the Volga and delivered into the burning city two tanks and General Vasili Chuikov who proceeded to relieve Lopatin of command. Chuikov was as tough a defensive fighter as the Red Army had. He was neither tired nor depressed. And he knew that reinforcements were on the way.

The Russian reinforcements did come. Battalion by battalion Chuikov fed them into the battle. Paulus' 6th Army came on in one bone-crushing attack after another. Yard by yard the Germans closed upon the Volga. Always it looked as though just one more heave and Stalingrad would be theirs.

By the beginning of October, Chuikov's main hold on the city was concentrated around three gutted factory complexes running for five miles along the Volga. Two thousand yards from the river the Germans massed for that one last heave. The German effort in Russia had finally focused down to this one small area. And that was precisely what Zhukov wanted.

FOCUS FIVE: THE BARENTS SEA

At the root of all Allied strategy around the world lay one objective, control of the seas. It had to be maintained so that the enormous industrial production of the United States could be carried to the Allied armies, no matter where they fought. This battle for the control of the oceans had started when the war started and it had continued, day and night, ever since. It was the basic battle of the war, for unless supplies continued to flow across the seas, there could be no Allied victories in the Solomons, in Africa or in Russia.

Winston Churchill was one man who never let this war at

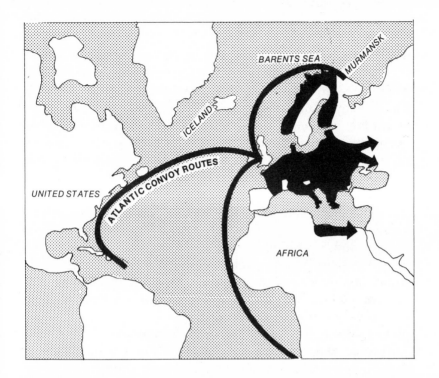

THE BATTLE OF THE ATLANTIC   All Allied operations depended on control of the sea lanes and their ability to move the products of American industry to the battlefields. The shipping routes crossing the Atlantic were under constant attack by the German U-boat fleet. In the far north, Allied convoys sailing through the Barents Sea to the Russian port of Murmansk were forced by the Arctic ice to sail close to northern Norway where the big ships of the German surface fleet were based. In the Barents Sea, the German Navy was looking forward not only to a victory but to a massacre as well.

sea out of his mind. Toward the end of 1940, after France had fallen and Britain was fighting Hitler alone, he wrote a letter to Franklin Roosevelt, just re-elected to a third term as president. In this letter, which Churchill quite accurately described as "one of the most important" he ever wrote, he reviewed the entire war situation as he then saw it.[24] In two areas Britain's position was critical.

"The decision for 1941 lies upon the seas. Unless we can establish our ability to feed this island, to import the munitions

[24] The complete text of the letter is reproduced in Winston Churchill's *The Second World War*, Vol. II, *Their Finest Hour*, pp. 475–482.

of all kinds which we need, unless we can move our armies
. . . we may fall by the way." Command of the seas, as it had
been since the time Drake had fought the Spanish Armada,
was one key to British survival. The other was money. United
States law prohibited the sending of American aid to Britain
except on a cash-and-carry basis and for Britain, wrote Churchill, "the moment approaches when we shall no longer be able
to pay cash." Britain was broke. Command of the seas, without
cash, would be valueless.

Churchill's letter was delivered to President Roosevelt as
he sailed the Caribbean on the cruiser *Tuscaloosa*, sunning
himself and, as his aides put it, "recharging his batteries."
Roosevelt read the letter and continued sunning himself. No
study commissions were appointed, no horde of advisers sent
for. The problem was not what to do. Obviously Britain would
have to be given what she needed without regard to cash. The
problem was how to put this over to the majority of the American people who, though sympathetic to Britain, wanted no part
of the fighting. This was a political problem and Roosevelt was
a master of political warfare. Without firing a shot he was to
win one of the war's decisive battles—and win it almost at one
blow.

"What I am trying to do is eliminate the dollar sign," he
told his press conference the day after he returned from his
Caribbean cruise. "Let me give you an illustration. Suppose my
neighbor's home catches fire and I have a length of garden
hose four or five hundred feet away. If he can take my garden
hose and connect it up with his hydrant, it may help him to
put out the fire. Now what do I do? I don't say to him before
that operation, 'Neighbor, my garden hose cost me fifteen dollars; you have to pay me fifteen dollars for it.' No! What is the
transaction that goes on? I don't want fifteen dollars—I want
my garden hose back after the fire is over." [25] Thus Roosevelt
proposed to lend or to lease to Britain what she needed in order
to fight.

[25] Robert E. Sherwood, *Roosevelt and Hopkins: An Intimate Biography*
(New York: Grosset & Dunlap, 1950), p. 225 and Churchill, *Their
Finest Hour*, pp. 483–484.

It was a masterstroke. The homey touch of the garden hose took the blood and thunder out of sending Britain the materials of war. The hose would simply be loaned to the neighbor. This was lend-lease. The Republican opposition thundered in outrage. One of its more pompous leaders, Senator Burton K. Wheeler, roared that lend-lease would mean "ploughing under every fourth American boy." [26] The isolationist element of the academic community also chimed in with President Robert Hutchins of the University of Chicago proclaiming that "the American people are about to commit suicide." [27] But the simile of the garden hose won out and on March 8, 1941, lend-lease passed the Senate.

And so "cash" was eliminated from cash-and-carry but the "carry" was not. No homey similes would cover getting the garden hose to the neighbor. German U-boats in ever-increasing numbers prowled the Atlantic. Seamen were roasted alive on burning tankers, scalded to death by live steam from exploding boilers, crushed by the collapsing iron of old freighters, were drowned or were condemned to the slow torture of death by thirst and exposure in an open boat. Nor was the fate of the U-boat men a pleasant one when the hull of their boat was finally opened by a depth charge.

The naval war had begun very slowly. Neither side was prepared for it, which was strange as the nearest the Kaiser's Germany had come to victory in the previous war had been when its U-boats had come within an ace of knocking Britain out of the war. Hitler, though, fancied himself a general, not an admiral. "On land I am a hero, but at sea I'm a coward," he told his naval chief, Grand Admiral Erich Raeder.[28]

The Grand Admiral was a rather stocky, stiff-necked, authoritarian product of the Kaiser's aristocratic navy. Outwardly he seemed a stern, thorough, but dull administrator, which he was; but he was also a first-rate naval strategist. Raeder could not accept Hitler's original strategic ideas, formed in the 1920's—conquest of Russia and Eastern Europe while in alli-

[26] Sherwood, p. 229.
[27] Sherwood, p. 264.
[28] Martienssen, *Hitler and His Admirals*, p. 2.

ance with Britain. Raeder knew that Britain instinctively fought any country which tried to dominate the continent, knowing that such dominance in the long run meant her own ruin. Raeder saw Britain as *the* enemy and her defeat a necessary preliminary to any adventure in Eastern Europe.

Raeder admired Hitler, was warmed by the Fuehrer's flattery and delighted by his assurance that the Navy would not be neglected in the rearmament of the Third Reich. He did not become a member of the Fuehrer's inner circle, for the gutter politicians who reigned there were hardly congenial companions for a man who had once been an officer on the Kaiser's yacht. He made an implacable and dangerous enemy of the number two Nazi, Reichsmarschall Hermann Goering, who, as Raeder noted with considerable accuracy, "was distinguished for his dishonesty, ignorance and selfishness—avaricious and extravagant, an effeminate and unsoldierly character." [29] Goering was also head of Hitler's air fleets, the Luftwaffe, and the feud between air power and sea power in Germany became a far more bitter and personal one than similar interservice feuds in Britain and the United States. The German Navy, due to Goering's enmity, would have no powerful air arm.

Assured by Hitler that there would be no war with England before the mid-forties, Raeder had started a long-range building program which by then would give him a fleet capable of, as Raeder put it, "settling the British question conclusively." [30] Included in that fleet were not only battleships and cruisers but some 200 U-boats. When, to Raeder's dismay, war with England came five years too soon, there were only seventeen U-boats deployed in the Atlantic.

The British naval staff did not particularly fear those seventeen U-boats, nor was there much reason for immediate alarm, except that their commander was Rear Admiral Karl Doenitz, a genius at undersea warfare. The thin, gaunt Doenitz had come from the very non-aristocratic world of U-boats and not from the quarterdecks of flagships as had Raeder. He could get along with the Nazi bosses, including Goering, and gave to Hitler unswerving devotion and obedience.

[29] Martienssen, p. 5.
[30] Martienssen, p. 20.

On the opening day of the war in 1939, Doenitz called for immediate expansion of the U-boat arm. Raeder agreed but Hitler didn't. Not until France fell in 1940, and Hitler found that Britain would not follow suit did the Fuehrer give the orders for building a truly powerful U-boat fleet. It is a long time between giving an order to having a U-boat at sea and ready for business. Thus Doenitz had to struggle through 1941 with insufficient forces.

He struggled pretty successfully as his boats sent down over 2,000,000 tons of shipping. The British had expected nothing like this. They had been prepared for underwater U-boat attacks and their convoy escorts were equipped with asdic, a device which sent out sound waves that, bouncing back from a submerged submarine, pinpointed its direction from the hunting ship. This was all well and good but Doenitz had no intention of using his U-boats for submerged attack. In the first war he had been extremely successful as a U-boat commander in attacking on the surface at night. The sound waves of asdic were so distorted on the surface of the ocean as to make it useless. A U-boat could do seventeen to eighteen knots on the surface as against three to four knots underwater. Its low silhouette made it almost impossible to see at night. And Doenitz had another wrinkle to add to these surprise tactics. The first U-boat to sight a convoy radioed its position and course and then settled down to shadow it. Doenitz would then concentrate every boat within reach, forming a wolf pack of U-boats. Once formed, the aptly named wolf pack would wait for night and then come in on the convoy from all sides with devastating results. But the wolf pack attacks were not decisive. There were not enough boats for that because of Hitler's failure to put U-boat production into high gear early enough. In the Battle of the Atlantic it was Hitler who was finding himself with "too little and too late."

Throughout 1941 the Royal Navy slowly built up its antisubmarine forces. Against the surfaced U-boat fast ships were necessary, equipped with radar as well as asdic. Not only did each ship's crew have to be trained, but it was found that each group of ships forming a convoy escort had to be trained as a group, for when the wolf packs attacked only a perfectly coordinated effort by the escorting forces could prevent a massacre.

Not only well-trained escort ships were necessary. Just as vital was the airplane. It could keep the U-boats submerged and, by depriving them of their surface speed, keep the wolf pack from forming. When equipped with radar and aerial depth charges, the airplane was a deadly enemy for a surfaced U-boat. But at the time the war started Britain did not have a single plane equipped for such duties.

Over-water operations by land-based planes were the responsibility of the Royal Air Force's Coastal Command, the Cinderella of the service. Coastal Command started the war with few planes and those equipped only for reconnaissance, their job being to keep an eye on Germany's surface ships which might break out into the Atlantic as commerce raiders. Big, long-range planes, such as were necessary for convoy escort, were just the types which the air marshals wanted for their strategic bombing of Germany and the growth of Coastal Command was, in consequence, a painfully slow process. Many of the myopic bomber generals forgot that every drop of fuel that their bombers used over Germany came to England by ship.

By the beginning of 1942 Doenitz was finally in command of a respectable fleet of U-boats but found himself unable to use them as he wanted. Hitler had developed considerable interest in both the Mediterranean and the Arctic and most of the U-boat fleet was sent to one or the other. It was a great disappointment to Doenitz who, with the United States entry into the war, found himself with one of the juiciest targets imaginable—American shipping off the Atlantic coast, sailing along as though there were no war at all.

So, in January of 1942, Doenitz started his operations off the American coast with only five boats and rarely during the following six months was he able to make it more than a dozen. With this minuscule force Doenitz inflicted on the United States Navy a far worse, and less excusable, defeat than had Yamamoto at Pearl Harbor. The United States admirals refused to initiate convoys, believing, contrary to all British experience, that "an inadequately escorted convoy is worse than no convoy at all." [31] What few destroyers they had were used on useless "search and destroy" missions. It was a long time before all ships doused their lights or ceased their idle wireless chatter. For months coastal navigational beacons remained lit as did the coastal cities whose bright lights silhouetted the merchant ships for the attacking U-boats. It was not until the mid-summer of 1942 that the United States finally got coastal shipping properly convoyed and organized on a wartime basis. Only then did the massacre finally end. And massacre it had been because in those six months, while losing only eight U-boats, Doenitz's men had sent 2,000,000 tons of shipping to the bottom. It was a loss that would bedevil Allied operations for the rest of the war.

Meanwhile, the U-boats which Doenitz had been forced to divert to northern Norway were also having their share of success. Their target was the Allied convoys which sailed through the Barents Sea, those gale-ridden waters between Norway's North Cape and the Arctic ice pack which was the path to the Russian ports of Murmansk and Archangel. Hitler's great aim in the summer of 1942 was the defeat of Russia and he wanted those Arctic convoys stopped. Nor did stopping them seem an overly difficult task. The polar ice cap forced the convoys to sail so close to Norway that they were well within range of Luftwaffe bases there. To the U-boats concentrated across their path was added the German surface fleet, including the giant battleship *Tirpitz*, waiting in the northern fjords ready to pounce. The Barents Sea was one place where the odds were all in Germany's favor.

To run convoys through such opposition was the height of military folly, but the decision had been a political one. Joseph Stalin demanded them and, to keep him fighting, Churchill and Roosevelt felt they had no choice but to agree. Stalin's hints that he might be forced to pull out of the war might be pure bluff, but it was a bluff the Western Allies were in no position to call.

Losses on the Murmansk run mounted, and by the sum-

[31] Roskill, *The War at Sea, 1943–1945,* Vol. II, *The Period of Balance,* p. 97.

mer of 1942 the price of military folly had to be paid. On July 4th, Convoy PQ-17, 33 merchant ships, was making its slow way around the North Cape. At the Admiralty in London there was information that German surface ships, particularly the awesome *Tirpitz*, were on the move. There was no definite information that they were about to attack the convoy but even the mere possibility caused the Admiralty, that evening, to order the escorts to withdraw and the convoy to scatter. Once scattered the ships of the convoy were little more than sitting ducks for the U-boats and planes just waiting for such an opportunity. Twenty-three merchant ships were sunk and with them 430 tanks and 210 planes went down, the price of a major land defeat.

The next convoy sailed in September and was more heavily escorted but thirteen of its forty merchant ships were lost, mostly to air attacks. The price of running the Arctic convoys was obviously too high. They would have to be suspended until the winter when the long nights would give them some measure of protection. Churchill himself broke the news to Stalin and was asked by the surly Russian dictator, "Has the British Navy no sense of glory?" [32] That Winston Churchill held his temper and, in effect, turned the other cheek, must be accounted one of the miracles of the war.

The answer to Stalin's question would have to come from the Royal Navy itself. Its losses in three years of war had been severe. Committed to action in the Indian Ocean, the Mediterranean and the Atlantic, there was precious little left over for the Barents Sea. In the shipyards of the United States a fleet far greater than Britain's was being built, and Britannia's long-held position as ruler of the waves was ending. Even so, on the last day of 1942, on those icy, Arctic waters the Royal Navy would show that, even in the twilight of its power, it was still the Navy of Drake and Nelson.

[32] Churchill, *The Hinge of Fate*, p. 433.

focus one: GUADALCANAL

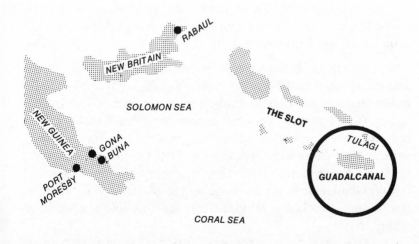

By October 4, 1942, the ships, the planes and the troops of the Axis and the Allies were assembling for battle. Japan's string of victories had been broken by the United States Navy at the battles of the Coral Sea and Midway, but at Guadalcanal the Japanese commanders could smell victory again. Only a a single, malaria-ridden division of American Marines protected a single air strip called Henderson Field. The battered, outnumbered ships of the United States Navy could offer them little protection—or so it seemed.

The Japanese attempts to retake Guadalcanal in August and September had been miserable failures. Japanese intelligence had grossly underestimated the strength of the United States forces ashore. Too few Japanese troops had been sent into the two attacks and they had been thrown forward in a series of headlong bayonet charges. This kind of action might have produced victories for the Japanese Army in China but not on Guadalcanal. Against the dug-in Marines, the Japanese troops had attacked with great courage but had simply been slaughtered.

As October came, Japanese Imperial General Headquarters at last realized that some real power would have to be put into the drive to retake the island. There was plenty of power around. The Imperial Navy had three big carriers in the area:

the *Shokaku* and the *Zuikaku,* both of which had missed the Midway battle, and the brand new *Junyo.* They had four fast battleships and plenty of cruisers and destroyers to go with them.

Even with all this strength the Combined Fleet commander, Admiral Yamamoto, was cautious. The Midway battle, which had cost him four big carriers, had given him a tremendous respect for the American dive-bomber. There were dive-bombers on Guadalcanal's Henderson Field and Yamamoto didn't want to tangle with them. Japanese ships could operate off Guadalcanal at night, but by daylight they preferred to be beyond the bomber's 200-mile radius of action.

There seemed no reason for the Imperial Navy to be unduly worried over Henderson Field as it had been assured by the Japanese Army that the field would be taken "in one blow." [1] The man who confidently gave that assurance was Lieutenant General Harukichi Hyakutake, Army commander for the entire Solomons area. Having shut down his offensive against MacArthur's Americans and Australians in New Guinea, Hyakutake could concentrate on Guadalcanal. Troops came in from China, the East Indies and the Philippines. His main force would be the 2nd Sendai Division under General Masao Maruyama. This was a crack outfit with some hard fighting in China under its belt. It had also shown considerable talent for rape, loot, pillage and the execution of prisoners, fully earning its title of "The Butchers of Nanking."

Maruyama was sure that once ashore they could do the job. He was to get some tanks and heavy artillery to help out. He was also to have Army Commander Hyakutake on the island as well. Both Hyakutake and Maruyama were highly thought-of officers with great courage and fertile brains.

To get the two generals and all their troops and equipment to Guadalcanal was the job of the Navy's Rear Admiral Raizo Tanaka, one of the best sea officers the Japanese Navy would produce in the entire war. It was Tanaka who had organized and led those night forays down the Slot, which the Marines had dubbed the Tokyo Express. At night his destroyers had brought down troops, disembarked them and then had

[1] Miller, *Guadalcanal, The First Offensive,* p. 137.

bombarded Henderson Field. By daylight he was usually well out of range of Henderson Field's bombers. It had not always worked so smoothly and there had been losses, but Tanaka had stuck to his job. With a good deal of grudging respect, the Americans called him "Tenacious" Tanaka.

The heavy ships of the Imperial Navy would have two tasks in the October offensive. Cruisers and battleships would add the weight of their guns to the bombardment of Henderson Field, hoping to keep it neutralized if not totally put out of action. Admiral Chuichi Nagumo, the victor at Pearl Harbor and the loser at Midway, would have his carrier forces waiting in the wings. Their main job would be to cut off the American retreat. They would swing into action when Hyakutake signaled that Henderson Field was in Japanese hands.

As the Sendai Division prepared to move south down the Slot, General Maruyama addressed his troops: "This is the decisive battle between Japan and the United States."[2] His superior, General Hyakutake, underscored the thought by pinpointing in his orders the exact spot where the Marine commander, General Alexander Vandegrift, would appear carrying the white flag of surrender.

Major General Alexander Archer Vandegrift, commanding all United States ground forces on Guadalcanal, was not the surrendering sort of general. A well-mannered, rather soft-spoken Virginia gentleman, he seemed like something out of Robert E. Lee's famous Army of Northern Virginia. But Vandegrift was all-Marine and quite at home with the tough, hard-drinking old timers of the Corps, who themselves were just as much at home fighting bandits in Nicaragua or sailors in a Shanghai bar. Like his men, Vandegrift was nothing if not a fighter.

His three Marine regiments were set up around a 22,000-yard-long perimeter extending from the Ilu River in the east to the Matanikau River in the west, four miles away. It was a long line for such a force to hold, and Vandegrift's regiments were not at full strength. Thus far casualties in the fighting had been fairly light, under a thousand, but the jungle was

[2] Morison, *The Struggle for Guadalcanal,* p. 143.

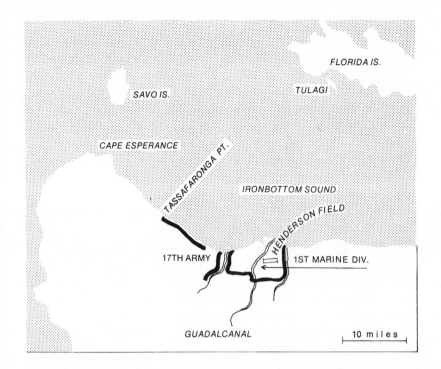

FLORIDA IS.

TULAGI

SAVO IS.

CAPE ESPERANCE

TASSAFARONGA PT.

IRONBOTTOM SOUND

HENDERSON FIELD

17TH ARMY

1ST MARINE DIV.

GUADALCANAL

10 miles

OCTOBER BATTLEFIELD   The key to Guadalcanal was Henderson Field. Its planes dominated the waters of Ironbottom Sound during the daylight. The Japanese Navy, forced to operate only at night, came in around Savo Island and landed small amounts of supplies and troops between Cape Esperance and the United States Marines' perimeter. The United States Navy was sending its cruisers to intercept these Japanese supply runs. The Japanese 17th Army felt it was already strong enough to burst through the American Marines and take Henderson Field. The Marines felt otherwise.

taking its toll in disease. There were bad fungus infections, dysentery and, most prevalent, malaria. The mosquitoes carrying the malaria germ would send almost 2,000 men to the hospital in October alone. The fact that the Marines were on short rations also contributed to the prevalence of disease.

In the middle of this ten-square-mile plot of ground held by the Marines lay Henderson Field, which was actually a 3,800-foot strip of ground, continually holed by Japanese bombs. It was covered with engine-choking dust when it baked under the tropical sun. Within minutes, though, heavy tropical downpours could turn it into a quagmire of mud the consistency of molasses.

To keep Henderson in operation was the job of Brigadier General Roy Geiger whose reputation for flawless profanity was matched only by his reputation as a flier. Geiger had been the fifth Marine to put up a pilot's wings, had won the Navy Cross in France during World War I and had flown everything from deHaviland biplanes to the latest Grumman fighters. Geiger had just the right touch of bravado to make him the perfect leader for Henderson's hard-pressed pilots. For his headquarters he selected a Japanese shack called "the Pagoda" which was only 200 yards off the runway, the prime target for Japanese bombers and destroyers.

Operating conditions at the field were desperate. It lacked almost everything. Its radio was usually good for only twenty miles. Gas had to be hand-pumped and bombs hand-hoisted onto the planes' bomb racks. Machine gun belts had to be hand-loaded. Spare parts were unknown and a damaged plane would be cannibalized on the spot and stripped down to a skeleton. Fuel was always short and so were planes and pilots.

Navy pilots from damaged carriers or some who simply came up to Guadalcanal on temporary duty were added to Geiger's Marines. The Army Air Force sent up some P-400's which had to be uncrated in the rear areas by mechanics who had never worked on a P-400 and then manned by pilots who had never flown one. The mechanics and the pilots learned on the spot but when the planes got to Guadalcanal, it was found that they were no good over 12,000 feet and, thus, useless against the high-flying Japanese bombers. But they could carry a 500-pound bomb over the Japanese lines—or sometimes a depth charge whose tremendous concussion could blow the clothes right off a Japanese, leaving him both naked and dead.

In the air the Henderson fliers had to meet the legendary Japanese Zero fighter, which in the first few months of the war had gained a reputation even greater than that of the British Spitfire or the German Messerschmitt. The Zero could indeed out-speed, out-climb and outmaneuver the Marines' Grumman fighters. But, as the Marines quickly found out, the Zero couldn't take it. Its performance had been achieved by sacrificing cockpit armor and its gas tanks were not self-sealing. The stubby little Grummans were tough planes and, as long as they did not tangle with a Zero in a single plane-to-plane dogfight, could more than hold their own.

To the American pilots it sometimes seemed that their own field was a worse enemy than the Japanese. One day, eight planes crashed on takeoff, only two of which were worth repairing. Pilots groused but Geiger had his own way of answering them. He climbed into a dive-bomber with a 1,000-pound bomb aboard, wove his way down the runway and took off over the Japanese lines. If a man nearing sixty could do it, so could the young pilots. And they did.

Almost a thousand miles south of Guadalcanal lay the large island of New Caledonia and on it the harassed headquarters of Vice Admiral Robert Ghormley, commander of the South Pacific Area. Guadalcanal was his responsibility, and it was one that was wearing him down. Ghormley was now pessimistic, and he communicated this pessimism to his boss, Pacific Commander Chester Nimitz, during the latter's early October visit to New Caledonia.

Ghormley had cause for worry. Everything was in short supply and arriving ships found a lack of dock space as well as all too few tugs, barges and cranes with which to unload. The Navy had not foreseen a protracted campaign on Guadalcanal and had even had to get 20,000 pairs of boots from the Army so that the Marines would not have to fight barefoot.

Supply shortages were not Ghormley's only worry. He seemed very preoccupied with his lines of communication to Guadalcanal. Indeed, at the moment he was planning on setting up yet another base further north to protect Guadalcanal's supply line. Hard objections to this scheme came from Ghormley's subordinate, Major General Millard Harmon, who commanded all Army and Air Force units in the South Pacific. Harmon pointed out that the main task, and certainly now the immediate task, was to get everything possible into Guadalcanal and to get the Navy into action in the waters off the island. Everything must be subordinated to holding Guadalcanal. Ghormley had to agree and the Army's 164th Infantry Regiment was alerted for shipment to Guadalcanal.

To clear the way for the transports carrying the Army

men to Guadalcanal, Ghormley dispatched a task force of four cruisers and five destroyers. It was due to arrive off Guadalcanal at the same time as elements of General Maruyama's Sendai Division, which was also being escorted by cruisers and destroyers. For the first time since August, American and Japanese warships were moving toward a head-on clash.

"Those are enemy cruisers, believe me!"

THE BATTLE OF CAPE ESPERANCE
OCTOBER 11, 1942

On October 9th the transports carrying the Army's 164th Infantry left New Caledonia for the four-day run to Guadalcanal. Far ahead of this convoy, cruising just south of Guadalcanal, was the "Screening and Attack Force" whose task was to see that the convoy got there. This force, officially designated Task Group 64, had been ordered by Ghormley "to search for and destroy enemy ships."

These orders were just what the Task Group commander, Rear Admiral Norman Scott, wanted. He had been riding a desk in the Pentagon when the war had started and had harassed his superiors into giving him sea duty. Scott wanted to fight and his Task Group was a powerful force.

With him, Scott had two heavy cruisers, the *San Francisco* with nine 8-inch guns and the *Salt Lake City* with ten, and two light cruisers, the *Helena* and *Boise*, each carrying fifteen 6-inch guns. This was a lot of gun power. Along with the cruisers were five destroyers. Scott had been training these ships in night-fighting for almost three weeks. This was a subject which had been almost totally neglected by the United States Navy in peacetime. The American admirals had always had a preference for a daytime fight with a well-ordered line of battle blasting away at an enemy at long range. But the Japanese Navy operated off Guadalcanal at night, and so a night fight it had to be.

Norman Scott had one great advantage for such a fight— radar. The Japanese did not have it. But radar was new and it was complicated. It was also highly secret and even rear admirals remained in ignorance of all its potentialities and limitations. All Scott's ships had a narrow-beam gunnery radar but only two, the light cruisers *Helena* and *Boise,* had the brand-new, highly effective SG search radar. But Scott chose the *San Francisco* as his flagship. She was the newer of the heavy cruisers and thus the traditional choice—but her search radar was of an old and inefficient type. There were rumors, false ones, that the Japanese had electronic devices which could locate a ship using this old-type radar and Scott ordered it not to be used. In 1942 there were very few fighting admirals who were even amateur scientists.

Though Scott was a fighter, he was also a man of conscience. He would enter any night engagement with one great fear—that of firing on his own ships and killing his own men. The normal way for a ship to identify itself as friendly was to flash its recognition lights. With an enemy around, that could be an invitation to instant destruction. To reduce the chances of confusion Scott had decided to fight in a long column. As long as his ships maintained such a formation, any other ships spotted to either right or left would be enemy.

Six hundred and fifty miles north of Guadalcanal lay Rabaul, Japanese naval headquarters for the Solomons area. In command was Vice Admiral Gunichi Mikawa who had led his cruisers down to Guadalcanal that past August to give the United States Navy such a beating. Since then he had had little trouble with the Navy but quite a bit from those fliers at Henderson Field.

Mikawa was confident of success. The job of getting the Sendai Division down to Guadalcanal had been going well. By October 9th most of the division had gotten there aboard the fast destroyers of Admiral Tanaka's Tokyo Express, as had Division Commander Maruyama and Army Commander Hyakutake. On the night of the 11th, Mikawa planned to send down some more troops as well as big guns and ammunition. To get all this down to Guadalcanal, the Express that night would have the usual destroyers, six of them, and two fast seaplane tenders, the *Chitose* and *Nisshin,* which would transport the heavy equipment. This would be an important run but Mikawa saw no reason why it should be a difficult one.

As for the Henderson Field fliers. Mikawa called on the

Naval Air Force at Rabaul to carry out a heavy raid on the field on the afternoon of the 11th. And just for a little icing on the cake, he ordered a second group of warships, the 6th Cruiser Division, to go down too and plaster the field that night. It all seemed very routine to Mikawa and he saw no reason to go himself.

Both groups of ships staged out of Shortland Island, the Japanese forward base only 250 miles north of Guadalcanal. The transport group, the two seaplane tenders and their escorting six destroyers, left Shortland at 8:00 A.M. on the 11th. They were scheduled to be off Guadalcanal soon after dark and to unload while night kept Henderson Field's planes grounded.

Not until six hours after the transports had left would the cruisers of the bombardment group leave Shortland. They were faster and needed less time for the run. Mikawa had not thought that the cruisers would have to protect the transports and had given them only the mission of bombarding Henderson Field. They were scheduled to arrive off Guadalcanal around midnight, a couple of hours after the transports had started unloading.

Rear Admiral Aritomo Goto commanded the three cruisers, the *Aoba*, his flagship, and the *Furutaka* and *Kinugasa*. They carried six 8-inch guns each and were all veterans of that August defeat of the Americans. Accompanying them were two destroyers. All the Japanese ships were superbly trained for night combat and had a superb weapon, their torpedoes, carried by the cruisers as well as the destroyers. But the Japanese force suffered from one very severe disadvantage. Admiral Goto was supremely overconfident. Since August United States warships had been absent from Guadalcanal waters after dark. Goto, like his superior, Mikawa, saw no reason to believe that this night was going to be any different.

First contact with the opposing forces came at 10:30 A.M. on October 11th. A United States Army B-17, flying long-range reconnaissance out of New Caledonia, sighted the Japanese transport force just south of Shortland. The two seaplane tenders were mistaken for cruisers and the B-17 radioed a report back to Henderson Field that two cruisers and six destroyers were headed down the Slot. Henderson Field passed the information along to Scott's cruisers.

First action came shortly after midday when the Japanese air raid on Henderson Field was put on. Thirty-four twin-engined bombers with a very powerful escort of twenty-nine fighters came over. Geiger's fighters went up to meet them. Four of the American fighters went down but they took four of the Japanese fighters with them, as well as seven of the bombers. The bullets of Geiger's fighter planes and some clouds which partially obscured the field made things difficult for the remaining Japanese bombardiers. Not a single bomb went anywhere near the field.

As soon as the ineffective Japanese raid was over, Henderson Field sent off its routine reconnaissance patrols. By three that afternoon the Japanese transport group had been sighted again. Again at 5:30 P.M. Henderson's fliers picked them up, now only a little over 100 miles away. But each time they were reported as two cruisers and six destroyers. Goto's cruisers remained beyond the range of the American fliers and were not reported.

All these sighting reports were what Norman Scott had been waiting for. Late in the afternoon he signaled his ships, "We are going in." [3] His Task Force sped up the west shore of Guadalcanal and at sunset the ships' loudspeakers bellowed, "All hands man your battle stations." Scott, unlike Goto, was taking no chances of being surprised. At ten he ordered his four cruisers to catapult their search planes. The *Helena* didn't get the message and the *Salt Lake City's* plane burned on takeoff so only two got into the air. The *Boise's* plane developed engine trouble and had to land at sea. That left only one.

By 10:25 P.M. Scott was abreast of Cape Esperance, the northwest tip of Guadalcanal. He ordered a turn toward Savo Island and simultaneously ordered his ships to take up their battle formation, a three-mile long column. Leading it was Scott's destroyer commander, Captain Robert Tobin in the *Farenholt*, followed at 500-yard intervals by the *Duncan* and *Laffey*. Then came the cruisers, Scott's flagship, the *San Fran-*

[3] Cook, *The Battle of Cape Esperance*, p. 20.

cisco, leading. She was followed by the *Boise*, *Salt Lake City* and *Helena*. The rear of the column was brought up by the destroyers *Buchanan* and *McCalla*.

At 10:50 Scott's single scout plane reported a contact. It reported one large and two small ships off Guadalcanal. These were part of the Japanese transport force which had been unloading for about an hour. Scott got the message but decided these were small fry. He could tend to them later. He continued on his patrol line from Cape Esperance to the small, volcanic cone of Savo Island. Here he could cut off the retreat of the Japanese already reported or intercept any other Japanese ships coming down from the north.

Admiral Goto's bombardment group was at that time coming down toward Scott. His three cruisers were in column, the flagship *Aoba* leading with the *Furutaka* and *Kinugasa* following. Slightly ahead of the cruisers were two destroyers, the *Hatsuyuki* off to the left and the *Fubuki* off to the right. Goto's only worry was the weather as his ships had been sailing down the Slot in the midst of continuous squalls. But as he approached Savo Island the weather cleared. Goto planned to sail between Cape Esperance and Savo Island and then proceed along the north shore of Guadalcanal to his bombardment position off Henderson Field. He had had no word from either the transport group or the Japanese radio on Guadalcanal that there were any Americans about and so he had not even bothered to order his crews to battle stations. By 11:30 P.M. Goto and Scott were 29,000 yards apart and neither admiral was aware of the other's presence.

On board the *Helena*, fourth in line of Scott's cruisers, contact had been made. Her new SG radar showed a small, glowing dot of light which could easily mean enemy ships. The contact report was phoned to the *Helena*'s captain, Gilbert Hoover, who was on the bridge, one deck above. Hoover had served in the Navy's Bureau of Ordnance in Washington and there had learned some of the secrets of the new search radar. He had also had a chance to try it out with the destroyer squadron he had commanded before coming to the *Helena*. Standing orders in the Navy then were for a ship's captain to confirm an enemy contact before reporting it on to the admiral. Hoover waited.

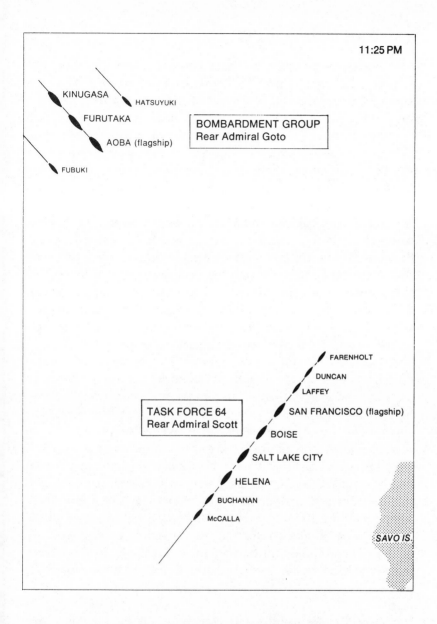

KINUGASA

HATSUYUKI

FURUTAKA

AOBA (flagship)

BOMBARDMENT GROUP
Rear Admiral Goto

FUBUKI

FARENHOLT

DUNCAN

LAFFEY

SAN FRANCISCO (flagship)

TASK FORCE 64
Rear Admiral Scott

BOISE

SALT LAKE CITY

HELENA

BUCHANAN

McCALLA

SAVO IS.

FIRST CONTACT As Task Force 64, four cruisers and five destroyers, reached the northern end of its patrol line between Cape Esperance and Savo Island, the cruiser *Helena*'s excellent search radar picked up the first indication of Japanese ships 29,000 yards to the northwest. Admiral Scott, whose flagship *San Francisco* had inferior radar, was unaware of the contact. Admiral Goto, commanding three cruisers and two destroyers, had no radar and sailed blindly toward the Americans on what he had been told was a routine mission to bombard Henderson Field.

For three minutes the radar contact was followed by the *Helena*'s radarmen until its course and speed could be estimated. During that time the small dot had slowly separated into three. Also the forward gunnery radar had been coached on to the contact. By now there was no doubt in Hoover's mind that there were at least three enemy ships bearing down on a southeasterly course at something between thirty and thirty-five knots. If Scott's column continued on its way to the northeast, the enemy would pass across its rear. The obvious move was for Scott's column to backtrack and head off the enemy. And at exactly this moment, 11:33 P.M., orders came from the flagship for the column to do precisely that. Hoover assumed that Scott had made contact too and was moving to put his ships squarely across the path of the oncoming Japanese. In this position the Japanese cruisers could only use their forward guns—twelve 8-inchers. The American cruisers could use their entire broadside, nineteen 8-inch guns and thirty 6-inch.

Hoover's assumption that Scott had ordered a counter-march to intercept the Japanese force was quite wrong. Scott's flagship, the *San Francisco*, had made no contact at all. Scott had planned to patrol between Cape Esperance and Savo. His ships were coming abreast of Savo and he simply wanted to reverse course and patrol back toward Cape Esperance.

The order Scott gave to accomplish the course reversal was a simple one, as was necessary with a task force which had been formed only three weeks before. Captain Tobin, leading the column in the destroyer *Farenholt*, would swing to his left through a half-circle and steady onto a southwesterly course. The ship behind him would follow right in the *Farenholt*'s track as would each successive ship in the column. It was like a game of follow-the-leader. But simple or not, it didn't work.

Scott's order went out by voice radio to each of his ships. But on board the flagship *San Francisco* it had to go by a makeshift intercom system up one deck from the Admiral's position to that of the ship's captain. In going from one deck to the next the order was garbled. The *San Francisco*'s captain got the order, not as meaning each ship would turn in succession, but as meaning that each ship should turn simultaneously. Thus, as Tobin in the *Farenholt* swung out to the left, so did the *San Francisco*.

Captain Moran of the *Boise,* next astern of the *San Francisco*, wondered why the flagship had pulled out of line but he followed in her wake. When in doubt, it was never a bad idea to follow the flagship. Then, after the *Boise,* came the *Salt Lake City* and *Helena* and the two tail-end destroyers. They all followed directly in the track of Scott's flagship.

Up ahead, Captain Tobin started to make his turn. Then, looking back, he saw that the *San Francisco* was turning independently. He slowed down, wondering what to do. Then he decided to complete his turn, pour on some speed, pass the column and pull into his proper position ahead of it.

As the cruisers turned on to the new course, Captain Hoover of the *Helena* wondered why there were no further orders from the flagship. The *Helena's* radar now showed the five ships of Admiral Goto's group closing the range at almost 1,000 yards a minute. At 11:42 Hoover, now absolutely positive of his contact, sent off a report to Admiral Scott. He waited for orders to open fire and none came. Two minutes later, at 11:44, Hoover heard the *Boise* report a contact, too.

Scott got the two reports. The *Boise's* confused him as she reported contacting "bogies," which could mean planes instead of ships. Scott thought it possible that both of them had contacted Tobin's three destroyers which he presumed were pulling up along the starboard side of the column. Over the voice radio he asked Tobin, "Are you taking station ahead?" Tobin answered, "Affirmative. Moving up your starboard side." [4]

Immediately after this exchange with his destroyer commander, Scott got another message from Captain Hoover on the *Helena*—"Interrogatory Roger." Hoover was asking permission to open fire. The word "Roger," standing for the letter R, meant, according to the Navy's Signal Book, to open fire. On voice radio it was also used simply to acknowledge a transmission. Hoover got a "Roger" to his message, meaning that it had been received, but he got no answer to his request to open fire.

[4] Morison, *The Struggle for Guadalcanal*, p. 156.

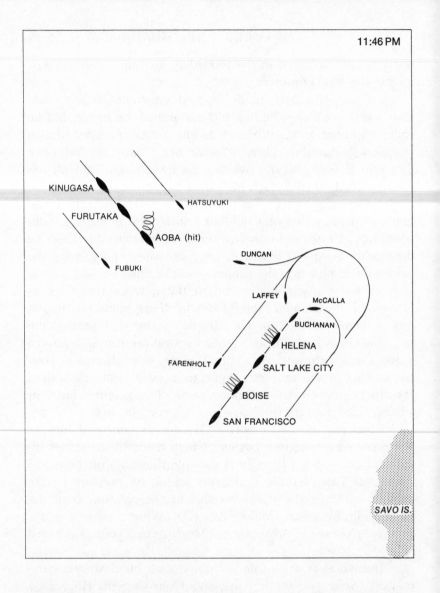

OPEN FIRE, RANGE 3,600 YARDS   At 11:33, Scott ordered his ships to countermarch and patrol back to the southwest. In confused execution of the order Scott's leading destroyers, the *Farenholt, Duncan* and *Laffey*, swung wide and tried to regain their position at the head of the column. As radar reports of the Japanese came in, Scott thought they referred to these American destroyers and withheld permission to open fire. The *Duncan* sighted the Japanese and turned to attack. At 11:46 the *Helena* sighted the Japanese ships and opened fire without orders. The *Boise* followed suit immediately and the Japanese flagship *Aoba* was badly hit and Admiral Goto mortally wounded.

Scott was pretty sure that both the *Helena*'s and *Boise*'s contacts were Tobin's destroyers. More of Scott's captains were beginning to think otherwise and all remembered Scott's verbal instructions before they had left base. A captain did not have to wait for orders to open fire when the enemy was located.

The *Helena* and *Boise* had contact. Now *Salt Lake City*'s old SC radar had picked up something. Scott had forbidden the use of this type but the *Salt Lake City* had not received the order. Her captain distrusted the report. But then a lookout, a man chosen because of his especially good night vision, made it emphatic—"Those are enemy cruisers, believe me! I've been studying the pictures. We got no ships like them." [5] The *Salt Lake City*'s ten 8-inch guns swung out and the gunnery radar locked on to the target.

On the destroyer *Duncan*, second in the column, a radar contact was made. The *Duncan*'s captain watched the *Farenholt* for a lead, not knowing that the *Farenholt*'s radar was out of commission. Japanese ships coming down on Scott's column as it was in the midst of a turn could mean disaster. Captain Taylor of the *Duncan* made his decision instantly. He swung out to his right, toward the enemy. No one on board the *Farenholt* saw him go. As the *Duncan* headed for the enemy the contact became visual. It was a Japanese heavy cruiser.

Finally the flagship *San Francisco* made contact with her gunnery radar. Her captain wondered if these were Tobin's destroyers. As it became clear by the contact's course and position that they couldn't be, Captain Hoover of the *Helena* was sending another "Interrogatory Roger," permission to open fire, to the Admiral. He got back a "Roger." It could have meant message received or open fire.

Captain Hoover didn't care now. The enemy was too close. At 11:46 he opened fire. The range was 3,600 yards—pointblank. The *Boise* instantly followed suit. This action resolved all doubts for the *Salt Lake City* and *San Francisco* and they joined in. The Battle of Cape Esperance had begun—without orders.

Scott was taken by surprise as his cruisers opened fire. The Japanese commander, Rear Admiral Goto, was aston-

[5] Cook, p. 49.

ished. Were these Japanese ships firing on him by mistake? Had he been sent on a routine mission by his chief, Admiral Mikawa, only to run into an American trap? Goto had no time to reflect on these questions. A deluge of shells hit his flagship, the *Aoba*, head-on. Shell fragments swept across the Admiral's bridge and Goto went down, mortally hit.

The *Aoba*'s captain acted fast. He called for hard right rudder and ordered a smokescreen. The *Aoba* began to turn, still taking a terrible pounding from the American guns. As she turned, the cruiser *Furutaka* followed in her wake and ran right into the same concentration of American fire. As the *Aoba* and *Furutaka* finally came round to a northwest course, the best line of retreat, both had been hit badly, the *Furutaka*, as it was to turn out, fatally.

The third cruiser in the Japanese column, the *Kinugasa*, swung out to the left. Her captain, Masao Sawa, had no intention of following the *Aoba* and *Furutaka* into that awful concentration of fire. Captain Sawa had saved his ship by his quick decision to turn left instead of right. He had also given his gunners and torpedomen a few minutes to recover from their surprise. It was all they were to need and, in a few minutes, they would come very close to evening the score with the Americans.

Scott's cruiser captains, all opening fire without direct orders, had just about won the Admiral's battle for him in its first minute. But Scott, half-blinded by the flashes of his flagship's guns going off right below his bridge, still thought they were firing at Tobin's destroyers. He sent out the order to cease fire. It went by voice radio to the other ships and the sound of the bombardment made it impossible to hear on some. On others, a deaf ear was turned to it.

Within a minute Scott ran up the ladder to the captain's bridge on the *San Francisco* and, with considerable heat, ordered the firing stopped. The *San Francisco*'s guns became silent and, behind her, the firing of the other cruisers began to slacken although it did not stop altogether.

Back on his own bridge, Scott radioed his destroyer commander, "How are you?" Tobin answered, "OK. We are going up ahead of you on your starboard side." To make sure, Scott

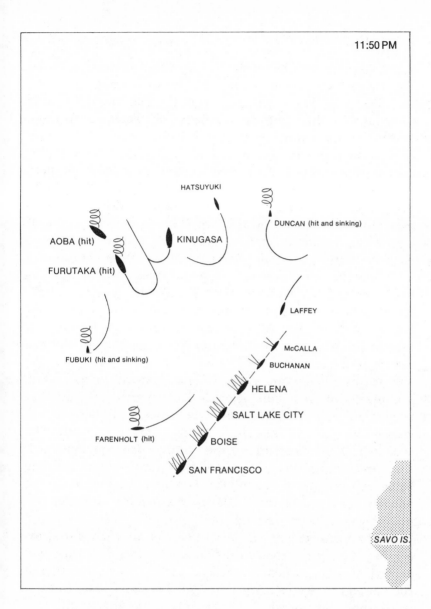

11:50 PM

HATSUYUKI

DUNCAN (hit and sinking)

AOBA (hit)

KINUGASA

FURUTAKA (hit)

LAFFEY

McCALLA

BUCHANAN

FUBUKI (hit and sinking)

HELENA

SALT LAKE CITY

FARENHOLT (hit)

BOISE

SAN FRANCISCO

SAVO IS.

JAPANESE DISASTER   Although the destroyers *Farenholt* and *Duncan* were both badly hit, the heavy guns of the American cruisers crushed the Japanese. The *Aoba* was severely damaged as she turned to retreat, and the *Furutaka*, following her, was battered into sinking condition as was the destroyer *Fubuki*. The cruiser *Kinugasa* and the destroyer *Hatsuyuki*, pulling out of the line of fire, escaped damage. Scott now ordered his ships to turn northwest in pursuit.

asked if Tobin was being fired at by the American cruisers. Tobin answered, "I don't know who you were firing at." [6]

Scott was now beginning to get the idea that there was something out there in the darkness besides Tobin's destroyers. The full truth was revealed to him within seconds. The *San Francisco*'s guns were still aimed at the ship they had been firing at when Scott had ordered the cease-fire. Her gunnery spotters could see it. One shouted to the bridge, "For God's sake, shoot!" [7] The *San Francisco*'s gunnery officer ordered a searchlight trained out on the target. In the dazzling beam of light was a Japanese destroyer only 1,400 yards away. It was the *Fubuki*, the right-hand destroyer of the Japanese force.

Now the *San Francisco*'s captain yelled, "Commence firing." Scott ordered the same thing. The *Fubuki*, a perfect target for the whole American column, was smothered by fire from half a hundred guns. An explosion tore her in half and, still held in the beam of the *San Francisco*'s searchlight, the *Fubuki* went down.

It was a bad moment for American destroyers as well as Japanese. Only moments after he had reported to Scott that he was OK, Tobin's ship, the *Farenholt* was hit. In her position between the two forces, she became a target for both. She tried to flash her recognition lights but they had been damaged. Two American shells tore into her forward section and one boiler was put out of action. The *Farenholt*, making only five knots, limped out of the battle. Scott's fears of firing on his own ships had been justified.

The destroyer *Laffey*, third in column of Tobin's destroyers, had not tried to follow the *Farenholt*. When the firing had started, she had turned and headed back to take up station at the tail end of Scott's formation. There she was safe. But not so with the *Duncan* which had been charging toward the Japanese when Scott's cruisers had opened up.

Within moments the *Duncan* was right in the midst of the Japanese formation. Captain Taylor maneuvered his ship violently and got off a torpedo at the second of the Japanese

[6] Cook, p. 72.
[7] Cook, p. 73.

cruisers he spotted. It was the *Furutaka*. As the *Duncan*'s torpedo sped straight toward its target, a shell smashed into the base of the *Duncan*'s forward funnel which crumpled, crushing to death those sailors stationed near it. More hits followed. Gunnery and torpedo control were knocked out. A bad fire started forward and the forward boilers were out of action. Captain Taylor ordered hard left rudder to get away but as the *Duncan* started to turn a shell crashed into her bridge. Captain Taylor was unhit although a man standing next to him was killed instantly. But Taylor was now unable to command his ship. The last hit had knocked out her steering and all communications to or from the bridge. The *Duncan* continued her left turn, out of control, burning and slowly sinking.

By 11:55 it had become clear to Admiral Scott that the Japanese force was retreating to the northwest. He ordered his column onto a parallel course to take up the pursuit. His four cruisers led the way with his three remaining undamaged destroyers following. At midnight Scott ordered another cease-fire and ordered all ships to flash their recognition lights. He wanted to make sure that all ships were in formation before the fight started again.

But now it was the turn of the Japanese to strike back. The flagship *Aoba*, although hit better than thirty times, had a few guns left in action. Behind her the *Furutaka* was a wreck, slowing down now and soon to sink. But Captain Sawa had his undamaged *Kinugasa* ready for action. At 8,000 yards he could make out the intermittent gun flashes from the American column and fired a spread of torpedoes at them.

On board the *Boise* a lookout spotted a torpedo's wake. He flashed the word to the bridge and Captain Mike Moran spotted it too. He swung his ship sharply to the right. The cruiser and the torpedo seemed on a collision course. But the *Boise*'s bow swung away and the *Kinugasa*'s torpedo missed. Another was spotted coming down the *Boise*'s starboard side. It missed her stern by a bare thirty yards. Captain Moran had made his turn with just about three or four seconds to spare.

No sooner had the *Boise* gotten back into the column after her wild maneuverings, than she spotted a Japanese ship off to starboard. It was the wounded *Aoba*. Moran ordered a

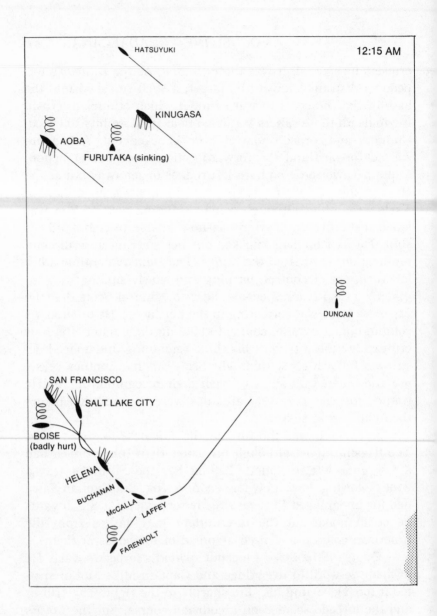

HATSUYUKI

12:15 AM

KINUGASA

AOBA

FURUTAKA (sinking)

DUNCAN

SAN FRANCISCO

SALT LAKE CITY

BOISE
(badly hurt)

HELENA

BUCHANAN

McCALLA   LAFFEY

FARENHOLT

JAPANESE REVENGE Leaving behind the sinking *Duncan*, Scott turned north in pursuit of the Japanese, hoping to complete his victory. But the undamaged *Kinugasa* aided by the damaged *Aoba* opened up with extremely accurate fire. The *Boise*, hit in the forward magazine and nearly destroyed, pulled out of line. Scott's column was thrown into some confusion, and he became afraid that his ships would start firing at one another. Thus, at 12:28 A. M., he called off any further pursuit and turned back toward his base.

searchlight switched on her and then opened fire. *Aoba* made what answer she could. But behind the *Aoba* was Captain Sawa's undamaged *Kinugasa* and it now gave the *Boise* a terrifying demonstration of just how well the Imperial Navy could shoot at night.

In tightly bunched salvos, right on target, came the 8-inch shells of the *Kinugasa*. Shell splashes erupted from the sea on either side of the *Boise*'s bow. Captain Moran on the *Boise*'s bridge knew he was in trouble. Some of the 6-inch guns forward of the bridge were no longer firing and a report of fire in the number one turret reached the bridge. Then came a shattering explosion and great fingers of flame leapt from the number one and two turrets. Below them was the forward powder magazine.

Many men on the bridge stood in stunned silence waiting for the next explosion which must surely tear the *Boise* to shreds. But not Captain Moran. He called for full speed and hard left rudder. The *Boise* swung out of the battle line. Seconds later another of the *Kinugasa*'s salvoes landed just where the *Boise* would have been had not Moran ordered her instant turn. And, as the *Boise* pulled out to her left, the *Salt Lake City,* next in column, swung to her right and passed between the *Boise* and the Japanese. She took some damage but it was not too bad.

On board the *Boise,* as she sheared out of the fight, Moran ordered the forward magazines to be flooded. It was the only way in which the ship could be saved. Word came back to the bridge that the flood valves would not work. The electrical connections to them had been severed. But just as it seemed that the magazines would go up and that the *Boise*'s destruction was inevitable, the fires suddenly started to abate. Damage control parties went forward and thrust hoses into turret openings jammed with some of the hundred bodies lying in the *Boise*'s two forward turrets.

What had saved the *Boise* was a piece of incredible luck. One of the *Kinugasa*'s 8-inch shells had hit her forward, nine feet below the waterline. Through this hole, water, 1,200 tons of it, had poured in and just fast enough to flood the forward magazine before the fires reached it. With twenty pumps at work bailing her out, the *Boise* limped off to safety, but she would not fight again for many months.

For five minutes after the *Boise* had pulled out of the column, Scott's ships had continued their pursuit of the Japanese. His ships, though, were in considerable disarray. Torpedo tracks had been sighted and the ships had swerved to avoid them; it had been extremely difficult in the dark to regain proper formation. Scott was afraid that the ships behind the *San Francisco* might take her for the enemy which, indeed, almost happened. At 12:20 Scott called off the pursuit.

Both sides attempted rescue efforts after the fighting was over. Scott detached the destroyer *McCalla*, which found the floating hulk of the *Duncan*. She could do nothing to save the ship which finally sank just before noon. But the *McCalla* did rescue 195 men from the water, including Captain Taylor. Forty-eight of the *Duncan*'s crew were lost.

The Japanese were not so lucky. A destroyer did manage to take off 513 men of the cruiser *Furutaka*'s crew before she went down at about 2:30 A.M. Two more Japanese destroyers searching for survivors were caught after daylight by Marine and Navy fliers from Henderson Field and both were sunk.

The Battle of Cape Esperance was over. Scott's task force had won a small victory. For the loss of the destroyer *Duncan*, they had sunk a Japanese heavy cruiser and a destroyer. But Scott had failed to accomplish his primary mission which was to derail the Tokyo Express, to stop Japanese men and supplies from reaching Guadalcanal.

While Scott and Goto had been fighting it out, the two seaplane tenders and six destroyers of the Japanese reinforcement group had been peacefully unloading tanks, heavy artillery, supplies and men. And what was obvious to South Pacific commander, Admiral Ghormley, and to every Marine private on Guadalcanal was that, unless the Japanese buildup of men and supplies could be stopped, sooner or later the Marine perimeter would be overwhelmed and the island lost.

"The situation is not hopeless, but it is certainly critical."

BUILDUP FOR BATTLE

OCTOBER 12–23, 1942

As Admiral Norman Scott's task force sailed southward toward its base during the daylight hours of October 12th, another Navy force took over the job of protecting the Marines' perimeter from the sea. But it was a pitifully inadequate force; only four pint-sized PT boats. It looked as though the United States Navy was scraping the bottom of the barrel.

On the following morning, the two transports bringing up the Army's 164th Infantry arrived and almost 3,000 soldiers disembarked to reenforce the Marines. The troops were green, not used to either the jungle or the Japanese, but they were welcome. So were the jeeps, trucks and ammunition which came with them, all things desperately needed on the island. But even more welcome to many malaria-ridden, jungle-weary Marines was a genuine American chocolate bar, something none of them had seen for what seemed like half a lifetime.

But the joy that 3,000 soldiers and chocolate bars had brought to the Marines was short-lived. Just before noon two dozen Japanese bombers winged in over the island. There had not been enough warning for fighter planes to get up to altitude and the Japanese tore up Henderson Field's runway, damaged some grounded planes and, what was much worse, burned up 5,000 gallons of aviation fuel. Gas for Geiger's planes was getting very scarce.

Later that afternoon another Japanese raid came in and added to the damage. During both raids the Japanese had lost only one bomber and two escorting fighters. Then, only a couple of hours after the Japanese bombers had finally left, the Japanese artillery, which had been landed while Scott and Goto had fought off Cape Esperance, opened fire. Their target, too, was Henderson Field, and the Marines, whose artillery was smaller than the new Japanese guns, could do nothing to stop them.

But all this was merely preliminary to the big show. At midnight that night two Japanese battleships, heavily escorted by destroyers, passed by Savo Island, through the waters where

Admiral Goto had fought only two nights before. Their mission was the same as his had been; to bombard Henderson Field. The battleships *Kongo* and *Haruna* had eight 14-inch guns apiece and carried over 900 rounds of bombardment shells, each weighing nearly a ton.

Just after 1:30 A.M. the battleships *Kongo* and *Haruna* were in position off Henderson Field. A Japanese plane flew over the field. Over the eastern end it dropped a green flare, over the middle a white one, and over the western end a red one. Then the sixteen big guns of the two battleships opened fire simultaneously. For an hour and a half Japanese shells raked the field. They literally tore it apart. Forty men were killed. Huge gasoline fires blazed through the night.

All the Navy could do was to send 35-ton PT boats against 30,000-ton battleships. The four PT boats did what they could, which was merely to annoy the Japanese. They scored no hits.

At dawn the Marines staggered from their foxholes and the results of what was ever after known simply as "The Bombardment" were all too apparent. Henderson Field was virtually wiped out. Of Geiger's thirty-nine dive-bombers, only five were fit to fly. Sixteen out of forty Grumman fighters were total wrecks, and every one of the remainder needed some sort of repairs before it could fly again. But the Japanese had not hit the new, grass-covered strip east of Henderson Field, officially called "Fighter One" but more appropriately called the "Cow Pasture" by the Marines. It was usable only in dry weather but it was, at least, something.

On the 14th, the day after The Bombardment, two of the five remaining dive-bombers went off on a reconnaissance mission up the Slot. They found six big Japanese troop transports with cruisers and destroyers escorting them, all headed for Guadalcanal. Geiger ordered whatever planes that could fly to attack. There were far too few and the Japanese force kept on its way.

That night two Japanese cruisers, the *Chokai* and *Kinugasa*, hit Henderson Field with better than 750 rounds of 8-inch shells. Under cover of this bombardment the Japanese transports arrived off Guadalcanal and began unloading. In the morning they were plainly visible to the Americans, only ten miles away.

General Geiger called for an attack but was told that there was no gasoline left at Henderson Field. "Then, by God, find some," he bellowed.[8] Gas was siphoned out of the tanks of two half-destroyed bombers that were lying there. Then someone remembered some drums of gasoline that had been hidden away months before. Geiger's bellow was heard all the way to the American bases far to the south and before the day was over, transport planes had dropped everything else to carry drums of gas to Henderson Field.

Once they had some fuel to fly with, Geiger's fliers roared off at the Japanese transports. They bombed and strafed and before the day was over three of the Japanese transports had been beached and were total losses. But about 3,500 Japanese troops had gotten ashore along with a good deal of their supplies. That night two more Japanese cruisers plastered Henderson Field again and by the next morning Geiger had only two dozen planes left and half of them needing some sort of repairs.

On October 15th, Pacific Commander Chester Nimitz summed up the situation. "It now appears that we are unable to control the sea in the Guadalcanal area. The situation is not hopeless, but it is certainly critical." [9] Nimitz was also beginning to get the idea that back in South Pacific headquarters there were many who did think that it was hopeless.

Early in the afternoon of October 18th a big Navy flying boat set down in the water off United States headquarters in New Caledonia. Aboard was Vice Admiral William F. Halsey, a rather gnome-like man who was, by reputation, the most pugnacious admiral in the United States Navy. It was Halsey who had commanded the carriers which had launched Doolittle's bombers on their Tokyo raid back in April, and it was that raid which had been the catalyst of the Guadalcanal campaign. After the raid, Halsey had been in hospital but now he

[8] Morison, *The Struggle for Guadalcanal*, p. 176.
[9] Morison, *The Struggle for Guadalcanal*, p. 178.

was fit and ready to take command of a carrier task force again.

As Halsey stepped from his plane to a waiting motor boat, he was looking forward to seeing Admiral Ghormley again. The two had been friends for almost forty years, since they had played football together at the Naval Academy. But as Halsey stepped into the boat, Ghormley's aide handed him a sealed envelope.

Halsey tore it open. There was another within it, marked "Secret." Halsey tore this open and read it. "Jesus Christ and General Jackson!" swore the Admiral, "This is the hottest potato they ever handed me." The message was from Pacific Commander Nimitz and it read, "You will take command of the South Pacific Area and South Pacific Forces immediately." [10] Instead of visiting with his old friend Ghormley, Halsey had to go over to headquarters and relieve him of command.

What Chester Nimitz had decided to do was to put the most aggressive commander he could find in charge of the whole Guadalcanal campaign—and aggressiveness was one thing Halsey had in full measure. There were those in the more erudite circles of the United States Navy who doubted Halsey's intellectual fitness for his command but none could deny that he had in full measure that rather mystical quality that the military call leadership. Even the dog-tired Marines on Guadalcanal were electrified by the news. "One minute we were too limp with malaria to crawl out of our foxholes," wrote one, "the next, we were running around shouting like kids." [11]

Halsey's strategy was simple. Stop all side shows and throw everything there was into holding Guadalcanal. When asked by a newspaperman just how he was going to win the campaign, Halsey's answer was: "Kill Japs, kill Japs, and keep on killing Japs." [12] It wasn't a bad answer.

---

[10] Halsey and Bryan, *Admiral Halsey's Story*, p. 130.
[11] Griffith, *The Battle for Guadalcanal*, p. 163.
[12] Halsey and Bryan, p. 123.

The Butchers are Butchered

THE BATTLE FOR HENDERSON FIELD
OCTOBER 23–26, 1942

As Henderson Field was being blasted by everything from Japanese bombers to battleships General Hyakutake was issuing orders for the ground offensive which he was now sure would capture Henderson Field and rout the Marines. He had 20,000 troops ashore. Most of these were from the Sendai Division, fresh and eager for action. After their victories they had indulged themselves in barbaric orgies, using individual prisoners for bayonet practice or roping large groups together and machine-gunning them. Any Marine who surrendered could expect this—or worse.

Hyakutake was considered a very clever general. His October plan of attack was too devious. Instead of massing his strength for one massive blow against the Marine perimeter, he decided to make three widely separated but supposedly simultaneous attacks. He even threw in a seaborne landing to the east of the Marine perimeter for good measure. As the grand climax, Admiral Yamamoto and the Combined Fleet would arrive off Guadalcanal, but only after they had gotten word from Hyakutake that Henderson Field was in Japanese hands.

One Japanese attack would go in across the mouth of the Matanikau River at the western edge of the American perimeter. Here Major General Sumuyoshi would attack with a regiment supported by sixteen tanks. Originally Hyakutake had planned on having a bridgehead across the Matanikau but his earlier attempts to gain one had been foiled. Sumuyoshi's attack would have to be made across the mouth of the river.

While Sumuyoshi was attacking at the river's mouth, another Japanese regiment, under Colonel Oka, would cross the river a mile and a half upstream. Once across, Oka would sweep down on the flank of the Marines already under attack by Sumuyoshi. These attacks across the Matanikau would serve to gain ground from which Japanese artillery could, at

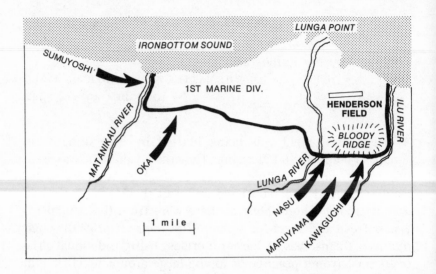

THE JAPANESE ARMY ATTACKS   General Hyakutake's plan to take Henderson Field called for subsidiary attacks to be made at the west end of the Marine perimeter where General Sumuyoshi's force would attack across the Matanikau River while another force under Colonel Oka would cross upstream to outflank the Americans. The main attack by three columns under General Maruyama was to be made east of the Lunga River. When Maruyama's men took Henderson Field, the Japanese Navy would move in to prevent any American troops from escaping.

shorter range, pinpoint their fire on the American airfields. They would also divert attention from the main attack.

This Japanese main effort was to be under the personal direction of the Sendai Division's commander, General Maruyama, and was to flow along the ridges just south of Henderson Field. The attack would be delivered by two wings. The left was to be under Major General Nasu, the Sendai Division's infantry commander. The right wing was under Major General Kawaguchi who had been in command of the unsuccessful Japanese attack along these same ridges in September. General Maruyama held back a full regiment under his own command, planning to use it to exploit a success by either wing.

By October 15th General Maruyama's column started on its fifteen-mile approach march to its attack positions. The fifteen miles were a nightmare. There was nothing but a sketchy path through the jungle, hacked out by axe and machete. There were no pack mules or horses and each soldier had to carry artillery or mortar shells or extra machine-gun ammunition as well as his own full combat equipment. The jungle floor was saturated by torrential rains and each step became a laborious effort. Soon the trail was littered by heavy equipment which the soldiers just could not carry. All artillery and mortars had to be left behind but General Maruyama was not unduly concerned. In the Japanese Army there was still a sort of mystical faith in their "devil-subduing, sharp bayonets."

As Maruyama's column crept along at a snail's pace, the date for the big attack was postponed to October 22nd and then to October 23rd. On that afternoon a big Japanese air raid came in over Henderson Field, to soften things up. Twenty Zero fighters came along to protect the bombers and all twenty were shot down by Marine and Navy fliers. It was a bad day for the Japanese in the air.

It was a bad day on the ground, too. General Maruyama had his left wing, under General Nasu, in position to attack but the right wing, under General Kawaguchi, was not in position. Kawaguchi didn't much like his orders anyway and proceeded to argue about them with General Maruyama. Kawaguchi was forthwith relieved of command and Colonel Shoji ordered to take over. Amid all this confusion there was nothing General Maruyama could do but postpone the whole attack for another twenty-four hours.

Now General Hyakutake's overly complicated plan of attack began to fall apart. Word of General Maruyama's last-minute postponement of the attack did not reach General Sumuyoshi down at the mouth of the Matanikau. Sumuyoshi, in a semi-coma from malaria, ordered his attack to go in. Both Sumuyoshi's tanks and his tank tactics left something to be desired. His little 18-ton tanks, which were twenty years out-of-date, moved out slowly along the sand bar at the river's mouth. There they were perfect targets for the Marines' little 37-mm anti-tank guns. Of the nine attacking tanks in the first wave, only one made it across the river, but once across was quickly knocked out. While Sumuyoshi's tanks made their abortive effort, the Japanese infantry milled about in its concentration areas waiting to follow. These areas were known to the Marine artillerymen, who plastered them with shells and killed 600 of Sumuyoshi's men. The attack further up the Matanikau by Colonel Oka's force did not come off. The ground he had to march across was far rougher than the Japanese had suspected and he was nowhere near his attack positions. The whole Matanikau attack had been a dismal failure.

Maruyama's postponed main attack did go in on the 24th, but not as planned. General Nasu's left wing was in position and his scouts reported that, as was indeed the fact, the Marines did not seem to be expecting an attack there. But Maruyama's right wing, now under Colonel Shoji, was not up and ready. Maruyama, his patience now at an end, ordered General Nasu's wing to attack anyway. A tremendous downpour of rain managed to postpone this attack from its scheduled five o'clock in the evening until midnight.

Facing Nasu's attack was a single battalion of Marines under an already legendary commander, "Chesty" Puller, a small, tough, bulldog fighter. Puller's battalion was a veteran outfit, but it was understrength and spread over a front that would normally have been held by two battalions. Behind Puller's men was a single battalion of the Army's 164th Infantry, green troops who were usually referred to as "doggies" by the rather scornful Marines.

At midnight a single rocket went up from the Japanese lines and their attack was on. The Japanese infantry now tried to make up with raw courage for the tactical failings of their generals. Nasu's men charged in on Puller's Marines and before long were putting an unbearable pressure on them. As the Marines fought with skill and determination, the soldiers of the 164th Infantry were fed up into the lines in small groups. They came forward in rain and dark into the midst of the howling Japanese attack, an awesome introduction to combat. But the veteran Marines and the green soldiers, often quite literally shoulder to shoulder, slowly mastered the Japanese attack and sent one wave of attacking Japanese after another reeling back into the jungle. If, by dawn, a Marine referred to a soldier as a "doggie," it was with affection, not scorn.

Only at one spot had the Japanese penetrated the Marines' line. Colonel Shojiro Ishimiya, whose infantry regiment had been the backbone of Nasu's attack, had led nine officers and men deep into Puller's position. There, around the regimental flag which they carried with them, Ishimiya and his men held out for two days before the Marines killed them all. Ishimiya's courage, which had to be admired, was, like so much of the Japanese bravery on Guadalcanal, wasted. It accomplished nothing and Ishimiya could hardly command his regiment effectively while cut off inside the Marines' line.

By dawn on the 25th, the worst problem facing the Marines and soldiers was the disposal of the thousand or so Japanese bodies that lay sprawled in front of their positions. Decomposition was rapid in the tropical sun and the work had to be done quickly. While it was, American reinforcements came up to the line and behind them more artillery and mortars moved into position. If the Sendai Division wanted to make any more attacks in this sector, they would be more than welcome to try. The Marines and soldiers were ready for them.

More attacks were just what Maruyama had in mind for that night, the 25th. But during the day a Japanese naval force appeared off Guadalcanal carrying some troops for a landing east of the Marine perimeter. By a confusion in signals, they thought that the Japanese Army had taken Henderson Field. They were quickly disabused of that idea, as American fliers sank a Japanese cruiser. The fliers also mauled Japanese planes attempting to bomb Henderson Field. A Marine Major, Joe Foss, shot down four Zero fighters that day, a not inconsiderable feat, but an incredible one considering that he had done exactly the same the previous day. So the daytime events of the 25th did not augur well for Maruyama's night attack.

That night the Sendai Division tried its best. Major General Nasu led his wing in person and was killed. Half the division's officers ended up dead or badly wounded before the night was done. It was a night of slaughter for the Sendai, the Butchers of Nanking, and as dawn broke it was clear that they were now the Butchered of Guadalcanal.

Late that night, as Maruyama's attacks were petering out, Colonel Oka finally came into action. His attack had been designed to support Sumuyoshi's across the Matanikau. Sumuyoshi's had failed two days before but Oka went on with his anyway. Like the others, it was beaten back with heavy Japanese losses. Now all of Hyakutake's complicated plan had failed. Sumuyoshi had attacked too early, Oka had attacked too late and Maruyama had attacked piecemeal. None of them had accomplished a thing.

October Postscript

THE BATTLE OF THE SANTA CRUZ ISLANDS
OCTOBER 26, 1942

All the time the Japanese Army had been trying to break through on Guadalcanal, the Japanese fleet had been milling about some 300 miles north waiting for word that Henderson Field had been captured. The nucleus of the fleet was three large carriers and one small one and they were supported by a plethora of battleships, cruisers and destroyers.

On October 23rd, when the Japanese Army attacks had started, Halsey had only the new, big carrier *Hornet* to set against the Japanese. The next day, the patched-up *Enterprise* arrived from Pearl Harbor, which brought the United States up to 171 in carrier-borne aircraft. The Japanese had 212 but that was all right with Halsey, and early on the 26th he sent out a three-word order—"Attack, repeat, attack."

The United States Navy drew first blood. Two scout planes, each carrying a 500-pound bomb in case they found anything, spotted the Japanese light carrier *Zuiho*. They got their bombs onto her flight deck and put her out of action for the day.

By 7:30 that morning, each side had located the other's big carriers, about 200 miles apart. Each side sent off its aircraft, the Japanese about twenty minutes before the Americans. Thus, the Japanese arrived over their targets first. The *Enterprise* found a rain squall to duck into but the *Hornet* was not so lucky. Twenty-seven Japanese planes went for her and only two survived the attack. The Japanese squadron commander, crippled by anti-aircraft fire, dove onto her flight deck where his two bombs exploded. Worse still, the Japanese got two torpedoes into the *Hornet* and they were fatal. The American carrier stayed stubbornly afloat for another sixteen hours, but it was impossible to save her.

While the *Hornet* was being attacked, her planes found the big Japanese carrier *Shokaku* and ripped up her flight deck with their bombs. The *Shokaku* didn't sink but she was out of the war for nine months.

The Japanese made every effort to get the *Enterprise* but could not. Sailing in close formation with the *Enterprise* was the new battleship *South Dakota* carrying dozens of anti-aircraft guns on her decks. The big battleship got at least two dozen Japanese planes, and damage to the *Enterprise* was held to three small bomb hits. She could be repaired in three weeks.

As the two fleets retired, the Japanese could claim a victory. They had sunk the *Hornet* and had not lost a carrier themselves. But the Japanese had lost about seventy veteran naval fliers and these could be ill-afforded. The real result of the Battle of the Santa Cruz Islands, as far as the Guadalcanal campaign was concerned, was that it cancelled out the carriers as a decisive weapon. Neither side could now put as many as 100 carrier planes into the air.

Yamamoto and Halsey both had plenty of other ships left, though, and neither considered the battle for Guadalcanal over by a long shot. If Yamamoto sent his battleships, cruisers and destroyers down the Slot, Halsey was ready to fight them off with his. The November battles would have to be fought with gun and torpedo at close range. They would be both bloody and decisive.

"Get the big ones!"

THE BATTLE OF FRIDAY, THE THIRTEENTH
NOVEMBER 13, 1942

The Japanese Army was nothing if not consistent. Each of their attacks aimed at Henderson Field had been larger than the one before. Their November plan was to try again and, this time, with a force double that used in October. General Hyakutake was to be reinforced up to a strength of 40,000 men and that, they thought, should do the job.

A good number of men were easily brought down to Guadalcanal on the fast destroyers of Rear Admiral Tanaka's Tokyo Express. But to supply 40,000 men on Guadalcanal was obviously going to be a job for more than destroyers. For the bulk of the troops, and especially for the 10,000 tons of supplies, food and ammunition which would be needed, big Army transports would have to be used. These ships were not as fast as the destroyers and could not come and go in a single night. At some time in their voyage they would be in range of Henderson Field during daylight hours. This would be fatal unless Henderson Field could first be put out of operation.

Yamamoto decided to send his battleships down the Slot again for another bombardment mission against the airfield. But with the United States Navy under Bill Halsey, it was a safe bet that there would be a lot more than four PT boats to meet as there had been in October.

As the Japanese Army and Navy were gathering their forces, the United States Marine commander, General Vandegrift, was busy himself. He attacked westward across the Matanikau with the objective of extending his perimeter and pushing the Japanese artillery back beyond range of his airfields. Vandegrift's Marines won a very neat little victory, pinning a Japanese battalion against the sea and eliminating it.

But after its initial success the Marine advance slowed down. Vandegrift brought up a fresh Marine regiment and threw it into the battle, but his advance remained stalled. Then, on November 11th, all the Marines were suddenly ordered back across the Matanikau to their original positions. Vandegrift had just gotten the word from Halsey that the biggest Japanese offensive yet was about to begin.

Halsey's staff, coming amazingly close to the mark, had figured Japanese strength at two carriers, four battleships, five heavy cruisers, thirty destroyers and some twenty troop transports. They read the Japanese plans as calling for massive air attacks on Henderson Field on the 11th, a bombardment by the Japanese fleet on the night of the 12th and a major troop landing covered by Japanese carriers on the 13th.

American troop and supply movements to Guadalcanal

were already in progress and Halsey decided there was time to complete them. Thus it was that the preliminaries began on November 11th. Three unloading American transports were jumped by a dozen dive-bombers from a Japanese carrier. One transport was shaken up by very near misses but got most of her cargo ashore before limping away with a destroyer for escort. Later in the day high-level bombers hit Henderson Field and its two satellite airstrips but without accomplishing much.

The next day, the 12th, things began to warm up. Four American transports carrying the Army's 182nd Infantry Regiment arrived at Guadalcanal. Rear Admiral Norman Scott, the victor of Cape Esperance, was already there with his flagship, the anti-aircraft cruiser *Atlanta,* and four destroyers. Along with the transports came the heavy cruiser *Portland* and four more destroyers. Close by was Rear Admiral Dan Callaghan, who had been Ghormley's chief of staff but now commanded the support group, his flagship, the heavy cruiser *San Francisco,* plus the light cruiser *Helena* and three additional destroyers.

Early in the afternoon word came in that Japanese bombers, torpedo planes and fighters were on the way. The transports scurried out into deep water where they could get room to maneuver. So well handled were the transports that not one was scratched. Anti-aircraft gunners splashed one Japanese torpedo bomber after another. Fighters from Henderson took care of anything the anti-aircraft gunners couldn't. The Japanese took their losses and came in. A wounded torpedo bomber smashed into the *San Francisco* knocking out her after control station and a fire control radar and leaving behind fifty casualties. An American destroyer, caught in the cross fire that had greeted the wave-hopping Japanese planes, was hit badly enough by friendly anti-aircraft fire to be ordered away that evening. The transports finished their unloading as soon as the air raids were over.

It was no time to lose the services of a destroyer or to have the flagship *San Francisco* damaged. Even before the Japanese planes arrived, the first of many scouting reports from Australian coast watchers, United States submarines and reconnaissance planes had started coming in. Two Japanese battleships with cruisers and destroyers were in position to sweep down on Guadalcanal during the night. No Japanese transports had been seen, so obviously this was a bombardment group with Henderson Field its objective.

Admiral Dan Callaghan was ordered to gather together every available warship and prepare to block the Japanese battleships. The best Callaghan could do was five cruisers, only two of them heavies, and eight destroyers. It was a pitifully weak force to send against battleships but there was no alternative. Halsey's big guns, the battleships *Washington* and *South Dakota*, along with his only carrier, the damaged *Enterprise*, were too far to the south to help. Callaghan's mission was clearly sacrificial. At whatever cost he must keep those Japanese battleships from knocking out Henderson Field.

By ten that night the American transports were safely on their way south and Callaghan ordered his ships to reverse course and head back for Ironbottom Sound. In two hours it would be Friday, the 13th, a date not easily missed by a man like Callaghan who, like so many Irishmen, was something of a mystic. He was a deeply religious, very likeable man, an extremely conscientious worker inclined to drive himself too hard. His months as Ghormley's chief of staff in the cupboard-scraping days of the past summer had been exhausting. In the two weeks he had had his new command he had driven himself almost beyond the limit. Dan Callaghan was a tired man but he did have the one necessary asset for going up against battleships—courage.

Approaching battle, Callaghan ordered his ships into the same single-file formation Scott had used at Cape Esperance. Leading was Commander Stokes' Destroyer Division 10—*Cushing, Laffey, Sterett* and *O'Bannon*. Only the rear ship, the *O'Bannon*, had good search radar but was in no position to use it. Next came the cruisers. First the *Atlanta*, an anti-aircraft cruiser bristling with sixteen 5-inch guns, very light stuff to throw at a battleship. Aboard was Rear Admiral Norman Scott, junior to Callaghan and thus second-in-command. Behind the *Atlanta* came Callaghan's flagship, the heavy cruiser *San Francisco* with a brand-new captain, Cassin Young, who wore a Medal of Honor won at Pearl Harbor. The *San Francisco* boasted nine 8-inch guns and these could hurt even a battleship if the range was close enough. Behind the *San Francisco* came Callaghan's other 8-inch gun heavy cruiser, the *Portland*, "Sweet P" to her crew, then the light cruiser *Helena* with her highly effective search radar so largely wasted at Cape Esperance. Finally came the *Juneau*, sister ship to the *Atlanta*, and uniquely numbering in her crew five brothers, the Sullivans. Behind the cruisers came Destroyer Division 12 under Commander Ralph Tobin, who had so narrowly escaped disaster at Cape Esperance—*Aaron Ward, Barton, Monssen* and *Fletcher.*

The column of gray fighting ships stretched for over five miles. It was an impressive display but few of the ships had ever worked together. This was a scratch force on a desperate mission. Callaghan had given his captains no battle plan and he was throwing away the enormous advantage of radar as had Scott before him.

Shortly after six that evening as the American transports had been hauling away from Guadalcanal, Rear Admiral Raizo Tanaka had sailed from the northern end of the Slot, 350 miles away. His destroyers were escorting eleven fast transports with the 38th Division's commander, General Tadayoshi Sano, aboard as well as 10,000 of his veteran troops, 10,000 tons of supplies and a Special Naval Landing Force of 3,000 men. To get those eleven transports to Guadalcanal was the whole purpose of the entire Japanese operation.

Japanese commander, Admiral Yamamoto, had assigned eight cruisers to cover the arrival of Tanaka's transports. Their arrival would be preceded by a battleship bombardment of Henderson Field, scheduled for the early morning hours of Friday, the 13th. It was necessary to knock out Henderson Field if the eleven transports were to get to Guadalcanal and unload their cargo. But Yamamoto, in keeping with the incurable Japanese habit of dividing their forces, failed to send as great a force as he could have on this vital mission.

Yamamoto's main force was Vice Admiral Kondo's 2nd Fleet, two carriers and four battleships. Yamamoto ordered Kondo to keep his carriers well north, out of range of Henderson Field, and keep two of his four battleships with them for protection. The two other battleships, a light cruiser and eleven destroyers under Vice Admiral Hiroaki Abe would carry out the bombardment mission. Yamamoto had studied Britain's great Admiral Nelson, and Nelson had said, "Only numbers can annihilate." But Yamamoto was sending only two battleships when he had four.

Vice Admiral Abe, leading the battleship force down the Slot, had a reputation in the Imperial Navy for caution, perhaps too much caution. He had been a good friend of Admiral Goto and had heard that his friend had died at the Battle of Cape Esperance mumbling, "the dumb bastards," thinking that it was Japanese shells that had killed him. Abe was, therefore, very concerned with making sure that his force was not going to be surprised by the Americans.

Abe's two battleships sailed in column, the flagship *Hiei* followed by her sister ship, the *Kirishima*. Directly ahead of them was the light cruiser *Nagara* with three destroyers fanned out on either side of her. Five miles ahead of this inner screen was another one formed by five more destroyers. Some of his captains thought this was just a cruising formation and that the Admiral would concentrate his destroyers for possible aggressive action before they arrived off Guadalcanal. Such was not the Admiral's intention.

During the afternoon Abe felt that his luck was in. His ships were enveloped by the dense, driving rain of a tropical squall. This was fine protection and the squall was proceeding right along Abe's course and at his speed. At eighteen knots his ships drove southward, though the visibility made such speed a bit dangerous.

As midnight approached Abe was nearing Guadalcanal. An Army radio on Guadalcanal told him the weather there was atrocious. The storm was probably passing over the island and the Admiral did not want to mill about, bombarding the airfield in any such weather. He signaled his entire formation to prepare to reverse course, each ship simultaneously. Now things started to go wrong for Abe. Two of the destroyers in his advance screen, five miles ahead, failed to acknowledge the order. Radio transmissions in such weather were never perfect.

While Abe waited for all ships to acknowledge the 180°

course change, the five destroyers of the advance screen had to change course anyway as they were in immediate danger of ramming right into Guadalcanal. Finally the order came from the Admiral and the ships turned. For a half hour they sailed away from Guadalcanal and at a reduced speed of twelve knots. Then, as the weather cleared, Abe ordered all ships about again, speed to be increased, and headed back toward the island.

The battleships *Hiei* and *Kirishima* were still in column with the cruiser *Nagara* ahead of them and three destroyers screening on either side. But the advance screen of five destroyers was in confusion. The emergency turn to avoid Guadalcanal, bad radio transmissions and the change in speed had split them. Only two, the destroyers *Yudachi* and *Harusame*, were ahead of Abe. The other three had ended up behind him. Nor did Abe now know exactly where any of those five destroyers of the advance screen were.

Around the 14-inch gun turrets of *Hiei* and *Kirishima* crewmen were stacking high explosive bombardment ammunition. Abe, as his ships steamed between Guadalcanal and Savo Island and made for the Marines' perimeter, had had no report of major opposition. His destroyers would be more than adequate to deal with the American PT boats if they showed up.

At 1:24 A.M. Callaghan's column was sailing past the Marines' position. A message came to the Admiral from the *Helena's* radar. "Contacts bearing 312 and 310, distance 27,000 and 32,000 yards." Rapidly the range closed as Abe and Callaghan approached each other at better than thirty yards a second. Callaghan, wanting close action, ordered his column onto a course of due north, a collision course with the Japanese. The minutes passed with no further orders from the *San Francisco*. The Japanese battleships with their bombardment ammunition piled out on deck were like powder magazines waiting for a match but Callaghan gave no order to open fire. He could not know the opportunity Abe had given him. He wanted no long-range duel with the Japanese 14-inch guns. He wanted to get in close. All this time Abe, without any radar, was sailing on in blissful ignorance of what was to come.

Seventeen minutes after the *Helena* had gotten the Japanese on radar, things became visual. Leading Abe's group was Commander Kiyoshi Kikkawa in the destroyer *Yudachi* with the destroyer *Harusame* astern. Kikkawa was peering intently into the starlit night. He wasn't looking for Americans but for those other three destroyers of the advance screen that were meant to be up front with him. At 1:41, off to his right and 3,000 yards away, he saw a destroyer. It was the *Cushing*, lead ship of Callaghan's column.

Kikkawa's ship was not ready for a fight so he got off an enemy-in-sight message to Abe and called for hard left rudder and full speed. Abe got Kikkawa's message. The Americans were 3,000 yards from the *Yudachi* but where was the *Yudachi*? After the confusing countermarches few of the Japanese captains knew the precise location of any other Japanese ship unless they could see it. Frantically the crewmen of the *Hiei* and *Kirishima* got those bombardment shells off the deck. Abe's battleships plowed on still half-blind.

Just as Kikkawa had sighted the *Cushing* so had Commander Stokes sighted the *Yudachi* and *Harusame*. He called for hard left rudder, both to avoid collision and to get into position to fire torpedoes. The *Laffey*, *Sterett* and *O'Bannon* followed with emergency turns. Behind them Norman Scott's *Atlanta*, bigger and heavier than the destroyers, had to swing hard. Over the voice radio to the *Atlanta* came Callaghan from the *San Francisco* right astern. "What are you doing?" "Avoiding our own destroyers," was the answer.[13]

The *San Francisco*'s officer of the deck shouted down the voice tube, "The *Atlanta*'s turning left! Shall I follow her?" "No. Hold your course." Then within seconds, "Follow the *Atlanta*." [14]

As the *San Francisco* swung into the *Atlanta*'s wake Japanese searchlights snapped on and the *Atlanta*, now swinging to her right and across the *San Francisco*'s bow, opened fire. The searchlights went off but not before gunners on the *Hiei* had gotten the range, about 5,500 yards, point-blank for the big 14-inchers. The *Hiei* swung a bit to her left to bring all eight big guns to bear and then she murdered the *Atlanta*.

[13] Morison, *The Struggle for Guadalcanal*, p. 242.
[14] McCandless, *The San Francisco Story*, p. 40.

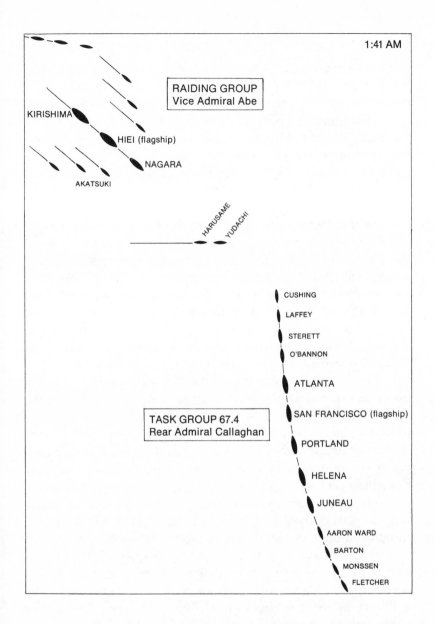

1:41 AM

RAIDING GROUP
Vice Admiral Abe

KIRISHIMA

HIEI (flagship)

NAGARA

AKATSUKI

HARUSAME

YUDACHI

CUSHING

LAFFEY

STERETT

O'BANNON

ATLANTA

SAN FRANCISCO (flagship)

TASK GROUP 67.4
Rear Admiral Callaghan

PORTLAND

HELENA

JUNEAU

AARON WARD

BARTON

MONSSEN

FLETCHER

ENEMY IN SIGHT The destroyers *Yudachi* and *Cushing* sighted each other simultaneously at 3,000 yards. Admiral Abe was caught by surprise, his two battleships the *Hiei* and *Kirishima* being ready to bombard Henderson Field rather than fight American ships. Admiral Callaghan ordered his ships to plow straight on into the Japanese, hoping that his cruisers could cripple the Japanese battleships at point-blank range. He was willing to sacrifice his task group to save Henderson Field.

Within moments the light cruiser was more of a slaughter-house than a fighting ship. On the bridge Rear Admiral Norman Scott and all but one of his staff were wiped out.

The Japanese destroyer *Akatsuke*, off the starboard bow of the *Hiei*, had the *Atlanta's* range too. Her torpedoes slipped into the water and ran straight to their target. There were a thousand pounds of high explosive in each of them and when they hit they lifted the *Atlanta* from the water and smacked her down a listing, burning, dying ship.

As the *Atlanta* was blasted out of the battle, Commander Stokes' four van destroyers came into action. The *Cushing*, in the lead, fired at the Japanese destroyers but was hit amidships and slowed to what seemed like a crawl. Then she spotted the massive bulk of the *Hiei* bearing down on her from the northwest. Slowly the crippled *Cushing* swung right to unmask her torpedo tubes. With the *Hiei* a bare 1,000 yards off, the *Cushing* let go with a six-torpedo salvo. At such a range it was impossible to miss. But nothing happened.

The *Cushing's* torpedoes had failed to explode, a not unusual occurrence with American torpedoes in the early months of the war. They had been equipped with an overly complex exploder device which the United States Navy's Bureau of Ordnance had developed in peacetime. This exploder was literally so complex that much of the time it didn't work. As peacetime economy had forbidden live torpedo trials and had permitted only dummy runs, the fact that the United States torpedoes were duds had been kept very quiet. Nor had anything been done to correct the situation in the Navy's torpedo factory at Newport, Rhode Island, where employment had been a matter of political patronage, where shoddy labor had been protected and where inefficiency had flourished. The gallantry of the *Cushing's* attack had been cancelled out by American corruption.

Coming up behind the crippled *Cushing*, the destroyer *Laffey* swung violently to avoid the *Hiei*, which passed so close to her stern that the *Laffey's* men could spray her with machine gun fire. The *Hiei's* captain was killed and Admiral Abe wounded by *Laffey's* fire. But as the American destroyer pulled away the *Hiei's* big 14-inch guns swung out and put two shells into her while a Japanese destroyer added a torpedo. *Laffey*'s captain ordered, "Abandon ship," an order which he himself did not follow, and many of her crew got off into the water. As the *Laffey* went down, her depth charges exploded and most of those in the water were crushed in the explosions.

Behind the *Laffey* came the *Sterett*. She had gotten the order to all ships Callaghan had sent out from the *San Francisco*—"Odd ships commence fire to starboard, even ships to port." The action with the *Hiei* was to port and the *Sterett* was an odd-numbered ship, being third in line. Dutifully she engaged to starboard but Japanese fire from port almost knocked her out. Her steering went out but, using her engines, the captain swung her around for a torpedo attack on the *Hiei* at 2,000 yards. Once again American torpedoes failed. The *Sterett*, her engines fortunately intact, limped off into the night.

Behind her the *O'Bannon* snaked her way past the crippled remnants of Destroyer Division 10 and took on the *Hiei* herself. She, too, fired torpedoes with no effect but her 5-inch guns peppered the big battleship's superstructure. The *Hiei* was beginning to burn and the *O'Bannon* was in so close that the *Hiei* couldn't aim her big guns low enough to hit her. The *O'Bannon* escaped to the southward still puzzled by an order she received, along with all other ships, from Callaghan. "Cease firing own ships."

The command had been meant for the *San Francisco* alone but had gone out to all ships by error. Callaghan's flagship had been firing at Japanese ships when the drifting *Atlanta* had come between them, right into the line of fire, taking some of the *San Francisco*'s 8-inch shells on board. But the *San Francisco* had already partially avenged the *Atlanta*, blasting the destroyer *Akatsuke* to the bottom with most of her crew.

Any thought of maintaining a cease-fire and of sorting out the wild melee of the battle vanished from Callaghan's mind. There was the *Hiei* crossing *San Francisco*'s bow and behind her was the *Kirishima*. Daniel J. Callaghan gave his last order—"We want the big ones. Get the big ones!" [15]

[15] Morison, *The Struggle for Guadalcanal*, p. 258.

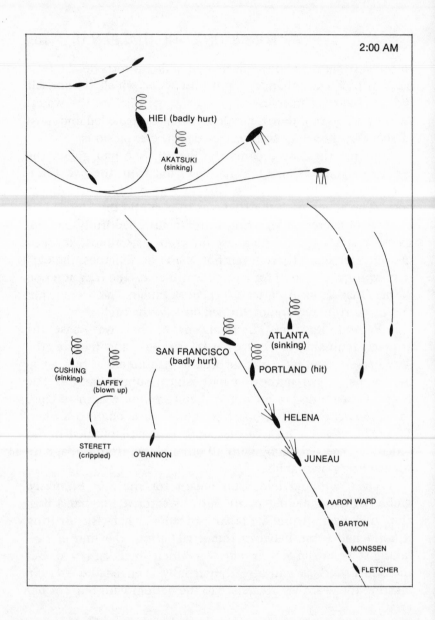

HIEI (badly hurt)

AKATSUKI
(sinking)

ATLANTA
(sinking)

SAN FRANCISCO
(badly hurt)

PORTLAND (hit)

CUSHING
(sinking)

LAFFEY
(blown up)

HELENA

STERETT
(crippled)

O'BANNON

JUNEAU

AARON WARD

BARTON

MONSSEN

FLETCHER

THE MELEE The leading destroyers *Cushing, Laffey, Sterett* and *O'Bannon* were beaten back after their defective torpedoes failed to explode. Callaghan's cruisers got in some crippling hits on the Japanese flagship *Hiei* but the *Atlanta* was torpedoed and left in sinking condition. The *San Francisco* and *Portland* were disabled, and Callaghan killed by Japanese guns. Japanese destroyers moved down to attack the rear of the American column where they torpedoed the cruiser *Juneau* and sunk the destroyers *Barton* and *Monssen*. But Admiral Abe, his flagship disabled, ordered a retreat and Henderson Field was saved.

The *San Francisco* got in the first salvo, slightly short but with one shell hitting the *Hiei*. Her gunnery officer went to rapid fire and her 8-inch guns, at about 2,000 yards, raked Abe's flagship. The *Hiei*, already hurt by Commander Stokes' four destroyers, was slow in firing and her first two salvos missed.

Only for moments did the *San Francisco*'s luck hold. The light cruiser *Nagara* began putting 5-inch shells into her from starboard, hitting with her second salvo from 3,000 yards. Then the battleship *Kirishima* opened up and the *Hiei*'s gunners got the range, not only with their big guns but the 6-inchers of her secondary batteries as well. It was a killing cross fire. Callaghan and his staff were killed, Captain Cassin Young mortally wounded. With her steering temporarily gone, the *San Francisco* swung away to port with forty-five hits on her. No Japanese torpedo had struck, though, and her wounds were not mortal, but she was out of the fight with over 80 crewmen dead and 100 seriously wounded.

The heavy cruiser *Portland* came up astern of the *San Francisco* and got a few damaging hits into the *Hiei*. Then a Japanese destroyer got a torpedo into the *Portland*'s stern, twisting it into a sort of grotesque rudder which forced the cruiser into performing aimless circles.

Admiral Abe had had enough by this time. The *Hiei* had taken more than fifty hits from the American cruisers and destroyers and was already a cripple. Abe ordered both battleships to retreat northward. The *Kirishima*, hit only once, pulled quickly out of action and headed north up the Slot to safety, but the *Hiei*'s steering was gone and all she could do was limp to the north of Savo Island where there was no safety.

As the Japanese battleships withdrew, the *Helena* came up with Captain Gilbert Hoover carefully picking his way through the wreckage. Behind the *Helena* came the *Juneau* and the four, tail-end destroyers. There were plenty of targets for now the Japanese destroyers had turned to attack the American column.

"Get ready, fishermen," ordered Tameichi Hara commanding the *Amatsukaze*.[16] Here was one of the best torpedo attack men in the Imperial Navy. He also had first-class torpe-

---

[16] Hara, Saito and Pineau, *Japanese Destroyer Captain*, p. 144.

does. His first salvo caught the destroyer *Barton* of the rear division. Two torpedoes broke her in half and she went down instantly taking her captain and nine out of every ten crewmen with her.

Hara doubled back to the north where he could make out the burning *Hiei*. Again he launched his torpedoes and this time one smashed into the light cruiser *Juneau*, astern of the *Helena*. The *Juneau* went dead in the water, out of the fight and struggling to keep afloat.

Nor did the other rear destroyers escape after the *Barton* had so suddenly gone down. Ahead of the *Barton*, the division leader, *Aaron Ward* was badly hit and barely underway while behind her the destroyer *Monssen*, taking thirty-seven hits, was a blazing wreck.

Tail-ender of the American formation, the destroyer *Fletcher*, was equipped with the latest search radar and had a skipper, Commander William Cole, who knew how to use it. At thirty-five knots he took the *Fletcher* through the shambles, picked his targets carefully and got his share of hits. Not a single Japanese shell or torpedo touched the *Fletcher*.

The battle rapidly petered out as the Japanese destroyers, their torpedo tubes empty, followed their battleships north in retreat. Callaghan's task force was a shambles with only the cruiser *Helena* and the destroyer *Fletcher* undamaged. But Henderson Field had not been obliterated as the Japanese had planned. Callaghan, now lying dead on the bridge of the *San Francisco*, had stopped them. That had been his mission.

At dawn the sea off Guadalcanal was littered with the wreckage of battle. The destroyers *Cushing* and *Monssen* were there, still afloat but burning and soon to go down. The Japanese *Yudachi*, who had made the first sighting of the American force, was there, too, abandoned but floating. The *Portland*, still steering in circles, poured some 8-inch salvos into the *Yudachi* and sent her down. North of Savo Island lay the rudderless *Hiei*, victim of eighty-five American hits. She could still shoot. At thirteen miles her big guns reached out for the engineless *Aaron Ward* but missed. A Navy tug finally towed the *Aaron Ward* out of the *Hiei*'s range and into the sanctuary of Tulagi harbor.

Almost off the Marine perimeter lay the crippled *Atlanta*, not quite dead. One Japanese bomber coming in too close was shot down. Efforts to save the *Atlanta* proved futile and after a day-long struggle her crew set demolition charges and in the early evening the *Atlanta* went under. But the *Portland* was saved. With the Navy tug *Bobolink* lashed onto her bow she could steer something resembling a straight course. That night she was eased into Tulagi.

The *Hiei* now paid for her failure to bombard Henderson Field. Joined by planes from the *Enterprise* moving up from the south, the Henderson fliers went after the big battleship with a vengeance. Even the big B-17's from rear bases came up to join in. Battleships are not good targets for high-level bombing and what counted were the torpedoes slammed into her. By early afternoon Japanese destroyers had taken off her crew and Admiral Abe. Then the "big boy" that Callaghan had wanted so badly went under.

The sad remnant of Callaghan's force was gathered together under Captain Hoover of the *Helena* and led slowly away from the battlefield. Hoover sent the destroyer *O'Bannon* ahead to radio Halsey the results of the battle. Behind the *Helena* came the badly crippled cruisers, *San Francisco* and *Juneau*. For an anti-submarine screen Hoover had only two destroyers. It was not enough. A Japanese submarine got off a spread of torpedoes at the formation. The *San Francisco* had a close call but the *Juneau* caught one of the torpedoes right under her bridge. There was an enormous explosion and in a cataclysm of fire and smoke, the *Juneau* disintegrated.

With Japanese submarines around, it was out of the question for Hoover to stay around and hunt for survivors. He radioed his position to a passing B-17 but, for some reason never discovered, the message was not relayed on to Halsey's headquarters. The handful of the *Juneau*'s men who survived the explosion had to fight thirst and sharks and one survived on a life raft for a week. He and nine others were all that lived of the *Juneau*'s 700-man crew. All five Sullivan brothers died with their ship, and after that the Navy refused to let so many members of one family serve together.

A final casualty of the night's battle was Vice Admiral Hiroaki Abe. He had failed in his mission and Yamamoto was in no mood to forgive failure. Abe ended up facing a court of enquiry and being deprived of any further command at sea. Most Japanese officers would have preferred the fate of Daniel Callaghan.

"Your objective, transports."

NOVEMBER 13–14, 1942

When word reached Yamamoto's headquarters that Abe had failed in his mission to bombard Henderson Field, Tanaka's eleven Japanese transports were turned around and headed back out of harm's way. With Henderson Field, which now boasted two adjacent fighter strips, still in operation, Yamamoto's whole schedule was thrown out of kilter. But there was one bright spot. Abe had failed to bombard, but he had all but wiped out the defending United States cruiser force.

Yamamoto ordered another bombardment of the American airfields for that night and ordered Tanaka to turn the transports around and, once again, head back for Guadalcanal. Tanaka knew that this was now a patched-up operation, and he had little confidence in patched-up operations. He obeyed his orders but with his faith in success severely diminished. But it would take a lot more than lack of faith to deter Tanaka, for it was not without reason that he was now being called by his enemies, "Tenacious" Tanaka.

As Tanaka's transports came down the Slot, what was left of United States sea power in the area was coming up from New Caledonia to meet them. The force was made up of the aircraft carrier *Enterprise* and the battleships *Washington* and *South Dakota* with supporting small ships. The force was proceeding north in the direction of Guadalcanal, but only very slowly. The *Enterprise* was still suffering from the bomb hits she had taken at the Battle of the Santa Cruz Islands. Her forward elevator was jammed and flight operations were difficult. What's worse, she had to contend with a southerly wind and that meant that, whenever taking off or landing planes, she had to reverse course to take advantage of that southerly wind. The battleships stayed with the carrier to give her the protection of their powerful anti-aircraft batteries.

Back in New Caledonia, Halsey's staff was putting together what scraps of intelligence it could and by late afternoon had reached the conclusion that the Japanese would be active off Guadalcanal again that night. Halsey sent out orders for the battleships *Washington* and *South Dakota* to be detached from their carrier escort duty and rushed up to Guadalcanal to take care of whatever the Japanese had in mind. But, due to that southerly wind, the task force was nowhere near as far north as Halsey hoped. The battleships were not close enough for a run in to the island that night. Guadalcanal would have to go it alone.

Fortunately for the Marines, Yamamoto was not sending battleships again. His bombardment force was two heavy cruisers. These two threw 1,000 shells into the Marines' airfields that night, but it was nothing like the awesome battleship bombardment of the month before. Less than twenty planes were total wrecks and Henderson had started the night with, for the first time, over 100 operational planes. When dawn came on the 14th, there were plenty of planes left.

In the morning the retiring Japanese cruisers got a going-over. Three were damaged but the *Kinugasa*, which had escaped the Battle of Cape Esperance with mere scratches, was sent to the bottom. Sinking a Japanese cruiser was a good beginning to the day, but *Kinugasa* was only an hors d'oeuvre for the fliers. Halsey made that quite clear with a three-word message, "Your objective, transports." [17]

Tanaka's force had been spotted early in the morning. He had his eleven transports formed in four columns, steaming southward at eleven knots. Ahead of them, Tanaka's eleven destroyers formed a V-shaped wedge, but with nothing but light anti-aircraft guns to fight with. Japanese air cover didn't amount to much.

It was for this moment that the Marines and soldiers had held their lines against the Japanese Army in October and for which Callaghan's sailors had sacrificed so much. Henderson Field had been kept in operation and now its planes roared up the Slot after Admiral Tanaka. Planes from the *Enterprise*,

---

[17] Halsey and Bryan, p. 130.

still far to the south, joined in and so did some big B-17's from Army bases on New Caledonia.

From noon until dusk the American planes hammered at the Japanese convoy. Torpedo planes came lumbering in low, barely missing the crest of the waves. Dive-bombers winged down from clouds. Marine and Navy fighters smashed the few escorting Japanese Zeros. Tanaka's destroyers, working at top speed, threw smoke screens around the madly zigzagging transports, while throwing up every bit of anti-aircraft fire they could. But the United States attack was overwhelming and it was pressed home inexorably.

Early in the afternoon, two of the Japanese transports were hit by the torpedo planes and went down. A third transport, with the commander of all the Japanese troops on board, took a terrible pasting from the bombers and limped off, back to the north, out of action. The eight remaining transports continued down the Slot but, with all their zigzagging and course changes, now well behind schedule.

Two more big American attacks came in during the early afternoon and three more transports went down burning from bomb hits. With superb seamanship Tanaka's destroyer captains maneuvered close to the burning transports and took off thousands of survivors. In the early evening yet another transport was lost, and as night finally offered its protection there were only four left.

These four, even at top speed, could not now arrive off Guadalcanal before dawn of the 15th, and Tanaka had reports that United States warships were gathering to hit him during the night. Orders to proceed came from Yamamoto, and Tanaka was told that powerful Japanese forces were coming down to help.

Powerful forces they were. This time Vice Admiral Nobutake Kondo was coming himself. The battleship *Kirishima* would be back with two heavy cruisers, the *Atago* and *Takao,* two light cruisers, the *Sendai* and *Nagara,* and nine destroyers. Kondo expected to find only United States cruisers opposing him. He intended to fight them off and then give Henderson Field the bombardment which Abe had failed to deliver.

The Washington *and Lee Stomp*

Detached on Halsey's order from Kincaid's group was Task Force 64, the battleships *Washington* and *South Dakota* with four destroyers screening—*Walke, Benham, Gwin* and *Preston*. By four in the afternoon, Rear Admiral Willis Augustus Lee knew that a big Japanese force was headed for Guadalcanal and he made ready for battle. His reliance was on his new battleships, each with nine 16-inch guns. But they had not sailed together before. His four destroyers were each from a different division and were given him only because they had more fuel aboard than any others. Lee's task force was a scratch force but it had one big plus—Willis A. Lee was a pro. He knew how to handle the big ships and he knew his radar.

By ten that evening Lee's task force with his four destroyers leading the battleships in column, having circled around Savo Island to the north, were headed southward. Lee knew there were Japanese coming but that was all.

They were coming—and right behind him. First was a screening force, the light cruiser *Sendai* and three destroyers under Rear Admiral Hashimoto. About three miles behind was another screen, the light cruiser *Nagara* and four destroyers under Rear Admiral Kimura. Behind that screen was Vice Admiral Kondo himself with his flag flying from the heavy cruiser *Atago,* screened by two more destroyers and followed by the heavy cruiser *Takao* and the battleship *Kirishima.*

Hashimoto in the light cruiser *Sendai,* sailing well ahead, was there to give warning of any American ships and at ten minutes after ten he did just that, but inaccurately. Peering through their night binoculars, Hashimoto's officers thought they made out two United States cruisers and four destroyers. They so informed Kondo who sent out his orders. Hashimoto with the *Sendai* and the destroyer *Shikinami* would keep after the Americans. His other two destroyers, the *Ayanami* and *Uranami* would peel off and head around Savo Island from the other side. Behind these two, Admiral Kimura would bring up the cruiser *Nagara* and four destroyers. Kondo, with the big bombardment ships, would mill about awaiting developments.

As Lee in the *Washington* turned to the west to sail be-

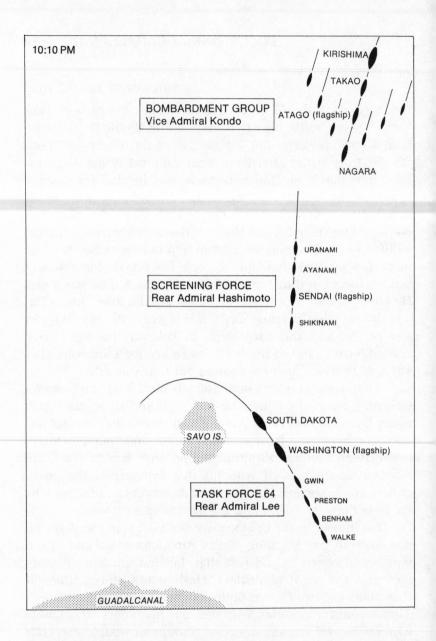

10:10 PM

KIRISHIMA

TAKAO

BOMBARDMENT GROUP
Vice Admiral Kondo

ATAGO (flagship)

NAGARA

URANAMI

AYANAMI

SCREENING FORCE
Rear Admiral Hashimoto

SENDAI (flagship)

SHIKINAMI

SOUTH DAKOTA

SAVO IS.

WASHINGTON (flagship)

GWIN

TASK FORCE 64
Rear Admiral Lee

PRESTON

BENHAM

WALKE

GUADALCANAL

JAPANESE ERROR The American task force of two battleships and four destroyers was sighted by the Japanese as it patrolled around Savo Island, but the Japanese screening force reported the ships as cruisers instead of battleships. Admiral Kondo decided to send his light cruisers *Sendai* and *Nagara* and seven destroyers to clear away the American ships while keeping the battleship *Kirishima* and two heavy cruisers *Atago* and *Takao* out of the fight. Kondo planned to use them to bombard Henderson Field later.

tween Savo and Guadalcanal, his radar picked up the *Sendai* and at 10:17 the *Washington* and *South Dakota* started throwing 16-inch shells at her. Hashimoto, realizing immediately that these were not cruisers, ordered his two ships to make smoke and get out fast.

Right after the American battleships opened up on Hashimoto the four destroyers ahead of them made out Hashimoto's two detached destroyers coming at them and then saw Kimura's force right behind them. The *Walke, Benham* and *Preston* opened fire and Japanese torpedomen took aim at the gun flashes. Both sides got some shell hits but then the big Japanese torpedos arrived. The *Walke* was hit in the bow, one of her guns blown 100 feet into the air and the whole front part of the ship torn away. In less than ten minutes she went down, taking her captain and seventy-five crewmen with her.

Behind the *Walke*, the *Benham* took a torpedo forward but with less disastrous results. She lost speed and began to settle by the bow, mortally wounded but with enough strength to pull away from the fight. Behind her, though, disaster came quickly to the *Preston* which tried a gun duel with the cruiser *Nagara* at rapidly diminishing ranges. The *Nagara*'s gunners fired with a precise fury that gutted the *Preston* in five minutes. Blasted and burning she rolled over and sank, going down with almost half her crew.

Tail-ender of the destroyers, the *Gwin*, picked her way through the debris, trading shots with the *Nagara* and her destroyers. The *Gwin*, hit in her engine room, was slowed to a crawl but went on firing as long as she was in range. It wasn't long as the action was now rapidly sweeping away to the west. Also limping away was the Japanese destroyer *Ayanami*. United States shells had put her in sinking condition, the only major Japanese casualty of the first minutes of the action.

The Japanese ships, attacking the Americans with Savo Island behind them, were obscure on the battleships' radar. Worse, Lee's fire power was cut in half. There was a failure of electric power throughout the *South Dakota*. Then, ahead of the *Washington*, loomed the wreckage of the destroyer force. Lee turned slightly south to steer around it. The *South Dakota*, running in foul luck that night, had to swerve right to avoid

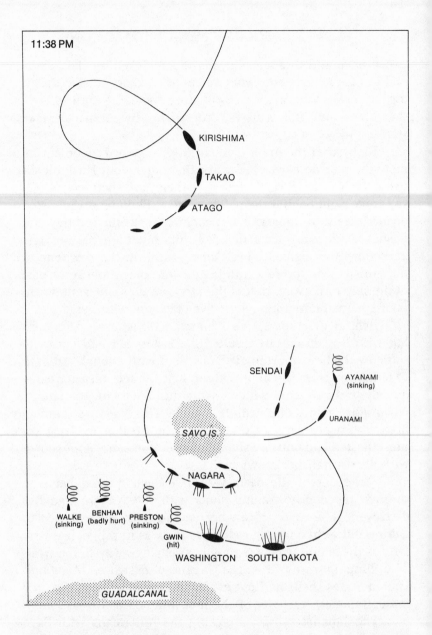

11:38 PM

KIRISHIMA

TAKAO

ATAGO

SENDAI

AYANAMI
(sinking)

URANAMI

SAVO IS.

NAGARA

WALKE
(sinking)

BENHAM
(badly hurt)

PRESTON
(sinking)

GWIN
(hit)

WASHINGTON   SOUTH DAKOTA

GUADALCANAL

FIRST ROUND TO JAPAN   The big guns of the American battleships sank the Japanese destroyer *Ayanami* but American gunnery radar was ineffective against the cruiser *Nagara* and four destroyers, as they had Savo Island directly behind them. As the Japanese heavy force to the north prepared to enter the battle, the American battleship *South Dakota* was silenced by an electrical failure. Of the United States force, only Admiral Lee's flagship, the *Washington,* was left in action.

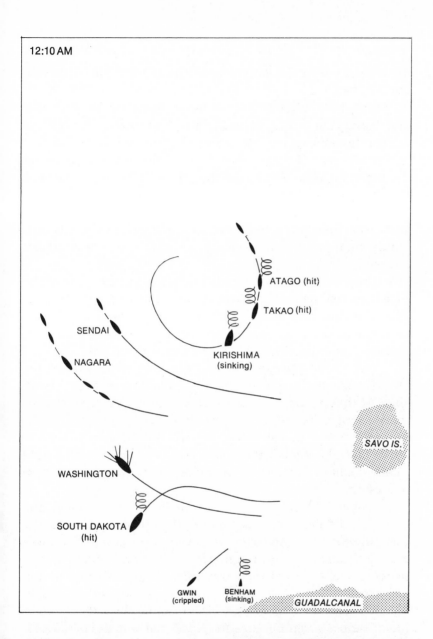

12:10 AM

ATAGO (hit)

TAKAO (hit)

SENDAI

KIRISHIMA
(sinking)

NAGARA

SAVO IS.

WASHINGTON

SOUTH DAKOTA
(hit)

GWIN
(crippled)

BENHAM
(sinking)

GUADALCANAL

LAST ROUND TO THE UNITED STATES NAVY With his destroyers out of action and the *South Dakota* hit by Japanese shells
and retreating, Admiral Lee took on the Japanese single-handed.
The *Washington's* nine 16-inch guns, firing at 8,400 yards put the
Kirishima out of action in seven minutes and damaged Kondo's two
heavy cruisers, the *Atago* and *Takao*. Kondo gave up the fight and
ordered a general retreat at 12:25 A. M. The *Washington* remained
in solitary possession of the sea.

the mortally hurt *Benham*. This maneuver put the flames of the American destroyers right behind the *South Dakota* silhouetting her. Admiral Kimura on *Nagara* got a good look at her and sent out an urgent call to Kondo. His men got off almost three dozen torpedoes but this time they all missed.

Vice Admiral Kondo, though, saw his chance and moved the main Japanese force into the attack. The *South Dakota's* electricity came back on but by now she had lost track of the *Washington*. She moved on steadily to the west, ignorant of what was ahead until suddenly, at 5,000 yards, she was brilliantly illuminated by the searchlights of Kondo's screening destroyers.

Then the *South Dakota* was hit by the 14-inch guns of the *Kirishima* and by the 8-inchers of Kondo's two heavy cruisers. The hits told. One of her 16-inch turrets was crippled and, even worse, her radar was destroyed. Fires were beginning to take hold and the *South Dakota* was in trouble.

Lee, in the *Washington*, had come out from behind his own wrecked destroyers and his radar had locked on to a large ship. At that moment the *South Dakota* was in a blind spot of the *Washington's* radar, and Lee could not be sure what ship his radar screen was showing. But when the Japanese searchlights had illuminated the *South Dakota*, Lee was no longer in any doubt. The target on his radar screen was the Japanese battleship.

Just as Callaghan had two nights before, Lee wanted "the big one." His flagship, *Washington*, thus proceeded to deliver upon the *Kirishima* the awesome destructive power of a modern battleship. In seven minutes her huge 16-inch armorpiercing shells gouged their way into the Japanese battleship at least nine times. The ten rapid-fire 5-inchers of the *Washington's* secondary broadside got in better than three dozen hits. In those seven minutes the *Kirishima* was disemboweled. She veered out of line, her decks a mass of flames, her steering gear wrecked.

Lee had lost contact with the *South Dakota*, whose radio was out. He hoped she was retiring and not sunk. His hopes were fulfilled as the *South Dakota* was indeed pulling away. Lee drove on and turned slightly toward the north. He wanted to draw the Japanese away from his cripples and block any transports coming down from the north. At twenty minutes past midnight Lee turned even more to the north and his radar screen now showed the Japanese cruisers and destroyers scurrying away from the battle area. The *Kirishima* had been abandoned and her sea valves opened to hasten her sinking.

The lone *Washington* now sailed the waters off Guadalcanal in solitary splendor. When it became obvious that if Tanaka cared to bring the last of the Japanese transports down to Guadalcanal, he would have to do it in daylight, Lee turned the *Washington* away to the south. He knew that the Henderson Field fliers could take care of them in the daylight.

Tanaka did keep on coming with the four transports which he had left. He knew, too, what the American fliers could and would do to him. He radioed back to headquarters for permission to proceed at full speed and ram his transports ashore. Admiral Kondo gave his consent and, at dawn, the four Japanese transports ran themselves onto Guadalcanal. They were beached only fifteen miles from Henderson Field and, almost immediately, began to take a tremendous pounding from the American planes. Marine artillery joined in at extreme range and very little was brought ashore by the Japanese. Later in the morning a United States destroyer arrived and pounded away at what few supplies had been landed.

When all the American bombing and shelling was done, it was time for the Japanese Army on Guadalcanal to assess the full measure of the Japanese Navy's defeat. The Navy had set out to deliver 10,000 troops and 10,000 tons of supplies to the island. What arrived were 2,000 troops along with 260 cases of ammunition and 1,500 bags of rice. It was the rice that was really important as the Japanese Army on Guadalcanal was beginning to starve. At a cost of two battleships, the Imperial Navy had delivered only one-twentieth of a bag of rice per man.

Back at headquarters, Admiral Halsey summed up the new strategic situation—"We've got the bastards licked!" [18]

---

[18] Halsey and Bryan, p. 130.

Guadalcanal Stalemate

NOVEMBER 18–23, 1942

Three days after the *Washington*'s guns had sunk the *Kiri-shima*, General Vandegrift started another offensive westward across the Matanikau against General Hyakutake's Japanese. Hyakutake's army was crippled by lack of supplies but it was far from dead. The courage of its infantrymen had been wasted by the stupidity of their leaders in the attacks of the past three months. But now that same courage was to be used on the defensive with tactical brilliance.

The American attack got underway on November 18th as two battalions of the Army's 182nd Infantry crossed the Matanikau. For two days their main opposition was more from the tropical heat and humidity of the jungle than from the Japanese. These troops, less than a week on the island, made slow progress.

On the morning of the third day, the 20th, the Japanese found a gap between the two battalions, hit it and broke the American lines. Army General Sebree, commanding the advance under Vandegrift, came forward himself. The retreat of the shaken battalions was stopped and they turned back to the advance. Sebree's men got back to their original positions but could go no further.

Sebree now brought up reinforcements, the jungle veterans of the 164th Infantry who had fought alongside the Marines in defense of Henderson Field in October. The two Army regiments attacked. They were now up against a Japanese position dug into the reverse slope of the hills where United States artillery and mortars could not get at them. Once the American infantrymen got over the crest of a hill they were caught in interlocking machine gun and rifle fire from positions so well camouflaged as to be invisible a few yards away. The Japanese positions, mutually supporting and organized in depth, were covered by the small Japanese mortars whose accuracy soon became something of a legend. The jungle across the Matanikau was cut by deep, sharply-sided ravines and was not easy ground for an attacker.

Sebree's Army infantry did its best but its gains were measured only in yards. Sebree was determined to move forward and called up his reserve, the 8th Marine Regiment. The 8th Marines, who had arrived on Guadalcanal early in the month, were cocky. They had heard stories that the Army men had panicked when the Japanese attacked. They were out to show the Army how it was done. On November 23rd, advancing behind a 2,600-shell barrage, the Marines went forward with the confidence of élite troops. All day they ran into the same deadly cross fire that had met the soldiers. The results were the same, gains measured only in yards. Vandegrift called off the attack.

The alternative to head-on assaults against the Japanese was to outflank them and for operations of this nature a good many more American troops would be necessary. It would be many weeks before they could be assembled on the island but when they all got there, they would find Vandegrift and the 1st Marine Division gone. These were the men who had come to establish a beachhead, seize and hold the airfield. That they had done against everything from bayonet charges to battleship bombardment. They were a ragged, sickly, miserable bunch as they boarded their transports. They were, after all, the men of a division where a man had to run a temperature of 103° before he was considered sick. They were the victors.

As the 1st Marine Division left, the new troops began to arrive. Two Army divisions and one Marine division would be assembled under Army Major General Alexander Patch. Supplies of every kind were coming in and finally Guadalcanal was no longer the shoestring operation it had been ever since August when the first landing had been made.

On the other hand, the Japanese situation was deteriorating. General Hyakutake had to worry about keeping his troops alive. Gone forever were the days of planning surrender ceremonies for the Americans. Now his front-line troops were eating coconuts, bamboo sprouts, roots and sometimes grass. Disease was already claiming a death toll almost equal to the strength of a division. Hyakutake's army was withering away.

Tanaka Wins—and Loses

THE BATTLE OF TASSAFARONGA

NOVEMBER 30, 1942

The slaughter of the Japanese transports in mid-November had shown that ordinary methods of supply were totally ineffective. Henderson Field, with its plane total approaching 200 by the end of November, was a going concern. Japanese destroyers could run in at night with some safety, but if they stopped to unload supplies they could not run far enough before dawn to be out of range of Henderson's bombers. The Japanese Navy came up with an ingenious plan to eliminate the unloading time. Supplies were loaded in large metal drums and the drums were loaded and roped together on the decks of destroyers. Offshore the drums would be tossed overboard and then hauled ashore by small boats and the troops already ashore. The destroyers would waste no time in hauling out of range of the American fliers. It was a makeshift supply system and could provide but a fraction of what the troops really needed. The Japanese felt, though, that anything was worth a try.

The first attempt was scheduled for the night of November 30th and the man picked to lead it was the redoubtable Raizo Tanaka. He would take eight destroyers, two ready for action and six cluttered with those metal drums full of supplies. It was a far cry from the vast assemblage of battleships, cruisers and destroyers that had come south only two weeks before.

Back in early October Nimitz's staff in Pearl Harbor had seen the necessity for the creation of a United States task force with the specific purpose of derailing the Tokyo Express. But the chance to put one together in the South Pacific came only after the mid-November battles. Four heavy cruisers, one light, and four destroyers were brought together and on November 24th, just six days before Tanaka arrived with his eight destroyers, Admiral Thomas Kincaid arrived to command what was now called Task Force 67. Kincaid, experienced in the South Pacific and a brilliant fighting admiral, was exactly the right man for the job.

Kincaid lasted exactly four days, just enough time to work out an operational plan but far from time enough to train his group in night tactics. Pearl Harbor had seen fit to order Kincaid away to the North Pacific which was in somewhat of a mess but which was a far from vital sector. So on the 28th the relatively inexperienced Rear Admiral Carleton Herbert Wright, for some reason nicknamed "Bosco," arrived to take over Task Force 67. It turned out to be an unfortunate change in command.

Late on the night of the 29th, his first full day in command, Wright led Task Force 67 toward Guadalcanal. At twenty-eight knots his ships plowed on all through the daylight of the 30th. Wright had little idea of just what he might meet. United States intelligence was indefinite. Tanaka, sailing at the same time as Wright, also lacked specific intelligence as to just what to expect. Each Admiral, though, knew pretty well that there was trouble ahead.

Tanaka made his intentions quite clear to his Destroyer Squadron 2. He signaled his captains, "There is great possibility of an encounter with the enemy tonight. In such an event, utmost efforts must be made to destroy the enemy without regard for the unloading of supplies." [19] To destroy the enemy Tanaka had sixty-four torpedo tubes. Wright was counting on his gun power, thirty-four 8-inchers and fifteen 6-inchers. Wright, like Callaghan and Scott before him, had the advantage of radar.

In the early evening Wright's task force passed a convoy retiring from Guadalcanal. On Halsey's orders two destroyers of the convoy, the *Lamson* and *Lardner*, were detached to join Wright. Since he had no chance to give them his operations plan and as they were only equipped with old-style radar, Wright simply let them tag along at the end of his column.

Soon after ten-thirty Wright's force was sweeping westward along the Guadalcanal shore toward Savo Island. Tanaka was approaching from the north, prepared to sweep south of Savo, close the shore to within two miles and get those metal drums overboard. Ahead of his destroyer column, which he led in his flagship *Naganami*, Tanaka had stationed the destroyer

[19] Tanaka and Pineau, *Japan's Losing Struggle for Guadalcanal*, p. 826.

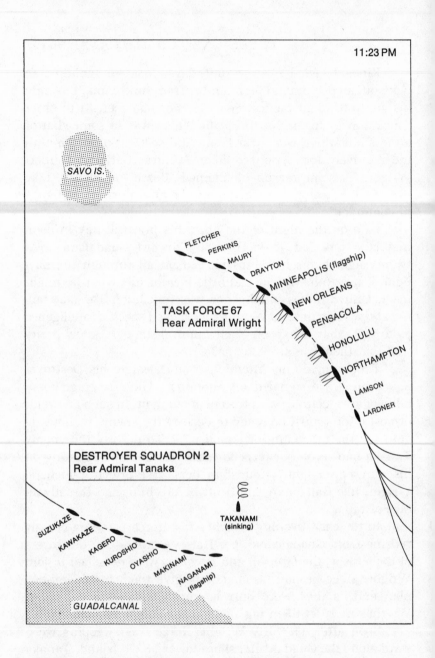

11:23 PM

SAVO IS.

FLETCHER
PERKINS
MAURY
DRAYTON
MINNEAPOLIS (flagship)

TASK FORCE 67
Rear Admiral Wright

NEW ORLEANS
PENSACOLA
HONOLULU
NORTHAMPTON
LAMSON
LARDNER

DESTROYER SQUADRON 2
Rear Admiral Tanaka

TAKANAMI
(sinking)

SUZUKAZE
KAWAKAZE
KAGERO
KUROSHIO
OYASHIO
MAKINAMI
NAGANAMI
(flagship)

GUADALCANAL

THE JAPANESE SURPRISED A powerful task force of five cruisers and six destroyers caught the Japanese destroyer squadron unloading supplies off Guadalcanal. The cruisers opened fire and destroyed the Japanese outpost destroyer *Takanami*. Admiral Tanaka ordered his ships to reverse course and counterattack with torpedoes.

Takanami as an outpost, a wise precaution. Kincaid's battle plan had envisaged sending two of his destroyers, those with the best radar, on ahead of the task force on a similar mission. This part of Kincaid's plan Wright had abandoned.

By eleven Tanaka had passed Savo Island and had closed the Guadalcanal shore. He slowed his ships to twelve knots so the drums could be jettisoned. The *Takanami* and the flagship *Naganami* were the only two unencumbered ships he had and they were ready to fight if they saw anything.

At 11:06 radar on Wright's flagship *Minneapolis* picked up Tanaka's force at 23,000 yards. Wright swung his ships simultaneously to the right bringing them into a column formation. Then he swung the column to the left to a parallel, but opposite, course to Tanaka's. Behind the *Minneapolis* came two more heavy cruisers, the *New Orleans* and *Pensacola*, then the light cruiser *Honolulu* and finally the heavy cruiser *Northampton*. Tagging along behind, a little like lost sheep, were the newly joined destroyers *Lamson* and *Lardner*. Two miles ahead of the cruiser column were Wright's own four destroyers, the *Fletcher*, *Perkins*, *Maury* and *Drayton* led by Commander William Cole in the *Fletcher*.

It was Cole's job to get in a torpedo attack and then haul clear while Wright's cruisers finished the job by gunfire. At 11:16, Cole, using the *Fletcher*'s first-class search radar, knew he was in the right position to attack. The Japanese were 7,000 yards on his port bow. He requested Wright's permission to attack. Wright hesitated. He asked Cole if the range were not too great. No, said Cole. Wright went on hesitating for four long minutes while the relative position of the two forces changed by two and a half miles. Finally Wright signaled Cole, "Go ahead and fire torpedoes." [20]

The four-minute delay was costly. The Japanese destroyers were pulling past Cole's and now the American torpedoes would have to chase the Japanese ships. What would have been an easy shot had become a hard one. Cole hoped that he had not been spotted by the Japanese and that his torpedoes would arrive as an unpleasant surprise. His four destroyers

[20] Jones, *Destroyer Squadron 23*, p. 13.

had twenty of them on the way to Tanaka. But then Cole, with utter astonishment, looked astern and saw Wright's cruisers open fire. Wright had waited too long to open fire with his torpedoes; now he just couldn't wait long enough to open fire with his big guns. Against the alerted Japanese, the United States torpedoes scored not a single hit.

Moments earlier, the outpost destroyer *Takanami* had flashed Tanaka an urgent message. "Enemy ships, bearing 100 degrees." Then, immediately after, "Seven enemy destroyers sighted." Tanaka had six destroyers behind him, all in the process of unloading those drums full of supplies. He did not hesitate. Tanaka signaled, "Stop unloading. Take battle stations." [21]

Then as Tanaka himself picked out the shapes of the American ships with his superlative night binoculars, star shells from the cruisers burst over his head. His destroyers cut loose the drums and worked up to top speed. There was no chance to form a perfect line of battle but that didn't make any difference. Tanaka knew that each of his captains was an expert at night torpedo attack. He did not question where they were or what they were doing. He just ordered, "Close and attack." [22]

The *Takanami*, out in front of Tanaka's column and closer to the Americans, was the biggest blip on the cruisers' radar screens. One by one the American ships opened on her but not before she had swung hard right and had launched her torpedoes. The *Takanami* was smothered by fire. The cruisers' heavy shells penetrated her thin hull with a red glow at the point of impact. "That's what I call shooting," exulted the gunnery officer of the *Pensacola*.[23] For the American cruisers it was the last good shooting of the night. But the *Takanami* was a dead ship.

Commander Cole's four destroyers had joined briefly in this firing. Then they veered away to the north around Savo Island. They were leaving Wright's cruisers a clear field of fire.

[21] Griffith, p. 220 and Tanaka and Pineau, p. 826.
[22] Griffith, p. 220.
[23] Jones, p. 15.

There would be no confusion about firing on friendly ships as there had been in the previous night battles.

The flashes from the cruiser guns that were tearing the *Takanami* apart were all the targets that Tanaka's expert torpedomen needed. His flagship, the *Naganami*, went into action instantly. Working up to forty knots, she swung right, steadied on a course parallel to Wright's and put eight torpedoes into the water.

Behind Tanaka, one by one, his other six destroyers came into action as quickly as they could. Against the dark background of Guadalcanal they made poor targets for the American gunners and none was hit. In the first minutes of the action they got off a dozen torpedoes to add to the eight Tanaka's flagship had fired. They were not long in arriving among Wright's cruisers.

These Japanese torpedoes came in at almost fifty knots, making them hard to dodge, and each one carried a half-ton of TNT as a warhead. Just as Wright's flagship, the heavy cruiser *Minneapolis*, got off her ninth salvo, she was hit by two of these big torpedoes. Her bow sagged, fires started and her speed dropped sharply. For a few moments her electric power held and her gunners got off three more salvoes. Then the *Minneapolis* staggered out of the battle, her pumps just barely keeping her afloat.

The *New Orleans*, next astern, swung hard to avoid a collision but as she did, took a torpedo in the forward magazine. At the stern a sailor reported she was passing over what he thought was the "sinking *Minneapolis*" but what he saw floating past him was 120 feet of the bow of his own ship. The *New Orleans*, too, was out of the fight with almost 200 of her crew dead.

Third in line, the *Pensacola*, saw the *New Orleans* swerve right and then catch a torpedo. The *Pensacola* swerved left and avoided the wreckage of the two heavy cruisers ahead of her. But the flames of the *Minneapolis* and *New Orleans* silhouetted her. Within ten minutes a Japanese torpedo got her, too. Sailors were trapped high on her foremast, a flaming torch from the burning oil tanks below. Only one man escaped from her after engine room. One hundred and twenty-five died.

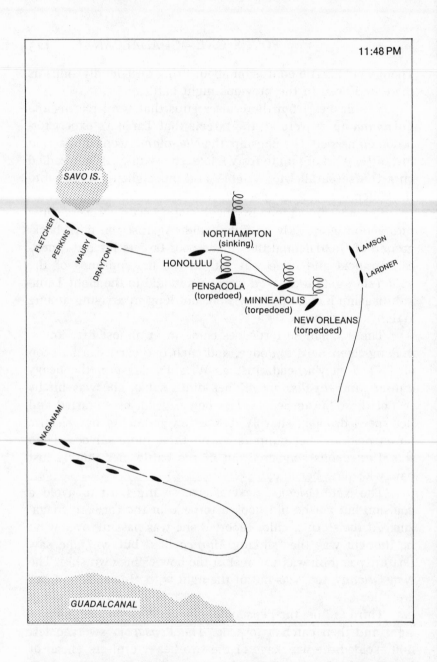

SAVO IS.

FLETCHER
PERKINS
MAURY
DRAYTON

NORTHAMPTON
(sinking)

HONOLULU

LAMSON

LARDNER

PENSACOLA
(torpedoed)

MINNEAPOLIS
(torpedoed)

NEW ORLEANS
(torpedoed)

NAGANAMI

GUADALCANAL

VICTORY FOR TANAKA'S TORPEDOES As the Japanese destroyers reversed course, the cruisers were unable to hit them. But Japanese torpedomen, with flashes of American guns to aim at, slaughtered the United States task force. Wright's flagship the *Minneapolis* and the cruisers *Pensacola* and *New Orleans* were crippled and the cruiser *Northampton* sunk.

Behind the *Pensacola*, the light cruiser *Honolulu* swung hard right, away from the Japanese, followed by the *Northampton*. The *Honolulu* dodged and swerved her way through wreckage and torpedo tracks, her fifteen 6-inch guns blazing like mad. She hit nothing, but then neither was she hit. The *Northampton*, though, heavier and slower than the *Honolulu*, couldn't dodge as fast. At 11:48, ten minutes after the *Pensacola* was hit, the *Northampton* took not one but two torpedoes and they were too much for her. She had two big holes in her and her entire stern was one big bonfire. But the *Northampton* sank slowly and all but fifty-four men were rescued.

At the tail end of the American formation the lost-sheep destroyers *Lamson* and *Lardner* swerved away from the damaged cruisers. They didn't even know the proper battle recognition lights for the night, and when shells came their way they simply hauled out. There was nothing they could do to help anyway. Tanaka was on his way home and the battle was over.

Of the United States cruisers only the *Northampton* went down that night. Since the August debacle off Savo Island, the Navy had learned a lot about damage control. Those lessons were now applied with both courage and efficiency. The *Pensacola, New Orleans* and *Minneapolis* were saved, but it would be a year before they were ready to fight again.

Tanaka made a clean getaway up the Slot with the loss of destroyer *Takanami* to mourn but a brilliant tactical victory to celebrate. But Tanaka's purpose that night had not been to sink American cruisers. It had been to deliver supplies to the Army and precious few of those metal drums got ashore. Naval victory or no naval victory, the hard fact was that the Japanese Army on Guadalcanal went right on starving.

MacArthur Makes His Move

BUNA-GONA

NOVEMBER, 1942

While the Japanese had concentrated their efforts on throwing the Marines off Guadalcanal, there had been no more interested spectator than General Douglas MacArthur, commander of the United States and Australian Forces, Southwest Pacific Theater. If Guadalcanal fell to the Japanese, MacArthur was sure that New Guinea would be next.

MacArthur was right. The Japanese summer attack over the Owen Stanley Mountains, which had come so close to MacArthur's headquarters at Port Moresby, had been called off in mid-September only because of the Japanese decision to concentrate all their resources on the recapture of Guadalcanal. The Japanese commander had been ordered to form a defensive perimeter around Buna and Gona on the north coast of New Guinea. When Guadalcanal was taken, he would then be reinforced for another advance on Port Moresby.

The Japanese withdrawal to the Buna-Gona area, however, was not the orderly affair which the Japanese planned. MacArthur ordered his Australian troops into the attack. Some of these were from Major General George Vasey's 7th Australian Division, veterans of the North African campaigns and just returned to the Far East. They harried and savaged the Japanese rearguards along the Kokoda Trail, back over the Owen Stanleys and into the coastal plain.

During the first half of November, MacArthur had built up his strength on the coastal plain preparatory to an attack to eliminate the Japanese in the Buna-Gona area. A master of improvisation, MacArthur had used air drops, then airstrips hacked out of the jungle underbrush to back up native porters back-packing supplies over the mountains. Around the eastern tip of New Guinea, more supplies came by outrigger canoes, rafts and coastal luggers. Just about everything that could move was pressed into service.

But all this time MacArthur had advanced over the Owen Stanleys with one eye cocked on Guadalcanal. Always, he kept a line of retreat open, for if there were a disaster at Henderson Field, MacArthur would have to pull back to Port Moresby, and quickly. In mid-November the news had come that the Japanese Navy had completely failed in its major attempt to get a large convoy through to Guadalcanal. The *Washington*'s guns battering the *Kirishima* had been like a signal to MacArthur that the time was ripe for an attack. A defensive battle had been won at Guadalcanal. Now on New Guinea, he would win an offensive one.

Besides Vasey's Australians, MacArthur now had two of the United States Army's 32nd Division regiments over the mountains and ready to attack. The Division's third regiment was already arriving at Port Moresby. This seemed like plenty, because all the generals on New Guinea seemed to be busily outdoing each other in underestimating the Japanese. On November 10th, General Willoughby, MacArthur's chief of intelligence, reported that the enemy had two depleted regiments to defend the Buna-Gona area. Four days later he downgraded that to one depleted regiment. Allied fliers could see few Japanese and little evidence of any fortifications.

What the fliers had missed was a Japanese line of defense so beautifully camouflaged that it was not only invisible to the aviators but, in many places, to an advancing infantryman three yards away. There were some concrete or steel pillboxes and a few large earthen blockhouses holding a garrison of thirty men. But, by the hundreds, there were the smaller coconut log bunkers. Foot-thick logs were used for supports and crossbeams. Walls were often reinforced by steel oil drums filled with sand and roofs covered not only with dirt and logs but sometimes with quarter-inch sheet steel as well. The bunkers were aligned in checkerboard fashion so that their fire would be mutually supporting. The line would have been a credit to the Western Front of 1914–18.

Out in front of the Japanese line was a defense almost as strong as those log bunkers, the malarial jungle swamp, in many places chest deep. There were drier patches where tall, stately coconut palms grew or, more commonly the four-foot high, sharp-edged kunai grass. Most areas were overgrown with scrub bush which was almost impenetrable. The rainy season had begun. Temperatures ran about 95° and the humidity about 85 percent. Those whom Japanese bullets missed could expect malaria, dengue fever, scrub typhus, dysentery or some form of jungle rot.

Instead of "one depleted regiment," the Japanese had 6,500 men, divided among three bridgeheads.[24] The battle zone was bisected by the swampy mouth of the Girua River with the Australians advancing to the west of the river, the

[24] Milner, *Victory in Papua*, p. 139.

Americans to the east of it. In the Australian sector the main Japanese position was around Sanananda Point where the Kokoda Trail terminated. Here Colonel Yokoyama had 3,000 men, half of them occupying a series of trail blocks three miles or so inland. Further west along the coast, at Gona, were a further 1,000 Japanese.

Immediately east of the river mouth, in the American sector, was Buna village, and the third Japanese bridgehead extended from there three miles along the coast to Cape Endaiadere. Navy Captain Yasuda was in command here and he had 2,500 men under him, 1,000 of them recently arrived veteran troops sent down from Rabaul. Japanese orders to the New Guinea commanders were explicit. They were to stand and fight until help could come. Yokoyama and Yasuda had every intention of obeying those orders whether help did or did not come.

For the assault of the Buna-Gona position the Allies were lacking some critical items. Medicines and food were in short supply. Even worse, for an assault on a powerful enemy line, there were few combat engineers, no tanks and almost no artillery. General Kenney, MacArthur's air commander, assured the foot soldiers that there was no need to worry. With superb overconfidence he stated, "The artillery in this theater flies." [25]

Of generals there were plenty. Above the two divisional commanders, Vasey of the Australian 7th and Harding of the American 32nd, was General Edmund Herring, an Australian, who commanded them both as C.O. Advance New Guinea Force. Over Herring was Sir Thomas Blamey, another Australian, who was commander of Allied land forces. Above Blamey was the Allied supreme commander, Douglas MacArthur, in Port Moresby.

Herring and Blamey were primarily interested in their Australians. Believing that there were few Japanese in the American area, they fixed their eyes on Sanananda and Gona. MacArthur did not disagree with this Australian estimate of the situation but his eye was fixed on General Harding's 32nd

[25] Milner, p. 135.

Division. What was wanted at MacArthur's headquarters was a smashing American victory. For MacArthur's headquarters, unlike the one Eisenhower was building in Europe, was not an Allied one. All staff section chiefs were American and they were all devoted MacArthur men.

These men were rather prone to see anti-MacArthur plots under every bed. There was always the Navy about which MacArthur had futilely warned General Marshall. Then there was General Marshall himself. When he was chief of staff in the thirties, MacArthur had exiled Marshall to the Siberia of the Illinois National Guard, and it was expected that Marshall, now with the upper hand, would take his revenge. This only demonstrated that they did not know Marshall.

But even higher up there was the commander-in-chief himself, Franklin Roosevelt. There were ugly innuendoes that Washington was keeping reinforcements away from MacArthur for fear that any great success might make him a powerful Republican candidate in the presidential election two years off. MacArthur had even tried to get his theater powerfully reinforced by going through Prime Minister Curtin of Australia who passed the word along through Churchill. This back-door approach had been thoroughly squelched.

MacArthur denied any presidential aspirations—"I have no political ambitions whatsoever . . . I started as a soldier and I shall finish as one." [26] He did little or nothing, though, to muzzle his subordinates.

Secretary of War Henry Stimson, himself a Republican, noted in his diary that "MacArthur, who is not an unselfish being and who is a good deal of a prima donna, has himself lent a little to the story by sending people here who carry a message that he is not a presidential candidate, thereby playing into the hands of people who would really like to make him a candidate instead of treating the matter, as a soldier like Marshall would treat it, never saying a word on the subject and assuming that all talk of one's candidacy was nonsense. These statements of MacArthur's have served to keep the story

[26]Statement issued by General MacArthur, quoted in *The New York Times*, October 29, 1942.

going." [27] Thus there was somewhat more than the usual pre-battle tension at Port Moresby when the Allied attacks began.

Vasey's Australians struck first at Gona where higher command echelons thought there might be no Japanese at all. On the 18th of November the leading Australian company found that there were. For a week the Australian 25th Brigade attacked. They went at the Japanese on the run, with bayonets fixed, but bayonets are of little use against coconut log bunkers. A softening-up by the little artillery available and by General Kenney's fliers accomplished nothing. The 25th Brigade, its casualties now over 20 percent, was spent, and Vasey ordered another brigade out of reserve to take its place.

With two of his three brigades committed at Gona, Vasey sent his remaining one, the 16th, against Sanananda. Rains there had turned the trail into a sea of mud. Air drops of food failed and one battalion lost fifty-seven men to heat, hunger and exhaustion before it even contacted the Japanese. The 16th Brigade had proven itself a crack outfit fighting across the Owen Stanleys. Now they proved it again.

When the Australians hit the first Japanese position across the Sanananda Trail, they used two companies to pin down the Japanese and threw a third company, ninety men under Captain B. W. T. Catterns, far around the enemy flank. At dusk Catterns' men surprised a company of Japanese soldiers at their supper, charged in and killed eighty of them. Then the Australians set up a perimeter defense in the rear of the Japanese position. The Japanese attacked all the next day. One by one Catterns' men dropped. Ammunition ran low but the remnant held on. By nightfall the Japanese gave it up as a bad job and retired toward Sanananda. Catterns had twenty-three of his ninety men left.

But this was only the Japanese outpost position and when the Australian brigade, down to half-strength, hit the main Japanese position further down the trail, they could make no headway. Vasey called for reinforcements. Herring, with MacArthur's approval, gave him most of one of Harding's two American regiments. It was still thought that there would be little opposition in front of Harding's 32nd Division.

[27] Pogue, *George C. Marshall*, p. 396.

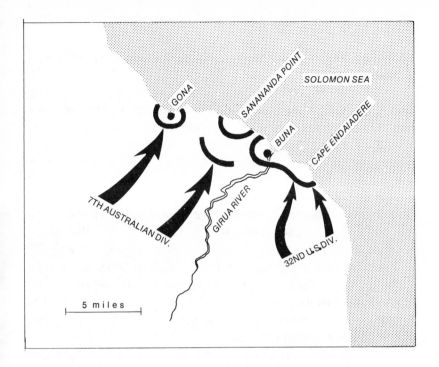

BATTLE ON NEW GUINEA Encouraged by the American victories at Guadalcanal, MacArthur ordered the American and Australian forces to take Buna and Gona. Allied intelligence grossly underestimated the Japanese strength and, instead of the quick and easy victory MacArthur expected, became involved in a two-month fight which eventually cost almost 6,000 casualties.

Harding was already having his troubles. His division, a National Guard outfit from Michigan and Wisconsin, had not been properly trained for the job ahead. Originally scheduled for Northern Ireland, they had been switched to Australia when it had been decided to leave one Australian Division in Egypt with the British 8th Army. There had never been any time to retrain the 32nd Division for jungle fighting. It had always been, as Harding put it, "getting ready to move, on the move, or getting settled after a move." [28] Now, with one regiment back in Port Moresby and one switched over to the Australian

[28] Milner, p. 133.

sector, Harding would have to attack the Japanese with only a third of his division.

Even before this truncated attack got going, the Japanese hit at Harding's tenuous supply line. It had been planned that after the necessary ground had been occupied, airstrips would be constructed and supplies flown in. In the initial phases of the attack Harding would have to depend mostly on coastal shipping consisting only of six luggers and a captured Japanese landing craft. Three days before Harding's attack was scheduled, Japanese Zeros, waiting until the Allied air cover had headed back to Port Moresby for the night, jumped a supply convoy bringing up heavy machine guns, mortars, ammunition, food and two small Australian cannon. Three of the luggers and the Japanese landing craft, which carried the cannon, were sunk. Harding, a passenger, had to swim to shore. Next day the Zeros got two more luggers, leaving Harding with only one.

On the 19th Harding's one regiment, the 128th Infantry, advanced. The men were cocky. The grapevine assured them that there were few Japanese around and that those were half-starved. Suddenly Japanese machine guns, unseen in the undergrowth, opened up. Casualties mounted and the United States infantry tried to fight its way forward. They had little idea where the enemy was. A machine gun would open from only a few feet away and rip a man in half. Occasionally they found a Japanese body and it was quite evident that the enemy here was no ragged detachment waiting to be mopped up.

At one point an American patrol managed to stalk and ambush a dozen Japanese. They tossed in a half-dozen of their Australian-made hand grenades. The grenades didn't work when wet and at Buna everything was always wet. But the grenades the Japanese threw back did work and half the American patrol were casualties. At the end of the first day the cocky 128th was badly shaken. They figured that they had walked into a trap. Possibly those on high didn't know exactly what they were doing.

Harding kept up the pressure. The next day a few machine gun nests were taken but the going was slow and very rough. For the following day Harding planned a three-battalion attack supported by General Kenney's "flying artillery." The air attack came over in the morning hitting both Japanese and American troops. The United States infantry had not gotten their orders in time and weren't prepared to attack. Orders finally got through and all was set again for midday. But then at midday the planes didn't show up. The whole thing was then laid on again for mid-afternoon. This time the planes showed up and plastered the two lead companies of Harding's infantry. This considerably delayed the start of the attack.

Harding's men finally went forward only to find the Japanese defenses hardly scratched by the air bombardment. They made slight progress and took heavy casualties. In one attacking company all officers were hit. One sergeant took over and was killed. Another sergeant followed him and was killed too. Nor was it simply a matter of the inexperience of the American infantrymen. An attached company of experienced Australian jungle fighters had no better luck in penetrating the Japanese lines.

Harding knew that his men had little chance without the proper weapons. The one chance he saw for immediate results was to use some of the light Stuart tanks that were back at Milne Bay. But when some were loaded on captured Japanese landing barges, the only craft available, they proved to be too heavy and the barges sank.

One battalion of the three sent to help Vasey's attack was returned to Harding and with four battalions he kept pushing. There was no chance of success. Not only were there not enough troops nor the right kind of weapons but the supply situation was critical. The American infantrymen were living on one meal a day, which was totally insufficient for the exertions required of them to move through the swamp and the undergrowth let alone fight in it. Medicines were scarce and dysentery and malaria were crippling the attacking battalions.

As it became clear that there was to be no quick, smashing success on either the Australian or American fronts, the aura of confidence vanished from the spacious rooms and wide, sweeping veranda of Government House in Port Moresby which was MacArthur's headquarters. In war, credit for victory climbs rapidly up the chain of command but discredit for defeat just as rapidly sinks down it. So it was to be now.

Only six days after the American attack had started, General Blamey, the Allied land forces commander, had visited MacArthur. The Australian general had discussed sending more troops forward. He wanted to use his veteran Australians, not the inexperienced Americans. He had a few disparaging remarks to make about the fighting qualities of the 32nd Division. To a man of MacArthur's intense patriotism, these were not remarks to be ignored. To back them up came rumors from over the mountains of panics and of poor combat leadership. As with all rumors flowing from a battle going badly, there were some elements of truth and many elements of exaggeration.

Two days after Blamey's visit, Colonel David Larr, deputy to MacArthur's operations chief, flew over the Owen Stanleys for a forty-eight-hour visit to the front. Larr came back with an extremely bad report of what he had seen. He delivered it orally and committed nothing to writing. The particular bugaboo to the officers at Port Moresby seemed to have been Harding's two field commanders, Colonel Mott, in charge of the attack on the left against Buna village, and Colonel Hale, who was pushing against Cape Endaiadere on the right. Mott, an irascible commander with whom Larr did not get along at all, had only been given his command on the day of Larr's arrival from Moresby so any judgment on him could hardly have been a considered one. Hale, the only regimental commander left in the division who was a National Guardsman, had only received command on the right four days before that. At Moresby the gross errors in intelligence and the Air Force's total inability to fulfill its "flying artillery" role were brushed aside. The best candidates for buck-passing seemed to be Colonels Mott and Hale.

This became clear to General Harding two days after Colonel Larr had gotten back to Moresby. Harding then had a visit from no less a personage than MacArthur's chief of staff, General Richard Sutherland. Harding wanted some reinforcements and asked Sutherland for all, or at least part, of his division's third regiment, then still back at Moresby. Sutherland said the supply situation would not allow it. There was some verbal sparring at lunch. Sutherland remarked that maybe Harding's division was not showing as much fight as it should. Harding bridled. The casualty list alone would refute that. Then Sutherland dropped his bombshells.

He told Harding that Colonel Larr's report had been very unfavorable and that, as a result, MacArthur had ordered Harding's direct superior, General Robert Eichelberger, to fly up to New Guinea from Australia. Eichelberger was commanding general of the United States First Corps which consisted of Harding's 32nd Division and the 41st which was still training in Australia. Harding knew that the only reason for bringing Eichelberger up at this time was either to ride herd on him or replace him. He had received a resounding vote of no confidence back in Port Moresby.

Then came the second of Sutherland's bombshells. What did Harding think of his top commanders, meaning Mott and Hale? But Harding was no buck passer and he put his own head on the block instead of theirs. He backed them up. Neither, he said, had had his job for over a week. Both were doing well with what little they had. That was not the answer Sutherland wanted. He flew back to Moresby and recommended to MacArthur that Harding be fired for keeping on incompetent commanders.

Just after Sutherland landed at the Port Moresby strip, Eichelberger's plane from Australia came in. The corps commander was quickly ushered onto the wide veranda of Government House. One look at Sutherland's grim face and Eichelberger knew what was in the wind. MacArthur strode back and forth along the veranda and then, speaking both in anger and in hurt pride, put it up to Eichelberger. "Bob, I'm putting you in command at Buna. Relieve Harding. I'm sending you in, Bob, and I want you to remove all officers who won't fight. Relieve regimental and battalion commanders; if necessary put sergeants in charge of battalions and corporals in charge of companies—anyone who will fight. Time is of the essence; the Japs may land reinforcements any night." [29]

He spoke of his personal humiliation at the reports that

---

[29] Eichelberger, *Our Jungle Road to Tokyo*, p. 21.

American troops had dropped their weapons and had fled the enemy. The honor of the United States Army was his honor. He spoke to Eichelberger as a consul of ancient Rome might have. "Bob, I want you to take Buna or not come back alive." [30]

Briefings were held that night. Right after breakfast the next morning, Eichelberger was to fly over the Owen Stanleys. But before he left, Eichelberger was taken aside by MacArthur, now in a much more pleasant mood. Eichelberger was told that if he took Buna he would get the Distinguished Service Cross as well as being recommended for a British decoration. And then came MacArthur's clincher—"I'll release your name for newspaper publication." [31]

Victory in New Guinea

BUNA-GONA
DECEMBER, 1942

On December 1st Eichelberger arrived at Harding's headquarters and the next day went forward with Harding to Colonel Mott's position. It was a cursory inspection at best and the condition of the troops who looked, as a medical officer reported to Eichelberger, "like Christ off the cross," was a shock.[32] That night Eichelberger relieved Harding and the next day Mott and Hale went, too.

Eichelberger learned quickly enough that something more than "inspired leadership" was needed at Buna. He found, and reported back to Moresby within three days, that the troops *were* fighting and that MacArthur could calm his fears on that score. Then, like Harding before him, he asked for both tanks and reinforcements. Unlike Harding, Eichelberger got them. For his mid-December attack he would have the 127th Infantry, now allowed to fly in from Port Moresby, as well as two Australian infantry battalions and tanks.

Before Eichelberger's attack was launched there were successes that began to swing the battle. Kenney's fliers might

[30] Eichelberger, p. 21.
[31] Eichelberger, p. 22.
[32] Milner, p. 207.

not have been successful artillerymen but they steadily increased the amount of supplies flown in over the mountains, performing the job under extremely bad weather conditions. More importantly, they cut off the Japanese from the sea. Reinforcements from Rabaul only dribbled in, and the Japanese food situation became more and more critical. By mid-December the westernmost and smallest of the Japanese bridgeheads at Gona had been wiped out. By December 9th, after extremely bitter fighting, the Australians had reduced the last Japanese bunker there. They took only sixteen prisoners, eleven of them stretcher cases, and buried 638.

Along the Sanananda Trail things had reached a stalemate. American troops had established a block on the trail behind the Japanese but found themselves under siege. They were forced to hold out for twenty-two days with supplies always running dangerously low while they beat off numberless Japanese attacks. The Sanananda front was obviously going to have to wait for a break on Eichelberger's Buna front.

There, five Australian tanks leading the assault on December 18th made all the difference. They were able to blast into the Japanese bunkers with their 37mm cannon and bit by bit the Japanese positions around Cape Endaiadere fell to the American and Australian infantrymen.

The swamps around the Buna end of the Japanese perimeter made the use of tanks very limited and the fighting came down to the old inch-by-inch digging out operation of the infantry. Eichelberger had the fresh 127th Regiment here and although the operation went slowly, it went surely. By the end of December the Japanese high command was issuing evacuation orders but it was too late for that. By New Year's the Japanese commanders were preparing themselves for hara-kiri, the ritual suicide by belly-slitting prescribed for an unsuccessful commander in the Emperor's service. It was obvious that once Buna had fallen, the fate of the Sanananda position would be the same, for then the full Allied weight could be thrown against it.

But the taking of Buna had been a bloody job, one for which the 32nd Division was never to get full credit. After the campaign was over General MacArthur's communiqué would announce that United States casualties had been low. They had not been. The 32nd Division had lost almost 2,000 men, killed and wounded, in the attack on the Buna position alone. All told, the campaign on eastern New Guinea cost more casualties than did the ground fighting on Guadalcanal— 8,500 as against 5,800.

"The darkness is very deep."

GUADALCANAL

DECEMBER, 1942

It was at Guadalcanal that, to the Japanese, defeat was the most bitter. For it was there that they had made their greatest effort.

Four days after his victory over Bosco Wright's cruisers at Tassafaronga, the tenacious Admiral Tanaka was trying again. This time he led another Tokyo Express down the Slot, seven destroyers loaded with those floating drums full of supplies. United States opposition was ineffective this night but so was the drum method of supply. Fifteen hundred drums went over the side, but only 310 arrived safely ashore. To try to supply a 40,000-man army by this means was sheer nonsense. When he got back to base Rear Admiral Tanaka went to his superior and told him precisely that. Tanaka also pointed out the inevitable conclusion to be reached. It was time to admit defeat and evacuate General Hyakutake's army from Guadalcanal. It would still take a bit of convincing for the Japanese high command to accept that conclusion.

On December 7th another effort to get those drums of supplies to Guadalcanal was made. One destroyer was badly damaged by American planes before it ever got there. The rest were so set upon by PT boats that they were not able to get even a single drum ashore.

Four days after that it was even worse. Tanaka again was leading. This time the PT boats got two torpedoes into Tanaka's flagship, the 2,500-ton *Teruzuke*. Tanaka was wounded and the brand new *Teruzuke* was sunk.

In desperation the Japanese admirals ordered submarines

to run supplies down to Guadalcanal. But the PT boats caught one on the surface in the act of unloading and sank her.

At last the Japanese admirals and generals were forced to face the ugly fact of defeat. Tanaka was relieved of his command and sent off to the backwaters of the war. This was his punishment for facing facts before his superiors were ready to.

On December 31st the commanders of the Japanese Army and Navy arrived at the Emperor's palace to seek his permission for the evacuation of Guadalcanal. They got it. On New Year's day—the Ninetieth Day—the Emperor's Rescript for the New Year had a rather depressing tone. "The Emperor is troubled," it announced. "The darkness is very deep." [33]

Dark, indeed, were the prospects for Japan's strategists. To hold Guadalcanal the Japanese Navy had expended two battleships, three cruisers, twelve destroyers, sixteen big transports and hundreds of planes—and had failed. If they could not hold at Guadalcanal, where could they? With American industry now pouring out everything from fleet carriers to hand grenades, the answer was quite clear—nowhere. The American advance on Tokyo that had started at Guadalcanal and New Guinea could be made bloody but it could not be stopped.

Isoroku Yamamoto put it into four lines of poetry during that gloomy December. On the first anniversary of his great victory at Pearl Harbor he wrote:

> The year has gone
> And so many friends
> The lost, the uncounted,
> The dead.[34]

---

[33] Morison, *The Struggle for Guadalcanal*, p. 317.
[34] Potter, *Yamamoto*, p. 319.

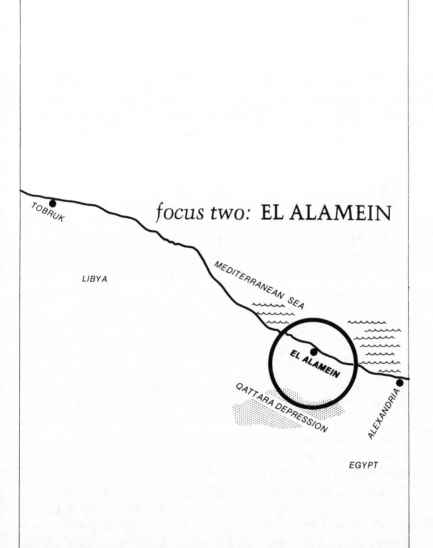

focus two: EL ALAMEIN

TOBRUK

LIBYA

MEDITERRANEAN SEA

EL ALAMEIN

QATTARA DEPRESSION

ALEXANDRIA

EGYPT

While the American defense of Guadalcanal had reached its "critical but not hopeless" phase in mid-October and while General Hyakutake had been preparing his decisive attack on Henderson Field, the war in the Egyptian desert had remained stalemated. After two years of seesaw fighting, the British and German armies faced each other across the minefields at El Alamein. But on the 23rd of October, only a few hours after Hyakutake started his ill-fated attack with nine ancient tanks, over 1,000 British tanks rolled forward into the last and the greatest of all the desert battles.

The relative quiet that had settled over the Egyptian desert after Rommel's attack of early September had been beaten back deceived no one. Along the thirty-five-mile front near El Alamein the German-Italian Panzer Army faced the British 8th Army, and every man on both sides of the line knew that a big battle was coming. Everyone knew it was the British who would now attack. The question was—when?

Winston Churchill, ever impatient, demanded a British attack in September. Both General Sir Harold Alexander, who commanded the whole Middle East Theater of Operations, and his subordinate, Lieutenant General Bernard Montgomery, who commanded the 8th Army, argued that they could not be ready until the full moon of late October. Preparations for battle took time, especially for a battle against Erwin Rommel who had so soundly beaten the British so often in the past. Churchill agreed to the delay. He waited and he fretted, for as he wrote Alexander, "All our hopes are centered upon the battle you and Montgomery are going to fight." [1]

This was not to be just another desert battle. Much more was at stake than the control of a few square miles of sand and rock. In early November, Operation Torch, the British-American invasion of French North Africa would begin. Of vital importance to the success of that venture was a minimum of French resistance as well as the neutrality of Spain which guaranteed the Allies the free use of Gibraltar and access to the western Mediterranean. A British victory in Egypt just before Torch could mean that, at least, the French and Spanish would continue to sit on the fence. A defeat in Egypt might mean they would throw in their lot with Hitler.

A victory by the British 8th Army was also essential for the relief of Malta. The supplies that had been fought through to the island in August were running low. Another convoy would have to arrive in November or Malta would be starving. To cover such a convoy, it was essential for the 8th Army to advance and seize the airfields inside Libya from which the convoy could be given air cover. To do this, the 8th Army must not only win a victory on the Alamein line, but must win it and then advance over 300 miles. And this must be done by mid-November.

That October, Malta was proving its value to the Allies. Its planes and submarines were sinking almost half of everything shipped to Rommel's army across the central Mediterranean. Scraping together 200 Italian and German bombers, Field Marshal Albert Kesselring, Hitler's commander-in-chief, South, opened what would be the last Malta blitz. But now Malta could boast 100 new Spitfires and Kesselring's bombers could accomplish little. By October 20th, as Axis bomber losses mounted past the fifty mark, the blitz was called off. Malta went right on sending out its planes and submarines. As the

[1] Churchill, *The Hinge of Fate,* 511.

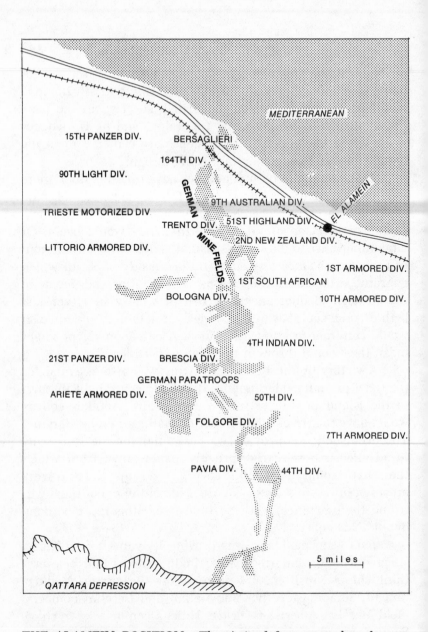

MEDITERRANEAN

15TH PANZER DIV.   BERSAGLIERI

                         164TH DIV.

90TH LIGHT DIV.

                                    9TH AUSTRALIAN DIV.

TRIESTE MOTORIZED DIV.

              TRENTO DIV. 51ST HIGHLAND DIV.

                              2ND NEW ZEALAND DIV.

LITTORIO ARMORED DIV.

                                              1ST ARMORED DIV.

                              1ST SOUTH AFRICAN

              BOLOGNA DIV.   10TH ARMORED DIV.

GERMAN MINE FIELDS

                              4TH INDIAN DIV.

21ST PANZER DIV.   BRESCIA DIV.

              GERMAN PARATROOPS

ARIETE ARMORED DIV.   50TH DIV.

              FOLGORE DIV.

                                              7TH ARMORED DIV.

              PAVIA DIV.   44TH DIV.

                                        5 miles

QATTARA DEPRESSION

THE ALAMEIN POSITION The Axis defense was based upon the minefields they had laid from the Mediterranean to the impassable Qattara Depression in the south. The key to defense was quick counterattacks by Rommel's veterans, the 15th Panzer Division and the 90th Light Infantry Division in the north and the 21st Panzer Division in the south. Montgomery's main attacking force was concentrated in the north, but every effort was made to make the Germans think that the attack would come in the south. The German command remained mystified until the battle began.

time for the desert battle neared, fuel for the German-Italian army was at a critically low level.

"Whole affair, about twelve days."

PLANS AND PREPARATIONS

OCTOBER, 1942

Panzer General Georg Stumme, sitting in for Rommel as commander of the German-Italian Panzer Army, was not pessimistic. Stumme was new to the desert, having come from command of a Panzer corps on the Russian front. He talked, not of static defense, not of simply halting a British attack, but of a German counterstroke. Stumme's optimism was based on what Rommel had called his "devil's garden," a half a million mines laid out in front of the main battle position.

The German minefield, or "the marsh" as some of the British soldiers called it, was mainly an anti-tank obstacle, 96 percent of the mines being set to explode only under the pressure from a vehicle's weight. But there were some 14,000 S-mines, man-killers, which, when a man stepped on them, would bounce waist-high and explode. The depth of the minefields ran to five miles and within the fields was an interlocking chain of small battle outposts. From them machine gunners, mortarmen and artillery observers covered the minefields and would make clearing them a deadly job. Within the minefields the British 8th Army was to be cut down to size.

Behind the minefields were the main infantry positions covered by dug-in tanks and anti-tank guns. Behind these were the Panzer divisions ready for immediate counterattack, as Rommel's plan called for any British penetration of his "devil's garden" to be thrown back instantly into the minefields.

The German-Italian line ran from the edge of the Qattara Depression to the sea, a distance of about thirty-five miles. At the southern end of the front the Italians held a cone-shaped 700-foot rock pile called Mt. Himmeimat from which they could observe what went on across the lines. From Himmeimat north for twenty-five miles the front was held by three rather mediocre Italian divisions reinforced by the first-class Germans of General Bernhard Ramcke's Parachute Brigade and the Italian paratroopers of the Folgore Division. Behind the southern sector lay the Italian Ariete Armored Division and the 21st Panzer.

The vital northern ten miles of the line which covered the paved coastal road was held in greater strength. On the line were the Italian Trento Division and the Bersaglieri, mountain troops from northern Italy and always her best. Intermingled with them was Carl-Hans Lungerhausen's 164th Infantry Division which had come over from Crete in the summer. Behind the front were the Italian Littorio Armored and the Trieste Motorized divisions plus the Afrika Korps' 15th Panzer and 90th Light Infantry divisions. The latter were the veteran infantry of the Afrika Korps, all desert veterans and with a first-rate commander in Graf von Sponeck. For ten miles of front this was a very powerful force.

It was precisely on this ten miles of the front that the new 8th Army Commander intended to break through. As the German line had no flanks that could be turned, the breakthrough would have to be a massive, carefully programmed affair like that which had smashed the Hindenburg Line in 1918. But it was in how to fight the rest of the battle that Bernard Montgomery differed from his predecessors.

Once the German minefields had been breached, the usual practice would have been for the British armor to charge through the gap and engage the German Panzers in a wild, free-for-all out in the desert. At this kind of fighting, Rommel's 15th and 21st Panzer divisions and his 90th Light Infantry Division, the old-timers of the Afrika Korps, were past masters. Such a fight was Rommell's meat. Montgomery, therefore, wanted no part of that.

After breaking through the German minefields, Montgomery wanted his armor to advance only a short distance and there assume a defensive posture and let the German Panzers do the attacking. If the German Panzers did not attack, Montgomery planned to chew away at the Axis infantry positions until Rommel was forced to commit his tanks.

In such a controlled battle Montgomery had two other advantages which he intended to use to the fullest. First was the Desert Air Force under Arthur Coningham, a New Zea-

lander and a brilliant commander of tactical air. The German
tanks would not move without taking a pounding from the air.
Second was the excellent British artillery with its unlimited
supplies of ammunition and a flexibility in fire control that
made it invaluable. For close-in work against German tanks
there was now the 57mm gun, the six-pounder, which, if
handled with nerve at close range, was a real tank-stopper.

In tanks Montgomery had a big overall superiority and
in the Sherman with its 75mm gun he had a tank to compare
with the German Mark IV. The latter, in a new version with
a long-barrelled 75, called the Mark IV Special, was the best
tank around but Rommel had only thirty. Montgomery had
250 Shermans. Counting the less powerful, mechanically unreliable British models he had better than 1,000 tanks. There
were 200 German tanks all told and 280 Italian, the latter
worthless against other tanks but useful against infantry.

To balance the British tank superiority Rommel had
eighty-six of his deadly 88mm high-velocity guns. Time and
again they had massacred the British armor and, in the
desert, the 88 was already a legend. Its sharp crack and
the high-pitched whine of its shell could terrify the bravest. To
add to these fabulous guns Rommel had almost seventy
captured Russian 76.2mm anti-tank guns which were only
barely inferior to the 88. These big anti-tank guns would
form the hard core of the 1,000-gun screen which the British
tanks would have to meet on the other side of the minefields.

The key factor for Montgomery was not in all these new
machines of war no matter how necessary they might be. In
his own words, the battle was to be a "dog fight," a "slogging
match" and for that the one indispensable ingredient was the
foot soldier, the assault infantryman with a rifle and a bayonet.
If he failed, not all the planes, tanks and guns in the Army
could retrieve the battle. For Alamein, Montgomery did not
have the numbers of infantry that a Staff College solution
would have called for, but what infantry he had were some
of the best in the world.

On the 19th and 20th of October, Montgomery assembled
the officers of the 8th Army including battalion commanders

in a movie theater and revealed to them the plan for the coming
offensive, now only a few days off. The General was a master
of exposition and he laid out the battle for them. There would
be very hard fighting and then there would be victory. His
notes read—"Whole affair, about twelve days." [2]

In the southern twenty-five miles of the front the plan
called for deception and feint attacks. Horrocks' 13th Corps
had two British infantry divisions, the fairly new 44th and
the veteran 50th. The latter had lost one complete brigade of
its three in the disastrous summer fighting near Tobruk. It had
been replaced with a Greek brigade who were avid night
patrollers and collectors of Italian ears. Horrocks' corps would
mount a feint attack using the 44th Division and the 7th
Armored, the old Desert Rats, who had been around since the
beginning. Horrocks hoped to turn it into the real thing but
was under a strict injunction from Montgomery not to waste
tanks that would be needed later. But what Horrocks must
do was to hold Rommel's 21st Panzer in the south until the
northern battle could develop.

To add to the enemy's confusion, the 8th Army put
Operation Bertram into effect in the south. Day-by-day a water
pipeline progressed into this sector. New concentrations of
guns were noted by the Germans as were dumps of supplies
and ammunition. On the air the Germans picked up the radio
traffic of another armored division in the south. These were
all fakes and very effective ones. Up until the beginning of
battle Stumme did not know where he was to be hit.

In the north, well back from the front, was the 10th
Corps, Montgomery's Armored. Its mass of 434 tanks was commanded by General Herbert Lumsden, an old cavalryman,
an expert horseman who had ridden in the man-killing Grand
National. He had a quick mind and a quick temper. He had
made it clear to Montgomery that he did not like the plan of
battle with his armored divisions engaged in the dog fight.
He wanted a clean breakthrough by the infantry before the
armor was committed.

The smaller but more expert of Lumsden's two divisions

[2] Playfair and Molney, *The Mediterranean and the Middle East*, Vol.
IV, *The Destruction of the Axis Forces in Africa*, p. 35.

was Raymond Briggs' 1st Armored. Its armored brigade, the 2nd, had 161 tanks, 92 of which were the new Shermans. His motorized infantry were the Rifle Regiments, long-time desert fighters and specialists in anti-tank fighting. Briggs himself was a competent, though unspectacular, tank commander and would earn the approval of the Army Commander, a rare honor for a tank man in those days.

Alec Gatehouse and the 10th Armored Division were quite another matter. He had two armored brigades in the division, one of which, the 24th, was new to the desert. His infantry brigade had come from the newly arrived 44th Division and were not the specialists that the Rifles of Briggs' division were. Gatehouse himself was one of the great characters of the old desert army. He was a fighter of enormous personal courage, a big rugged man with an incongruously high-pitched voice. He was a tank man to his fingertips. He did not get along at all with either Lumsden, his corps commander, or Montgomery, the Army commander.

All was not happy within the 10th Corps. It would go into the battle with its thinking not quite in line with Montgomery's. The British armor would soon find Montgomery as rough an opponent as Rommel. But in the infantry it was a different story.

Thirtieth Corps, five infantry divisions, was the assault force in the north. Montgomery had brought his own man out from England to command it. General Oliver Leese was a big, bluff Guards officer. He knew and loved soldiering and soldiers of all types, a necessary attribute in a corps whose divisions came from four different continents.

South of the low ridge called Miteirya lay the 4th Indian Division which had opened the desert war with a successful attack on the Italians two years before. As the main advance was to be against the Miteirya Ridge and the ground between it and the small, rocky hill of Tel El Eisa in the north, the 4th Indian Division would have little to do in the first stages of the battle.

North of the Indians lay the 1st South African Division under Dan Pienaar who could be a difficult man at times and would need deft handling as the battle progressed. The South

Africans' objective was the southern end of Miteirya Ridge. Their part was a small one but it was essential that it be well carried out.

Faced with the main assault of the Miteirya was the New Zealand division, veterans of Greece and Crete as well as the desert. Its commander, Bernard Freyberg, had started as an officer in the Grenadier Guards, gone on to fight in the Mexican Revolution and had come out of World War I with twenty-seven scars and a Victoria Cross. An instinctive fighter, he was greatly admired by Churchill and soon would be by Montgomery. The men of the division considered themselves, not without some justification, as the best in the Middle East. Past battle casualties had left the division with only enough men for two, instead of the normal three, infantry brigades but a full armored brigade, the 9th, had been added to the division.

The 9th Armored Brigade was made up of three former cavalry regiments, only one of which was a veteran outfit. The other two had been trained with ferocity by the Brigadier, John Currie, who was no less a fighter than Freyberg himself. Currie's tankers would draw the bloodiest assignment of the battle.

On the right of the New Zealanders and forming the center of the main assault was a division fresh out of England. If it was without combat experience, it carried a name of enormous reputation, for it was the 51st Highland Division and the names of its regiments—the Black Watch, the Gordons, the Seaforths, the Camerons and the Argyll and Sutherland Highlanders—bespoke the red-coated romance of British military tradition. It was a thoroughly professional outfit, beautifully trained by its commander, Douglas Wimberley, known as "Big Tam" to his men. The original 51st Division had been lost in the disastrous summer of 1940 in France, pinned against the sea by the 7th Panzer Division of Erwin Rommel. The new 51st was understandably eager for the battle. Its presence in the desert was no secret, for in the cool, crisp morning air the sound of the bagpipes at reveille carried far.

On the extreme right of the 30th Corps was the last of the Australian divisions to stay in the Middle East, the 9th.

Instead of pulling them back with the 6th and 7th Divisions, the Australian government had, after the war with Japan had begun, agreed to leave them if an American divison was sent to Australia. This was to be the Australians' farewell appearance in the desert. They were, including the very Australian Leslie Morshead commanding them, veterans of the great siege of Tobruk and their nick-of-time arrival at the front the past summer had saved the Alamein position. Their farewell performance would not suffer by comparison. "Be bloody, bold and resolute," one battalion commander, quoting Shakespeare, told his men.[3] They would be.

On October 18th an intelligence officer from the Foreign Armies West section of Hitler's staff arrived at Stumme's headquarters. His news was that the British would not attack that month. Many of the Afrika Korps were not so sure. In five days the moon would be full and that was the time to fear an attack. On the 19th the Germans had more visitors. British, South African and Australian planes roared in over the forward German fighter fields and gave the Luftwaffe a terrible pasting. The attacks continued and by the 23rd the Luftwaffe had been badly hurt.

Most of Montgomery's infantry assault force had taken their positions on the night of the 22nd. All day on the 23rd they had to lie in their shallow holes, fighting off flies and keeping an eye on their watches to see how long it was until 10:00 P.M.

On the morning of the 23rd General Stumme visited the central section of the Axis front. A ceremony was held attended by Italian and German brass for the purpose of decorating several Italian soldiers with the Iron Cross. Two of them had declared their intention to refuse. One had had a father and the other a brother killed fighting the Germans in the first war. Their generals managed to persuade them to humor their German allies and the ceremony proceeded without a hitch. The wrath of the bemonocled Stumme was something which no Italian general cared to face.

[3] Phillips, *Alamein*, p. 42.

It had been a fairly routine day for the temporary commander of the Panzer Army and early that evening the routine report went out to Hitler's headquarters—"Enemy situation unchanged." [4]

From the other side of the line the single word, "Zip," went out from Middle East Headquarters to Churchill. It meant that at twenty minutes to ten 882 guns of the 8th Army had opened fire and that the situation would never be the same again.

The First Day

ALAMEIN

OCTOBER 23–24, 1942

The opening crash of the Alamein barrage was like nothing the desert had ever known before. At the forward headquarters of the 164th Division, Lungerhausen and his staff were taking a nightcap. The table jumped, a bottle rolled to the ground and the officers ran to the slits looking toward the British lines. The horizon was rippling to the flashes of the guns. Slowly the flashes merged into a steady glow as the exploding shells raised an immense curtain of dust from the desert floor, in the midst of which the night's battle would be fought.

For fifteen minutes the British artillery pounded away at every known German and Italian gun position. There was no reply. Ammunition was not plentiful in the Panzer Army. Stumme would give the order when, from the midst of the dust storm, came the necessary information. Was it a full-scale offensive? Where was the main effort? The barrage cut phone wires, and special electronic equipment flown by the RAF over the German lines jammed their radios. Stumme peered into the dust cloud and waited through the night.

Montgomery listened to the guns and then, quite early, went to his caravan. There he read from the great martial prose of Shakespeare's *Henry V* and went to sleep.

Fifteen minutes after the guns had opened fire they stopped. For five minutes silence returned to the desert. In

[4] Phillips, p. 148.

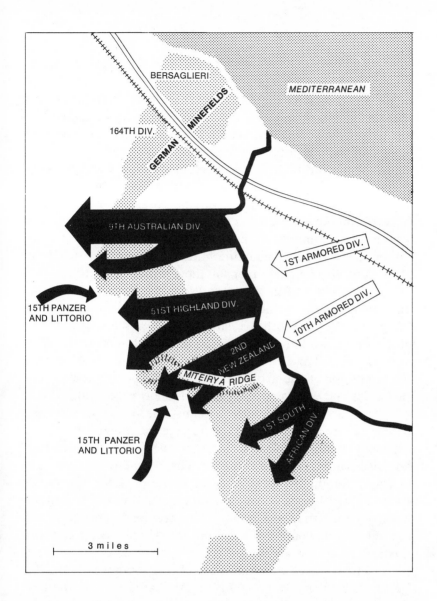

MONTGOMERY'S INITIAL ATTACK Four infantry divisions of the British 30th Corps—the Australians, Highlanders, New Zealanders and South Africans—bulged into the German positions on the first night of the battle. Montgomery's plan to clear two large corridors through the German minefields that night for the use of his armored divisions proved too ambitious, and few British tanks got through the minefields by dawn. German and Italian armored counterattacks were beaten off, however, and the British held their forward positions. Rommel, on sick leave in Austria, began his flight back to Africa to take charge of the battle.

those five minutes the platoons of the attacking divisions moved to their start lines just inside no man's land. Equipment was adjusted for the hundredth time. Safety catches clicked off rifles and watches were stared at. At precisely ten o'clock whistles blew, orders were shouted and the first lines stepped off into the minefields. And the guns began again. This time their fire was put down 100 yards in front of the advancing infantry. Every three minutes the fire would be lifted another 100 yards and the infantry would bound forward hoping to catch the enemy with his head still down. To the great rumble of the barrage was added the ripping sound of the German machine guns which were manned, as always, by the toughest men of the German infantry.

To the south of the Miteirya Ridge the Indians raided out into the minefields, something at which they were quite expert. On their right the South Africans, assaulting the southern end of the ridge, ran hard up against a strong German battle position which had not been spotted and had thus been spared the attentions of the artillery. The South Africans took heavy casualties and were stopped 500 yards short of the ridge.

The check to the South Africans was not vital. The purpose of the infantry advance was to take the minefields so that corridors could be cleared through them for the armored brigades waiting well to the rear. The southern corridor was to run through the New Zealand division sector up to the crest of the Miteirya Ridge and through it was to come Gatehouse's 10th Armored Division. The northern corridor would run along the boundary between the Highlanders and the Australians to Kidney Ridge.

At first the New Zealand attack had gone easily on the approaches to the Miteirya Ridge. Attacking on the right of the division the 23rd Battalion, keyed to an almost unbearable pitch, had reached their first objective with far too much ease. Reg Romans, the battalion commander, his jacket off, sleeves rolled up, wouldn't halt. "We can't stop here. We haven't fought yet." [5] And he led the battalion right through its own supporting gun fire and on to the foot of the ridge

[5] Phillips, p. 164.

itself. Far out ahead of the whole army, the 23rd Battalion waited for them to catch up.

Beyond the first objective Romans had found all the fight he wanted and so did the other New Zealand battalions coming forward to assault the ridge itself. The Germans and Italians in their battle outposts fought hard, only 300 of them falling prisoner. The New Zealanders were unstoppable and by dawn carried the crest of the low ridge. On the division's left they had to pull back to link up with the South Africans. It had been a great performance, but its cost had been very high. In the assaulting infantry companies killed and wounded ran to almost 50 percent, but the ridge had been taken.

On the far right of the British attack, Leslie Morshead's Australians had much farther to go than the New Zealanders, about four miles, and in addition had to set up a blocking position facing north from what, by dawn, would be a huge bulge in the German position. On the right the attack went well and the blocking position was set up. South toward Kidney Ridge and along their boundary with the Highlanders there was a good deal of trouble, mostly from Lungerhausen's 382nd Regiment. In the final stages of the Australian advance there was only one battalion for a one-mile front. It was not enough power and on the division's left the Australians dug in some 1,000 yards short of their final objective.

Between the Australians and the New Zealanders, the Highland division advanced to the sound of the pipes, each company and battalion commander being accompanied into action by his own piper. That wild battle music, the tunes of glory that had been heard at Ticonderoga, Lucknow and at Waterloo, pierced the roar of the barrage and, as it always had, steadied the men new to battle. The Highland division was out for blood.

As in the other sectors, the Highlanders' first objectives were reached without much trouble. From then on the fight became bloody. This ground between Tel El Eisa and the Miteirya Ridge was a natural avenue of attack and Rommel had seen to it that it was particularly well-mined and guarded by battle posts far stronger than most. Here German artillery barrages were fired and the soldiers simply had to walk through them. Always beneath their feet were the mines. In the Argylls, a man's foot touched a trip wire and a buried 250-pound aircraft bomb exploded wiping out a twenty-man platoon. One of their companies lost all its officers. On the division's right a company of the Gordons lost four of its five officers and 84 of 102 men. Here the Highlanders, like the Australians, dug in some 1,000 yards short of their final objectives.

On the far left of the division, bordering the New Zealanders, the final objective was the northern tip of the Miteirya Ridge. The halfway line was taken by the Camerons and then the Black Watch passed through for the final assault. Four companies marched out and after 1,000 yards they halted, their strength almost halved. The battalion commander formed a composite company out of the remnants of two companies and, with their piper still playing, they stormed up the deadly ridge and over it. There, not a single unwounded officer left, forty able-bodied men stood upon the objective and there they stayed.

Montgomery's infantry had driven a huge bulge into the German minefields. But behind them lay thousands of anti-tank mines. To make it possible for the British armored divisions to advance, it was necessary for two corridors to be cleared through these mines. One was along the dividing line between the Australians and the Highlanders, the other through the middle of the New Zealanders' sector. To clear the mines the sappers, combat engineers, followed hard on the heels of the infantry. Working with a coolness and nerve that was not the least remarkable feature of this night, they moved slowly and methodically along their allotted paths. Standing erect to use the Polish mine detector, which looked like a housewife's floor polisher, or kneeling to prod with a bayonet, they kept on under artillery and machine gun fire. It was an agonizingly slow process.

Behind the sappers came the two armored divisions of General Lumsden's 10th Corps, the 1st Armored Division through the northern corridor and the 10th Armored Division along the southern corridor. In the whole of the 10th Corps there were, from jeeps to tanks, 5,000 vehicles and they added in vast profusion to the enormous dust cloud that hung over the battle. Tank commanders and drivers could see only a few feet ahead if they could see at all.

Montgomery's plan had called for the British armored divisions to be through the German minefields by dawn. They were not. Early in the day Montgomery and his generals came forward to assess the situation. What Montgomery most feared was the 8th Army's becoming bogged down in the midst of the minefields. The momentum of its advance must be kept up.

So on the second night of the battle the infantry of General Leese's 30th Corps was to continue its advance. The rest of the minefields must be seized and the two corridors completed. The armor of General Lumsden's 10th Corps was to pass through the infantry, out beyond the minefields. There it would draw upon itself the German armor and start the business of destroying the German tanks.

What Montgomery made clear to Lumsden was that, regardless of what success the infantry had, the tanks must fight their way out of the minefields. If this meant heavy tank losses, then so be it. Tank crews, as often as not, managed to escape from disabled tanks and the 8th Army had a large reserve of tanks in the rear. The Germans had no such reserve. The British could afford to lose tanks and the Germans simply could not.

Early that same morning the Axis commander, General Stumme, decided, as had Montgomery, to go forward for a look at just what was going on. The reports he had gotten throughout the night were fragmentary and confusing. With a driver and his intelligence officer he drove off toward the Kidney Ridge area in the sector of the Australian division. Suddenly enemy infantry appeared in the desert ahead of him. A machine gun opened fire and Stumme's intelligence officer was shot and killed. Stumme leaped from the car. His driver gunned the engine and skidded around through the sand to escape. Stumme jumped for the car and clung to its side. Moments later the General's driver looked over his shoulder, but General Stumme was nowhere to be seen. Some German armored cars came up to rescue him but it was too late. Lying on the desert was the body of the German-Italian Panzer Army's Commander. Stumme was dead of a heart attack.

The command of the Axis forces now went to General Ritter von Thoma whose tank fighting experience went back to the thirties when he had fought for General Franco in the Spanish Civil War. He was an old hand at desert warfare and was not dismayed. He knew the British had broken into the minefields but had not broken through them. Far to the south, near Mt. Himmeimat, the British had attacked too and had been held. Von Thoma decided to leave the German and Italian armor in the south where it was. He had enough reserves, he thought, to handle what might develop in the north.

That afternoon, the Highland division had sent forward a battalion and it had managed to advance right to the edge of the German minefield. Sappers cleared the last mines and some of General Briggs' 1st Armored Division tanks at last lumbered up through the corridor and deployed out beyond the mines.

Von Thoma's reaction was instinctive and immediate— counterattack. Late in the afternoon, with the sun behind them shining into the eyes of the British tank gunners, the Panzers advanced. But Briggs was not to be suckered into a wild charge against the Germans. Keeping his tanks under tight control, he fought a purely defensive battle. As dusk came both the British and the Germans had lost two dozen tanks. This was a beginning of the kind of fighting that Montgomery wanted. He could afford two dozen tanks and the Germans could not. But it was only a small beginning.

At noon on that first day Field Marshal Rommel had received a telephone call at his mountain retreat. Adolf Hitler was on the line. "Do you feel capable of returning to Africa and taking command of the army again?" [6] Rommel, although his health was still below par, agreed to go. He ordered his plane readied for takeoff at dawn the next day.

---

[6] Freidin and Richardson, *The Fatal Decisions*, p. 110.

Hat, Boat and Bottle—The Second Day
OCTOBER 24–25, 1942

Montgomery's main effort for the second night of the battle, October 24th, was to be a repetition of the previous night's assault, but on a smaller scale. The difference was that it was to be made against an enemy fully alerted as to what to expect. This attack of Montgomery's was to come at the left of the bulge driven into the German minefields, from the Miteirya Ridge, with the objective of breaking out to the southwest.

The New Zealanders had seized the Miteirya Ridge during the first night's fighting. When British tanks had attempted to advance beyond it, they had driven right into the line of sight of German guns and, in one spot, had lost a tank a minute for five minutes. They discovered that a German anti-tank gun screen had been established roughly along the crest of another ridge, the Wishka, about two miles beyond Miteirya Ridge. These anti-tank guns had made any daylight advance by the British tanks impossible. Between these two ridges the barren desert sloped down only about ten to fifteen feet but in the flatness of the desert ten or fifteen feet could seem like a mountain.

To attack this German gun screen on the Wishka Ridge was the second night's objective of the 8th Armored Brigade of Alec Gatehouse's 10th Armored Division. The 8th Brigade was his veteran outfit. His other armored brigade, the inexperienced 24th would attack on the right of the 8th, linking up with Briggs' 1st Armored Division to form a screen against any German attacks from the north.

On Gatehouse's left, to the south, the 9th Armored Brigade of the New Zealand division would attack southwest and open the way for the New Zealander infantry. The 9th, fighting alongside the New Zealanders on the first night, had already lost one-third of its tank strength.

Gatehouse knew that the key to the operation was the 8th Armored Brigade's attack in the center against the Wishka Ridge. He stationed himself directly in their rear. He did not like this attack at all. To him using tanks like some sort of battering ram was all wrong. He was afraid that at dawn his tanks would be caught in the open and massacred by the

German guns. But Montgomery had made it clear that he expected the tanks to fight their way through, taking heavy losses if they had to.

When darkness fell, the sappers started their work of lifting mines out in front of the 8th Armored Brigade. They were ordered to clear three narrow corridors through the mines, code named from left to right Hat, Boat and Bottle. The sappers were given very little time for their task. At 10:00 P.M. a 300-gun barrage was to begin and the tanks were to go forward, one regiment, about eighty tanks, through each corridor.

In the corridor named Hat, the southernmost, things started to go wrong right at the beginning. The commanding officer of the sappers went ahead to reconnoiter the route and got a German bullet through the head. More sappers came up but found themselves under the direct fire of a German 88. Hat route was effectively blocked. The 3rd Royal Tanks, who were to use this route, were shunted off to use the center route, Boat, instead. Boat was already being used by another tank regiment, the Sherwood Rangers, so this meant overcrowding, congestion and a tempting target.

Promptly at ten o'clock the British barrage came down. Behind it, through Boat route in the center, a great mass of tanks, guns, trucks, jeeps, and command cars began to crawl forward. Hardly had the movement begun when the entire scene was brilliantly illuminated by German flares. Then a handful of the bombers the Luftwaffe had left in flying condition started their attack. The bombs came down right on target. The British force could not disperse as they were neatly penned in the narrow corridor through the minefield, which was only wide enough for two vehicles abreast. The British were trapped.

As the German bombs burst, artillery shells began to pour into the area and then, from close by, German infantry began to pour in rifle, mortar and machine gun fire. Within a few minutes twenty ammunition and fuel trucks were on fire. Using these as an aiming point the German guns poured in an accurate fire for hours. Thus, in a welter of flames, explosions and utter confusion, Boat route was slammed shut.

There, two of the 8th Armored Brigade's three tank regiments were stopped.

But on the right of the brigade one route through the mines remained, Bottle. There the British tanks were making some progress. This was the route of the Staffordshire Yeomanry whose men wore the red triangle of the Bass Brewery where so many had worked before the war. A couple of their tanks went up on mines but the regiment was only sideswiped by the great concentration of bombs and shells pouring down on Boat route. As the night wore on, the Staffordshires were moving out of the mines and across the open toward the slopes of the Wishka Ridge.

Alec Gatehouse was up right behind the 8th Armored Brigade with his advanced headquarters in two tanks. Too far advanced, some of his staff thought. He kept urging the 8th Brigade forward and was distinctly unhappy over the very slow rate of progress of his 24th Brigade on the right of the 8th. There were plenty of mines there and progress was at the pace of a man crawling forward and prodding the earth with a bayonet to find them. Few details were known at division headquarters as radio communication was particularly bad that night.

Shortly after midnight a messenger arrived from the rear and Gatehouse was told that the corps commander, Lumsden, wanted to talk to him. Telephone communications to the rear were no good and Gatehouse had to travel back eight miles to a usable field telephone. When he got there he laid it on the line to Lumsden. Daylight, he said, would find his armor somewhere between the Miteirya and Wishka ridges and there the German gun screen would blow them apart. The disasters of the night were bad enough, but Gatehouse foresaw even worse for the next day. He wanted to withdraw his armor back behind the Miteirya Ridge before daylight.

Lumsden agreed and so reported to 8th Army headquarters where Montgomery was sound asleep. Montgomery's Chief of Staff hesitated to wake the General. It was Montgomery's contention that an army commander was paid to think, not dash about twenty-four hours a day. But the Chief of Staff was understandably worried and he conferred with Oliver Leese, the infantry corps commander. Montgomery must be awakened. It was 3:30 A.M.

The 8th Army Commander thus faced his first crisis of the battle. He listened to Leese and Lumsden relate how the battle had become bogged down. Montgomery's reaction was quick. At all costs the momentum must be kept up. The armor must drive ahead. Lumsden wanted the Army Commander to talk with Gatehouse personally.

Montgomery, knowing nothing of the communications problems, was shocked to find Gatehouse some eight miles behind his tanks. He said so and he said he wanted the attack pushed. Gatehouse balked and came close to outright insubordination. Montgomery could relieve Gatehouse but this would compound confusion. He compromised. Of the 8th Armored Brigade's three regiments, only the Staffordshires would continue forward but the 24th Brigade on the right must continue its advance and link up with Briggs' division. Then Montgomery went back to bed and Gatehouse went back to his tanks.

When dawn came, the Staffordshires, as Gatehouse had foreseen, found themselves in a suicidal position. As soon as it was light enough to see, the German anti-tank gunners picked off ten tanks. The regimental commander came back to the Miteirya Ridge and asked Gatehouse for permission to withdraw. By then more than half his tanks were gone. Gatehouse, acting on his own, approved the withdrawal and the attack of the 8th Armored Brigade was over, all three of its regiments being back behind the Miteirya Ridge where they had started.

Gatehouse's 24th Brigade, on his right, had finally cleared the mines, had rolled ahead and reported itself as on the objective. Actually, they were a bit short but they were out in the open and in due course would link up with Briggs' tanks.

To the left Currie's tanks of the 9th Armored Brigade had gotten through the mines but, like the Staffordshires, found themselves in a badly exposed position in front of the German guns. Shielded by smoke shells fired by the New Zealand artillerymen, Currie held his ground, losing a few tanks but getting a few enemy ones in return.

That morning, at Wiener-Neustadt airfield outside Vienna, Rommel's plane was refused permission for its scheduled 7:00 A.M. takeoff, bad icing conditions at 18,000 feet. "We're taking off," said Rommel.[7] Shortly before noon he was in Rome talking to the German military attaché, General Rintelen. What Rommel heard of the progress of the battle was not too bad but what appalled him was the fact that in the whole African theater there were only three issues of fuel for his army. That meant only three days of mobile warfare. In a bitter mood, the General flew on to Crete and from there to the African desert.

The Battle Swings to the North

OCTOBER 26–27, 1942

As Rommel's plane droned across the Mediterranean, Lieutenant General Montgomery was reassessing his battle. The big push by the 30th Corps had gouged a great salient into the German minefields. Only two armored brigades, one of Gatehouse's and one of Briggs', were barely through the mines. Ahead of them was the German gun screen and on that second morning Briggs' armor had taken serious losses attacking it in the Kidney Ridge area. To many this looked a bit like a stalemate, and a stalemate would be a defeat for the British.

To Montgomery it was simply the time to start his crumbling operation, his wearing down of the German infantry, and he looked about for a good place to start it. The New Zealand infantry, understrength when the battle began, had taken heavy casualties and must now be set aside for an exploitation role later. The Highland division had suffered more heavily but, having started at full strength, still had plenty of power left. The Australians, though, had had a comparatively light casualty list and the day before Montgomery had talked with Morshead, the division commander. Morshead was ready for a fight. Montgomery would make his next move with the Australians.

Morshead's Australians held the right flank of the great bulge which had been driven into the German lines. Attacking

[7] Carell, *The Foxes of the Desert*, p. 289.

from the forward part of this salient toward the sea, they would threaten Rommel's most sensitive point, the coastal road, which was both the German supply route and their line of retreat. Montgomery reasoned that any attack here was bound to provoke a violent reaction from the Germans. Here, therefore, would be Montgomery's main effort for the third night of the battle, the night of the 25th. Only subsidiary small attacks would be made along the line to the south.

The British armor would be reshuffled. Gatehouse was ordered to hand over his 24th Brigade to Briggs' 1st Armored Division which would then have two armored brigades operating in the Kidney Ridge sector. Gatehouse, with his 8th Armored Brigade that had been so badly battered in the Hat, Boat, and Bottle battle, were to pull back out of the line to re-equip. Currie's 9th Brigade would remain attached to the New Zealanders but would pull back over the Miteirya Ridge.

During the day of the 25th, Briggs' constant pushing brought the usual reaction from von Thoma, a series of armored counterattacks. The 15th Panzer Division and the Littorio came on in greater strength than before and pressed their attacks right up to the British and Australian anti-tank guns. They were stopped and badly hurt. The 15th Panzer Division, which had started the battle with 119 tanks, had only thirty-one still in action by the evening of the 25th. On each side the defense had mastered the attacking tank. The German tankers had one additional problem. Wherever they tried to move, they left that telltale plume of dust on the desert floor, and Coningham's Desert Air Force was sure to pounce on them. The Luftwaffe, after its smashing up of Gatehouse's attack the night before, had been reduced to hit and run raids, unpleasant on the receiving end but now too small to be effective.

Northward, toward the sea, from the tip of the Australian penetration, lay Point 29, a hillock rising about twenty feet from the desert floor surrounding it. It flanked the Germans holding the hill called Tel El Eisa, and it was invaluable in that flat country as an artillery observation post. It was a mile and a quarter from the Australian lines and strongly held by Panzer Grenadiers of Lungerhausen's 164th Division. It was the objective for the night of the 25th and was assigned to the 48th Australian battalion.

The 48th was commanded by a former cavalryman, Dick Hammer, and his method of assault was as unconventional as it was successful. He had a good idea of the setup of the German defenses as an Australian patrol had captured two German officers complete with maps. The initial preparation for Hammer's attack included 115 tons of bombs dropped by the RAF and the fire of seven regiments of guns. Hammer's two leading companies advanced behind the artillery fire for 900 yards, taking the covering minefield. The sappers went to work immediately clearing gaps.

When the gaps were cleared, Hammer's third company was loaded on Bren gun carriers—small, open, tracked vehicles that looked like miniature tanks with the top half cut away. They were 1,000 yards from their objective. Down went an artillery concentration right on Point 29. Off went the carriers at top speed in a column of fours. Nine minutes later they arrived just as the artillery ceased fire. The Australians jumped out of the small carriers, right on top of the German defenders and overwhelmed them at close quarters, rifle butts and bayonets being freely used. Another battalion then advanced through Hammer's and extended the penetration to the north and east.

That night had been Rommel's first back in the desert and it was not a happy one. "Dearest Lu," he wrote his wife the following morning, "Arrived 18:30 yesterday. Situation critical." [8] Rommel decided to throw everything he could get his hands on into an effort to drive the Australians out of their newly won positions. It was a bad move.

As the German and Italian forces gathered to attack the Australians, they were chopped up by the RAF light bombers of the Desert Air Force who carpeted the desert floor with their bomb patterns. As they drew closer to the Australian lines, the beautifully handled British artillery came into action. The German and Italian fliers tried to come to the aid of the at-

[8] Hart, ed., *The Rommel Papers*, p. 308.

tacking troops but better than half a hundred British fighters stopped them cold. Rommel's attack fell apart and the Australian grip on Point 29 was not loosened. Losses were mounting disastrously in both the 15th Panzer and the Littorio divisions so Rommel decided that he must bring the 21st Panzer Division up from the south.

To Montgomery, the German sensitivity to the Australian success in the northern salient was encouraging. His plan now was to increase the pressure by the Australians in the north and thus draw the Germans more and more to that sector and, hopefully, into bigger and costlier counterattacks. At the same time he wanted to pull the New Zealand infantry and some of his tanks out of the line. There they would be rested and re-equipped for another major attack like the one which had opened the battle.

This meant a considerable reshuffling of the 8th Army's infantry divisions, which was not simply a matter of the 30th Corps Commander, Leese, calling a meeting and issuing orders. Three of the infantry divisions were Commonwealth divisions, those from New Zealand, Australia and South Africa. The commanders of those divisions could refuse an order that they thought might imperil their troops and demand to be allowed to consult their home government.

Leese knew this and when he called his division commanders' meeting, he knew where the most likely trouble spot would be—the South Africans. There had been two South African divisions with the 8th Army but, that previous June, one of them had been in Tobruk, had been overrun by Rommel's tanks, and the entire division had been captured. It was a disaster not of the South Africans' making but it had left its bitterness as well as a justifiable fear among the South Africans of their being once again overrun by German tanks.

So, Leese assembled the division commanders and explained the plans. The Australians would concentrate all three of their brigades for their coming attacks in the north. Leslie Morshead, the division commander, agreed heartily. The Highlanders would have to sideslip to their right to cover some of the ground held by the Australians. The New Zealand division, in turn, would sideslip northward and take over some of the

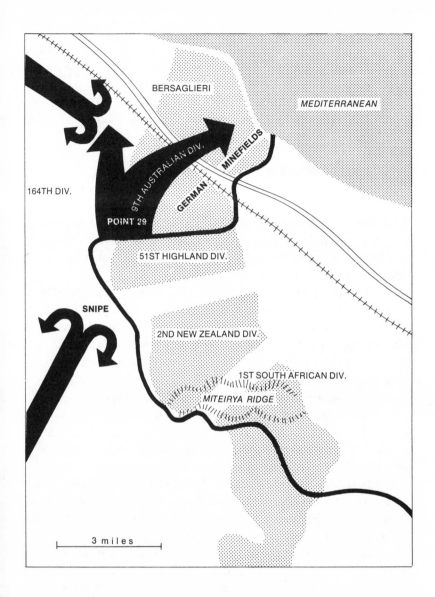

BERSAGLIERI

MEDITERRANEAN

MINEFIELDS

9TH AUSTRALIAN DIV.

GERMAN

164TH DIV.

POINT 29

51ST HIGHLAND DIV.

SNIPE

2ND NEW ZEALAND DIV.

1ST SOUTH AFRICAN DIV.

MITEIRYA RIDGE

3 miles

MONTGOMERY ATTACKS TO THE NORTH   After his efforts to
advance from the Miteirya Ridge failed, Montgomery switched his
main effort to northward attacks by the 9th Australian Division.
These convinced Rommel that the decisive battle was in the north
and he brought his 21st Panzer Division and some of the Italian
Ariete Armored up from the south. Their attack was smashed, particularly by British anti-tank gunners at an outpost called Snipe.
Rommel's attempt to throw back the Australians with his 15th
Panzer and 90th Light Infantry divisions was also a failure. Montgomery was now gaining the upper hand.

ground held by the Highlanders. This would be very tricky as, while doing this, the New Zealand infantry would be relieved by a British brigade brought up from the south. Also the division's 9th Armored Brigade would be pulled back from its Miteirya Ridge positions so as to be brought up to full tank strength.

Then Leese got down to the delicate part of the move. The South Africans would have to sideslip to their right onto the Miteirya Ridge and take over from the New Zealanders. And they would be on that bloody ridge without the tanks of the 9th Armored Brigade to support them. Dan Pienaar, a stubborn and prideful man, commanded the South Africans and all eyes were on him. Pienaar objected.

The South African explained that he didn't think he had enough transport to make such a move. Was it this or a fear of German tanks? Freyberg of the New Zealanders, with all his prestige as a hero of the first war as well as this one, applied the needle to Pienaar. "Is it only transport that's worrying you, Dan? No other difficulty?"

"No," said Pienaar. "Just not enough transport."

Now it was Pienaar's pride that Freyberg played on. He knew the South African and instead of giving him an argument, Freyberg gave him an offer of assistance. "Can we help you then? I'll give you any transport you need." [9]

Freyberg's thrust worked. Pienaar said that the South Africans could manage on their own. They didn't need New Zealand help. Freyberg had shown himself as fine a diplomat as he was a fighter.

The reshuffle of the 8th Army started. It was going to have to be completed in forty-eight hours, as the Australians were scheduled to attack on the 28th. Staff officers drew up the orders and soon 60,000 men started on a confused, sleepless, dust-ridden move that looks easy only on the map.

Rommel Attacks

OCTOBER 27, 1942

While the 8th Army reshuffled its forces, Rommel moved fast. The 21st Panzer Division was put on the move up from

[9] Phillips, p. 259.

the south. The 90th Light Infantry Division, Rommel's best infantry, was moved out of reserve. All four of his German divisions were now concentrated in the north. There, he planned to attack the dangerous British penetrations, the Australian salient and Briggs' 1st Armored Division in the Kidney Ridge area.

Against the Australians Graf von Sponeck's veterans of the 90th Light Infantry formed up for their attack. They were hit time after time by the RAF. German fighters could offer no effective cover now. The most awesome sight to the German infantry was the flight of eighteen RAF light bombers who always came over flying in perfect formation as though on a peacetime review. This formation flying gave their bomb pattern a tightness and a deadliness that the Germans had not known in previous desert battles. The Germans called them the "pig-headed" eighteen; the British called them the "imperturbable" eighteen. The 90th Light Infantry could make no progress against Morshead's Australians and the German attack in the far north foundered just as it had on the previous day. Rommel himself had watched and the superiority of the Royal Air Force made a deep and depressing impression on him.

Further to the south, Rommel's attack on Briggs' 1st Armored Division was to be backed up by the fresh 21st Panzer Division coming up from the south. But the Germans had a surprise waiting for them. The night before, Briggs had ordered an advanced anti-tank outpost set up well out in front of the British lines in an area code-named Snipe just south of Kidney Ridge.

To man this outpost, Briggs assigned the men of his division's armored infantry, the Rifles. These were veteran troops, used to tank fighting and armed with their own small 57mm anti-tank guns and backed by some from the division's artillery. The 57 was new to the 8th Army. It was small, but at close range very deadly. In all, 300 men and nineteen of the small anti-tank guns made up the task force. Their commander, Lieutenant Colonel Victor Turner, had no illusions about their mission. "A last man, last round assignment," he called it.[10]

[10] Phillips, p. 271.

The Riflemen got well out into the desert without more than the ordinary troubles of a night movement close to the enemy. They got their guns up and took possession of a slight hollow in the ground. It was not actually their objective but it was close enough for their purpose. Even before the first light a German self-propelled gun and one of their big Mark IV tanks rolled right up to the Rifles' position. At thirty yards the British gunners chewed up the Mark IV and the self-propelled gun was easily destroyed.

As daylight came, the British found they were right in the middle of the German armor. As the Panzers started to move, the anti-tank guns opened up on them at ranges of 600–800 yards. The gunnery couldn't have been better and in minutes there were sixteen tanks and guns burning out in the desert. Eleven of them were badly enough hit not to be worth towing away for repair. German shells poured in on the British gunners now that they had given away their position, and three British guns were wrecked.

Then the 24th Armored Brigade arrived about 2,000 yards behind them but, thinking the anti-tank guns were German, opened fire. Turner's battalion intelligence officer took a Bren gun carrier and went out to get them to stop. Finally the 24th Brigade started to advance against the German tanks, and the Rifles picked off three of the Germans opposing them.

The tanks of the 24th Brigade now took up positions alongside Turner's guns and this drew a tremendous fire down on the position. Fifteen of the British tanks were blazing away in a short time and the 24th Armored Brigade pulled back. Turner, glad to be rid of the British tanks, set about his fight. Two of his guns had been destroyed while the British tanks were with him. He had fourteen guns left.

Later in the morning Italian infantry came in for an attack but were easily beaten off by the light machine guns mounted on Turner's Bren gun carriers. Italian tanks had a try and lost four. German tanks then came on but, caught in a cross fire between Turner's guns and the 24th Brigade's tanks in the rear, lost eight. But two more of Turner's guns were knocked out as well.

Then, from the southwest, eight Italian tanks and a self-propelled gun came in to the attack. At this point on the British perimeter there was only a single British gun left in action and it was manned by only one man, Sergeant Charles Calistan. Turner and Lieutenant Jack Toms ran over, and the three men opened fire at a range of 600 yards. The Italians kept coming. Six of their tanks were hit and set on fire and their self-propelled gun blasted out of action. There were three Italian tanks left and they were manned by brave men who now sensed that victory was theirs. They were close enough to the British gun to spray it with machine gun fire. At the gun, itself, there were only two rounds of ammunition left.

Lieutenant Toms jumped into a jeep and drove to a disabled gun, piled in some ammunition and came roaring back. The Italian tanks' machine guns caught the jeep as it arrived and set it on fire. Toms leaped out, Turner ran over with a corporal who had just joined the makeshift gun crew. The three of them lugged the ammunition away from the burning jeep with the Italian machine guns on them the whole time. At the gun Sergeant Calistan kept his sight on the Italian tanks and waited.

A bullet creased Turner's skull and he fell bleeding beside the gun. The ammunition was now there and Calistan aimed with cool deliberation. For him the range was now point-blank and with three shots he destroyed the three Italian tanks. Then the magnificent sergeant suggested that they use the burning jeep to brew some tea.

Turner, though badly hurt, refused to stay out of action, but his head wound was too much for him. In the heat of the afternoon he thought the attacking tanks were warships and his officers forced him to lie down in the small headquarters dugout.

In the early afternoon Briggs' 2nd Armored Brigade appeared on the horizon and like the 24th before them thought Turner's guns were the enemy and gave them a good shelling. It was only a prelude to the big German attack still to come, for Turner's Riflemen were standing right in the path of the oncoming 21st Panzer Division.

Thirty German and ten Italian tanks plowed steadily along past Turner's gunners. Five British guns came to bear on this mass and, opening fire at less than 300 yards, crippled a dozen tanks in two minutes' shooting. The German commander swung some tanks to charge the guns, one getting to within a hundred yards and its machine gun bullets penetrating the gun's shield before it was knocked out. Three of Turner's guns were knocked out, but these German tanks finally pulled away.

A second group of tanks then came on, fifteen German Mark III's, making right for Turner's position. Only three of the 57's could be brought to bear on them, and these three guns had only thirty rounds of ammunition left, ten per gun. At 200 yards the three guns opened fire. One was manned by a lone sergeant. Six German tanks went up in flames, the last within 100 yards of the guns. The rest drew back. There were then only nine rounds of ammunition left.

With only six guns left in usable condition Turner's small group waited for a relief force. The relief force missed them in the dark and Turner's men had to make their own way back from where they had come the night before. There was only transport enough to bring out the men and one gun. Behind them they left thirty-two totally destroyed enemy tanks plus half again as many badly damaged.

Rommel's attack of the 27th had been beaten off all along the line, but on the following day he was granted a momentary respite. He was hammered from the air but on the ground action was limited. Gatehouse's 10th Armored again came up to Kidney Ridge but in a defensive role. Briggs' 1st Armored Division was now to reform in the rear. But the respite in the battle was short-lived and on the night of the 28th, the sixth night, it ended as the Australians attacked in force.

Supercharge

OCTOBER 28–NOVEMBER 2, 1942

The new Australian attack was to be made north from Point 29, sweeping around a large fortified area known as Thompson's Post and then hopefully crossing the coastal road and reaching the sea itself. But the real objective of the attack was not any particular piece of ground, no matter how valuable.

The purpose was to draw in the Axis reserves, grind them up and thus set up the Panzer Army for the kill.

On the first night, October 28th, the initial objectives were taken but bitter fighting developed later. Casualties for the attackers were very heavy. One Australian battalion ended the night with a strength of a hundred men, and a British tank regiment supporting the attack ended up with only eight tanks. But one battalion of the 125th Panzer Grenadiers was all but wiped out, and Rommel was being forced to commit more and more of his reserves.

The next day was a gloomy one in London. Churchill felt that the battle was petering out in a lot of inconclusive fighting. He prepared a message for the Middle East, a real blast. General Alan Brooke, chief of Britain's Army and also chief patron of Bernard Montgomery, got a look at Churchill's message and was horrified. He had doubts of his own but was keeping them strictly to himself. So had Montgomery but expressed them only to Brooke.

Churchill harangued Brooke, "Have we not got a single general who could even win one single battle?" [11] Brooke explained that he was sure that Montgomery's pulling divisions out of the line only meant he was preparing for new attacks. At last Churchill's old friend, Jan Smuts, the great leader of South Africa, spoke. He backed up Brooke and the Prime Minister's anger subsided. The harsh telegram composed in the early hours of the morning was not sent. One went out that amounted only to a gentle prod.

Rommel, too, was feeling the full load of command in what, to him, was fast becoming a hopeless situation. "At night I lie with my eyes wide open," he wrote his wife, "unable to sleep for the load that is on my shoulders. In the day I'm dead tired." [12] The only move possible seemed to be a retreat to another position about fifty miles to the rear. There was not enough transport, though, in the Panzer Army to move all his infantry, but if he stayed on he risked losing everything. It was a Hobson's choice.

[11] Bryant, *The Turn of the Tide*, p. 417.
[12] Hart, ed., *The Rommel Papers*, p. 317.

On the 29th and the 30th the Australian pressure eased and Rommel breathed easier. He also caught up a bit on his sleep. On the night of the 30th he started to pull the 21st Panzer Division out of the line to form a reserve. But that night Morshead's men came on again.

It was a bloody night for the Australians. Their infantry strength had been whittled down during all the previous fighting, and there were not enough men to form more than long skirmish lines. The men of Graf von Sponeck's 90th Light Infantry Division came up to stiffen the battered remnants of Lungerhausen's regiments. Thompson's Post held out. The Germans, the Italian Bersaglieri and some of the Italian artillery, using guns which had fought against the Germans twenty-five years before, fought with skill and stubbornness. Only the tip of the Australian advance reached the coastal road and their hold there was tenuous at best. But they had won their battle, for on the last day of October they had forced Rommel to send his 21st Panzer and most of the 90th Light Infantry back into the attack against them.

The German attackers were the cream of the old Afrika Korps, and they had their successes against the thin Australian lines, but nowhere was a decisive penetration made. The British tanks suffered badly. They went out alone beyond the coastal road and died there. All day long the British artillery hammered at the Germans, and the RAF put on almost continuous bombings. Local successes were all that the 21st Panzer and 90th Light Infantry could claim, and at this point in the battle local successes were not enough.

While the Australians drew down the weight of Rommel's best about them, Montgomery was shuffling his army again for what he hoped would be the clinching attack—code named Supercharge. He had been thinking of trying for a breakthrough directly along the coast road but as Rommel had concentrated there, Montgomery now decided to hit a bit to the south toward the Rahman track and Tel el Aqqaqir.

To command Supercharge, Montgomery picked his toughest fighter, Bernard Freyberg, for no one saw this new assault as any easy breakthrough. Supported by 360 guns Freyberg was to use two infantry brigades on a 4,000-yard front.

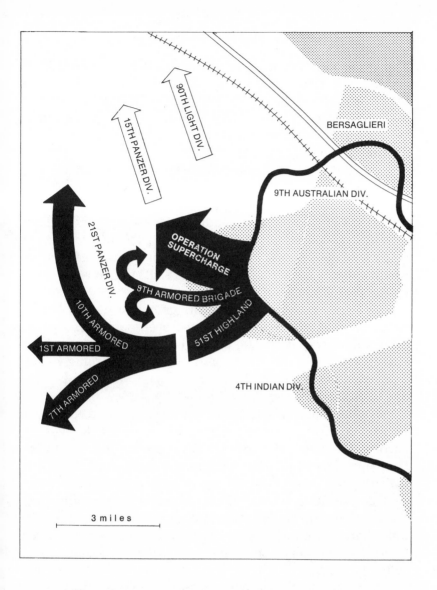

90TH LIGHT DIV.

15TH PANZER DIV.

BERSAGLIERI

21ST PANZER DIV.

OPERATION SUPERCHARGE

9TH AUSTRALIAN DIV.

9TH ARMORED BRIGADE

10TH ARMORED

51ST HIGHLAND

1ST ARMORED

7TH ARMORED

4TH INDIAN DIV.

3 miles

MONTGOMERY'S BREAKTHROUGH Again switching the main axis of his advance, Montgomery tried another great night attack, Operation Supercharge, similar to the one that had opened the battle. Once again, however, the British armor could not get through the minefields quickly enough and the 9th Armored Brigade, attacking at dawn, was slaughtered by Rommel's anti-tank guns. Then Montgomery attacked even further south with the 51st Highland Division, reinforced by Indian troops. Rommel had nothing left to stop this attack, and Montgomery's three armored divisions broke out into the open desert while Rommel, forced to delay his retreat by a stupid "stand and die" order from Hitler, only escaped westward with a small remnant of his army.

They were to advance 4,000 yards to objectives named Neat and Brandy, about 1,000 yards short of the Rahman track. On the right this was the job of the Durham Brigade, which had been brought up from the British 50th Division in the south. On the left the Seaforths and the Camerons of the Highland division got the assignment.

After the infantry objectives were secured, Currie's 9th Armored Brigade was to charge across the Rahman track and onto the low Aqqaqir Ridge just beyond it. The hope was to break the German gun screen during the last minutes of darkness. Currie pointed out to Freyberg that such an attack could mean a 50 percent loss in the tanks of his brigade. "The army commander," Freyberg told him, "has said that he is prepared to accept 100 percent." [13]

If Currie got through, then Briggs' 1st Armored Division would be ready to sweep on into the open desert. The whole thing was a very desperate enterprise. The moon was rising later every night and the infantry advance, needing moonlight, could not begin until after 1:00 A.M. Currie's tanks were due to go through them at 5:45.

The British artillery opened fire on time and the infantry stepped off. Once again the skirl of the pipes cut through the barrage, this time to be answered by a hunting horn from the Durhams. The Highlanders' advance was close to perfection with the Neat objective line taken right on schedule. There were dug-in German tanks along the way and two were taken intact in grenade attacks. But once on their Neat line, a half-mile short of the Rahman track, the Highlanders were lashed by German artillery and in the undiggable, rock-hard desert suffered badly.

On the right, the Durhams met with stiffer resistance than the Highlanders had, quite a bit more than had been foreseen. Casualties began to mount up early in the attack but the battalions pressed on. By 1:00 A.M. they had a tenuous hold on their Brandy objective. Unlike the great advance which had opened the battle nine nights before, this one had been met by heavy fire from the German artillery; yet the infantry had gotten through.

[13] Phillips, p. 336.

Now it was the turn of the tanks of Currie's 9th Armored Brigade. They had an eight-mile approach march to make and it was a horror. With a waning moon, there was little light and as the brigade's three regiments each made its way, two abreast, through its own minefield corridor, a head wind blew the fine desert dust right into the eyes of the tank drivers. They plowed on as they knew little darkness was left, and to attack the Axis gun screen after first light would be suicidal.

By 5:45, the appointed hour for Currie's attack, the 3rd Hussars on the right were up as were the Royal Wiltshire Yeomanry in the center. Currie's left-hand regiment, the Warwickshire Yeomanry, was still on the way. First light was getting much too close but Currie wanted all three regiments up for the charge. Fifteen regiments of field artillery were ordered to hold their fire for half an hour. By 6:15 Currie was ready and, in the van, standing on his tank, gave the order to go forward. "Driver, advance."

Right behind the barrage the British tanks moved ponderously ahead, 100 yards in three minutes. Suddenly they were in among the machine gunners and light anti-tank guns of the German front line. German and Italian prisoners started to filter to the rear. In the center the Wiltshires were across the Rahman track itself. But the big enemy guns, the 88's, were beyond the track. Behind the tanks the first traces of dawn brought a thin ribbon of light to the horizon. Against this ribbon of pale light the stark silhouettes of the British tanks now became visible to the German gunners. Immediately they opened fire.

The execution done by the big German guns was prompt and efficient. Entire troops of British tanks seemed to burst into flame simultaneously. For the British there was no thought of pulling back and it was impossible to stand still. The attack was pushed on. Between the Warwickshires on the left and the Wiltshires in the center, there was a slight gap. With superb skill, the 21st Panzer Division got a battle group into the gap and, using flanking fire on the British tanks on either side, knocked out one tank after another.

As the light increased so did the fury of the battle. Currie, still outside his tank, allowed no faltering and the attack was

pressed right up the muzzles of the Axis guns. The courage of
Currie's tankers was matched at the gun positions of the Germans and Italians. Small gaps were made in the line of guns,
some thirty-five were knocked out, but the gun screen held.
When seventy-five of the ninety-four attacking tanks had been
lost, the remnants of the 9th Armored Brigade pulled back
into defensive positions where they went on fighting.

The two brigades of Briggs' 1st Armored Division were
now coming up, having had an even worse approach march
than Currie's brigade. Currie himself was anxious for them
to plow right on in his path. The 2nd Armored Brigade came
up and its commander saw no gap for his tanks. In fact, the
scene of the battle looked like a British defeat.

To Rommel, it didn't look like a British defeat at all. The
British armored attack had been repulsed, but, once again, the
British infantry had driven a dangerous bulge into the German
line. Any British breakthrough now could mean complete disaster to the German-Italian Panzer Army. Rommel could not
allow the British to gather strength for another big attack. The
bulge created by Operation Supercharge must be wiped out,
and wiped out immediately.

Down from the north, where Rommel had expected the
8th Army would attack, came every available tank of the 15th
and 21st Panzer divisions. Orders went down to the south for
the Italian Ariete Armored Division to move north. The Panzer
Army was preparing to make its last great attack in the Western Desert. As the Axis tanks moved up, they were hammered
again and again by the RAF. "Air raid after air raid after air
raid," Rommel wrote his wife.[14]

By midday the German Panzers came on in force with the
thin-skinned Italian tanks in support. One hundred and twenty
Axis tanks went into action and all afternoon the desert
sounded like some gigantic blacksmith shop with the hard
armor-piercing shot banging against the hulls and turrets of
the tanks.

The British tanks now sat in defensive positions, taking
advantage of every fold in the ground to show as little of their

[14] Hart, ed., *The Rommel Papers,* p. 317.

bulk to the advancing Germans and Italians as possible. Rommel's tanks came in slowly, probing, advancing in short bounds. At one time they burst into the northern side of the British bulge but were thrown out. All the courage and skill of Rommel's men could not break the British grip on their newly won ground. Seventy-seven German tanks were knocked out, forty Italian. By the end of the day von Thoma would report to Rommel that his total German tank strength in both Panzer divisions was thirty-five.

Desert Victory

NOVEMBER 3, 1942

Rommel realized that it was time to leave. The Alamein position was broken. Only that very thin line of guns across the tip of the British bulge now held the 8th Army at bay. Rommel's orders went out to start the retreat. He was not a moment too soon, for that night Montgomery ordered small attacks south from the tip of his new bulge. They went off with surprising ease and more importantly met with little but light Italian resistance. Already a regiment of British armored cars had slipped around to the south of the Germans and was well in Rommel's rear.

On the morning of November 3rd, Rommel noted with great relief that the British attacks from the tip of their bulge were small and not pushed hard. The Italian infantry, for whom there were no trucks, were ordered out along the coastal road but were hit by RAF fighter-bombers. But at least the retreat had been started. Something would be saved from the wreckage.

At midday Rommel drove back to his command post, dodging bombs most of the way. He was in time to receive a personal communication from the Fuehrer:

> The German people join with me in following, with full confidence in your leadership and in the bravery of the German and Italian troops under your command, the heroic defense of Egypt. In your present situation nothing else can be thought of but to hold on, not to yield a step, and to throw every weapon and every fighting man

who can still be freed into the battle. . . . It would not
be the first time in history that the stronger will has tri-
umphed over the enemy's stronger battalions. You can
show your troops no other road than to victory or death.

Adolf Hitler [15]

The night before Rommel had detailed his desperately
bad position in a report to the Fuehrer and this, he thought,
was his answer. Actually, Rommel's wire had arrived after
Hitler had gone to bed, and there were no one who dared wake
him up. Rommel was not used to this kind of stand-or-die
order, and, although it was senseless, he could see no possible
course but to obey. Orders cancelling the retreat already in
progress went out, although some Italian columns had, luckily
for them, already retreated far enough to be out of touch. One
of Rommel's staff officers was sent off by plane to the Wolfschanze to try to get the Fuehrer to listen to reason.

All day the signs had been read in Montgomery's headquarters. It looked as though Rommel were preparing a withdrawal. There was, though, not to be another head-on crack by
the British but rather a deft sideslipping to the south to get
around the German flank and out into the clear. It had to be
laid on quickly and expertly. The task was given to Wimberley's Highland division.

The first objective was a point on the Rahman track about
two miles south of Tel el Aqqaqir, and the Gordon Highlanders
and a tank regiment were sent out. The 1st Armored Division
claimed that they already had tanks on the objective and the
Gordons could merely advance and occupy the ground. But the
1st Armored Division was off in its map reading, a very easy
thing to do in that featureless wilderness. A strong enemy
position barred the way. Better than half the tanks were shot
up and the infantry badly hurt. The attack was a failure.

When the corps commander talked of laying on the next
attack, even Wimberley hesitated. There seemed no end to the
pattern of attack without breakthrough. But the next one went
in, put on this time by part of the 4th Indian Division brought
up from the south. One Indian battalion got bogged down in
soft going on the way up. The attack was postponed for an hour

[15] Playfair and Molney, Vol. IV, pp. 475–476.

and not until 2:30 A.M. did two other battalions go forward with their supporting tanks. Their objective was a point on the Rahman track, about two miles south of where the Gordons had been stopped.

It was a long way, through what was to the troops a strange and unknown piece of desert. But the 4th Indian Division was a thoroughly professional, veteran outfit, and they had not gone through the long bloody battling of the past twelve days. Their attack went off perfectly, tanks and infantry working smoothly behind the barrage. Three hundred and fifty prisoners were taken and Rommel's Tel el Aqqaqir position was flanked. At first light the British armor moved through the Indians and, finally, out into the open beyond. There had been twelve days of fighting, as Montgomery had predicted, and now, at last, here was the breakthrough.

Rommel was indeed pulling back with his German divisions formed as a rearguard. The Highlanders poured into Tel el Aqqaqir itself and the front was smashed. Lumsden's 10th Corps, with all British tanks under command, roared out into the desert. The Italian Ariete Division was caught, and its old-fashioned tanks and even older guns could do nothing to stop Lumsden's armor. The Italians fought well but fruitlessly and the Ariete was quickly overwhelmed.

Then the British armor surged against the last position of the Afrika Korps. Von Sponeck's 90th Light Infantry remained unbroken but, down to less than two dozen tanks, the 15th and 21st Panzer divisions could not hold. Von Thoma, Rommel's second-in-command, came forward into the fighting. His tank went up in flames, but he lived to be captured and sent back to meet General Montgomery. By mid-afternoon Rommel had decided that the Fuehrer's "victory or death" order must be disobeyed. He ordered full retreat and as fast as possible. Hitler's authorization for the retreat came through the next morning.

The 8th Army gathered itself for the pursuit but only with great difficulty. The vast majority of Rommel's mines were still there and there were still corridors to be negotiated, many clogged with the wreckage of battle. Above all, after twelve days of hard fighting, the 8th Army was bone-tired, from the infantry private and the tank gunner right up to the highest staff officer. They had taken 13,500 casualties and there was no fresh force left for the pursuit.

On the day after the battle, November 5th, Montgomery sent Lumsden's armor out on a series of short left hooks, attempting to cut through to the coastal road behind Rommel. The Panzer Army, what was left of it, was doubling back at terrific speed and the left hooks mainly fell into empty space. Freyberg's New Zealanders, with armor attached, got into the traffic jam in the minefield corridors and was slow getting under way.

By the afternoon of the sixth, rains came to the desert and little but the paved coastal road was usable. There Rommel's rearguards fought with stubbornness when necessary, and his engineers with their mines and booby traps made the going hard for their pursuers.

Far to the south, out in the desert, the Italian divisions, who had held the southern part of the Alamein line, had no hope of escape. Some fought it out but most surrendered. The only Germans left on that part of the front when the battle ended had been General Ramcke's paratroop brigade. They had pulled back on foot and then stumbled across a British supply column. In moments they had captured the trucks and were racing to the rear. Six hundred of Ramcke's men got through.

By November 8th Rommel was gathering the survivors of Alamein along the Egyptian border. They would be organized only for further retreat as there was no possibility of making a fight for the Cyrenian bulge. He had only some five thousand German fighting troops and half as many Italians. There were less than two dozen tanks and about 150 guns of all types. Such was the measure of Montgomery's victory.

By eleven o'clock that morning Rommel knew that it was no longer a question of holding some line in Libya. The question now was whether anything in all of Africa could be held. He had gotten the news of vast American and British landings in French North Africa thousands of miles in his rear.

It had been only sixteen days since Stumme had sent his signal to Berlin—"Enemy situation unchanged." Then the

German-Italian Panzer Army had stood within easy striking distance of the great British naval base at Alexandria, as well as the Nile Delta and the Suez Canal. Now that army was in full retreat, 30,000 of its men and almost all of its tanks lost. British and American troops were landing in French North Africa in its rear. Now British convoys could go through to Malta protected by aircraft flying from Libyan airfields.

To Rommel, it was far worse than just a lost battle. Africa, the scene of so many German victories in the past, had suddenly become a vast trap. Rommel sensed what his enemy, Winston Churchill, was to put into words: that the battle of El Alamein "marked, in fact, the turning of the 'Hinge of Fate.'" [16]

[16] Churchill, *The Hinge of Fate*, p. 524.

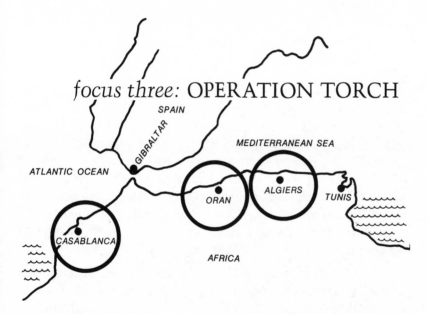

focus three: OPERATION TORCH

SPAIN

GIBRALTAR

MEDITERRANEAN SEA

ATLANTIC OCEAN

ORAN

ALGIERS

TUNIS

CASABLANCA

AFRICA

On the day before Montgomery's 1,000-gun barrage had opened the battle of El Alamein, the first of the convoys of Operation Torch, the invasion of French North Africa, had sailed. As Alamein was being fought, 107,000 British and American troops had been moving across the Atlantic. Ahead of them, in Algiers, one American diplomat had been trying to talk the French into not opposing the landings. No one knew if the French would fight, but everyone knew that what had started at Alamein as the battle for Egypt was now about to become the battle for the Mediterranean.

In the fall of 1942 Africa was still to almost all Americans "the dark continent," illuminated only by the French Foreign Legion of P. C. Wren's *Beau Geste* and the Tarzan adventures of Edgar Rice Burroughs. Generals and diplomats had shown interest only in continental Europe. One exception, and a most important one, was Robert Murphy, who since late 1940 had been President Roosevelt's personal representative in French North Africa. As a young diplomat Murphy had witnessed, in 1923, the farcical Munich beer hall putsch when Adolf Hitler, an almost unknown political agitator, had tried to seize power in Bavaria. He had attended Hitler's trial and sentencing and had prophetically reported that "the nationalist movement behind it is by no means extinguished in Bavaria.

It has simply been delayed. . . ." [1] After his tour of duty in Germany, Murphy had gone to France and, in time, had watched that "nationalist movement" of Hitler's crush the Third French Republic in 1940.

The French Army's defeat in the spring of 1940 had been complete. At the end of a six-week campaign, France was no longer a European military power. The French Army, which many people had thought the most powerful in the world, had disintegrated. France, and a good deal of the rest of the world, was stunned. To most Frenchmen one fact was clear— Hitler had won the war. Most thought that Britain would now have to sue for peace or, in the words of one French general, "have her neck wrung like a chicken."

Under the terms of the German-French armistice, concluded in June, the Germans occupied all of northern France including Paris as well as a strip of the French Atlantic coast running down to the Pyrenees and the Spanish border. All that was left of France was a small section of the south, and there a government was set up under the octogenarian hero of World War I, Marshal Henri Philippe Pétain, with its capital in the city of Vichy.

The men of the Vichy government were soon to be reviled by the peoples of Britain and the United States as traitors, villains, men willing to do anything to help Hitler win the war. Such, however, in most cases was not true. Most of them, convinced of Hitler's coming victory, were simply trying to salvage for France something out of the wreckage. Some, like the notorious Pierre Laval, thought that they could outfox Hitler and gain for France, and themselves, a position of power in a Nazified Europe.

Marshal Pétain played a smarter game. He knew that the Germans could march, unresisted, into Vichy France any time they wanted to. The Germans also held at their mercy hundreds of thousands of French prisoners. But Pétain had the French fleet, most of which was concentrated in the Mediterranean port of Toulon. Hitler did not want that fleet to sail off and join the British. There was also the French overseas empire,

[1] Murphy, *Diplomat Among Warriors*, p. 22.

which Hitler, having no fleet, could not touch. With these bargaining points, Pétain stalled. That October, Hitler offered Pétain various concessions to get more French cooperation in his war with Britain. A complex program was worked out but, as Pétain said to a friend, "It will take six months to discuss this program and then another six months to forget it." [2] Pétain was right, because a year from that October Hitler's armies were far from France. They were hundreds of miles inside Russia.

President Roosevelt kept close diplomatic ties with the Vichy government. He was severely criticized by those who considered the Vichyites as Nazis in French clothing, but Roosevelt was extremely interested in the French colonies in North Africa. If the Allies could get the use of the big French bases at Dakar and Casablanca on the west coast of Africa, they could more effectively fight the German submarines operating in the South Atlantic. If the Allies could get the French Mediterranean bases at Algiers, Oran and Tunis, they could control the Mediterranean. It was for these reasons that Robert Murphy had gone to Africa in late 1940.

On September 4, 1942, Murphy had been summoned to see Roosevelt at Hyde Park. The President told him that the invasion of French Africa was on. He impressed upon Murphy the necessity for secrecy—"Don't tell anybody in the State Department about this. That place is a sieve." [3] Nor were the de Gaullists, the Free French headquartered in London, to be let in on the secret. Neither Roosevelt nor Churchill had any liking for the often arrogant, always difficult de Gaulle. What was more important, his bungled attempt to take Dakar on the Atlantic coast of Africa two years before had been bitterly resented by the French officials in Africa. Murphy knew that to a great extent in the French Army, and almost unanimously in the Air Force and Navy, de Gaulle's name was anathema. There were, however, Murphy said, important Frenchmen willing to cooperate with the Allies.

[2] Bullock, *Hitler: A Study in Tyranny*, p. 606.
[3] Murphy, p. 102.

To Roosevelt, with his great feel for political intrigue, this was good news. To General Marshall and Secretary of War Stimson, it made little difference. They wanted an invasion strong enough to beat down any French resistance and were convinced that if there was too much talking with pro-Allied Frenchmen the secret of the invasion would get back to Hitler. Marshall was adamant on the point that Murphy must not confide the actual invasion plans to any Frenchman until the very last moment.

Marshall did decide, though, that Murphy must go see Eisenhower. But if the United States' leading African expert were to show up at his London headquarters, German intelligence could certainly put two and two together. "We'll disguise you in a lieutenant colonel's uniform," said Marshall. "Nobody ever pays any attention to a lieutenant colonel." [4]

So, in mid-September a mysterious Lt. Col. MacGowan landed at Prestwick in Scotland. An old friend who recognized the Colonel as Robert Murphy was rushed off under temporary arrest, and the Colonel proceeded to a small cottage on the outskirts of London, nestled between two golf courses, where Eisenhower had his retreat from the bustle of his downtown London headquarters.

Under a tall pine Eisenhower and his experts listened with no little horror to Murphy's recital of the intricacies of French colonial politics into which they were about to be thrown. Murphy described an area of over 1,000,000 square miles with a population of over 16,000,000. Within this population were political and religious divisions which threatened explosion at any time. There were the Moslem tribes and city dwellers, the vast majority. They had little use for the native Jews. Nor were most Moslems convinced of the benefits of French colonialism with its ever-present troops and immensely wealthy French landowners. The European population had been swollen by about 200,000 war refugees of every shade of political persuasion. Eisenhower's lines of communication would run through this turbulent area for 1,200 miles, from his westernmost port at Casablanca to Tunis, the ulti-

[4] Murphy, p. 102.

mate objective of the campaign. The French, through a combination of administrative miracles and 120,000 troops, had
managed to keep order. Eisenhower had no intention of taking
over this policing function from the French as he would need
his troops for the advance from Algiers to Tunis. He must
invade French territory but make French friends at the same
time.

Of vital importance, then, were the men who controlled
this empire in the name of the Vichy government and its
chief, Marshal Henri Philippe Pétain. Not only was the aged
Marshal's portrait a popular wall decoration for the houses
and apartments of the French inhabitants, but he himself
was very definitely a figure of veneration and genuine respect
to the men who ran the colonies. To them he had kept the
French fleet at Toulon and Casablanca out of German hands
and, especially, he had maintained French control in Africa.
He was also a Marshal of France and to a military man that
was no empty title.

Number two man to Pétain was a five-star admiral, Jean
Charles François Darlan, who acted as commander-in-chief
of all the French forces. The Admiral was rabidly anti-British
and, in 1940, had collaborated with the Germans, not because
he was pro-Nazi, but because he saw them as the victors in
the war. Now his mind had changed and, by 1942, he had
been making very discreet overtures of friendship to the Americans.

In Africa, Darlan was a very important man. He was
chief of the armed forces and the armed forces ran Africa. In
Algeria there was a governor general, Yves Chatel, but the
real power was vested in Admiral Raymond Fénard, a protégé
and good friend of Darlan. Overall Army command was held
by General Alphonse Juin who was something of a political
enigma. He had been captured by the Germans in 1940 and
paroled after giving his word that he would not fight against
them during the remainder of the war. The Allies thought that
Juin might regard this pledge as having been given "under
duress" and thus consider it invalid. He could be counted on as
sympathetic to the Allies but was certainly not a man to lead a
break with the authority of the Vichy government.

In Tunisia where the Allies did not plan to land, but into which they did intend to make a rapid advance, the head man was another admiral loyal to Darlan, Jean-Pierre Estéva. As Resident General, he ruled in the name of the native Bey of Tunis, a figurehead. As the French commander nearest the Germans, Estéva was an understandably nervous man.

In Morocco, where the major American landings were to be made, the real power, as in Tunisia, was not in the hands of the Sultan but in those of the Resident General, Auguste Noguès, a dapper, shrewd general who had perched delicately on the fence while pronouncing a policy of defense against all comers. Actually, he was ready to bow to a superior force, whether Allied or Axis.

The naval commander in Morocco was Admiral Michelier, very definitely unfriendly to the Allies, but the Army division in Casablanca was commanded by a very pro-Allied general, Émile Marie Bethouart. Here, at least, was a situation with possibilities.

The importance of Admiral Darlan was obvious but there was no Allied leader who could bring himself to trust him. What they had been searching for was a French leader who was above the intricacies of politics and who could marshal all Frenchmen behind him to renew the fight with Hitler's Germany. Back in April, Churchill had wired Roosevelt expressing great interest in General Henri Giraud. The General had just managed to escape from a German prison, a feat he had accomplished in the First World War as well. He had a fine military record and, undeniably, was a hero and not associated with the Vichy government. He seemed just the man to the romantic natures of Roosevelt and Churchill. The cynical, tough, rather bitter leaders of French Africa were not, however, romantically inclined.

Colonel MacGowan, leaving Eisenhower and his staff with much to think about, left for Washington and then Africa again. He had at least set the General straight on the fact that he would need winter underwear for the coming campaign and that Algiers was more like Paris than a set for a Tarzan movie. He had not, however, left with a completely clear picture of just what the military operations were to be but with very clear instructions that he was to reveal nothing to his French contacts until the last minute.

By mid-October Murphy, having shed his Colonel Mac-Gowan disguise, was back in Africa. In Casablanca he made a desperate effort to get Noguès onto the Allied side but the General was not interested. He told Murphy it was too late for France to get back into the war and threatened to oppose any landings with force. Noguès' great worry, like that of the other French commanders, was that the Allies would land only a small raiding force which would be quickly evacuated when the Germans struck back. With Murphy forbidden to disclose any details of the strength of the coming invasion, Noguès' mind could not be relieved.

Murphy, however, hoped that in Casablanca General Béthouart, commanding the Army division, could at least temporarily checkmate his commander, Noguès, and that there might be a peaceful landing. With the heavy Atlantic surf to contend with, the thought of a peaceful landing there was a comforting one. Béthouart became a willing conspirator.

The prospects of help in the landing at Oran, inside the Mediterranean, were far dimmer than at Casablanca. The Chief of Staff of the French Army's Oran division was entirely sympathetic but was not high enough in the chain of command or daring enough to be a really effective conspirator. Murphy would have to make his main effort in the capital, Algiers.

Here Murphy had contacted Admiral Fénard, Darlan's number one man in Algeria, as well as Darlan's young son, Alain, a junior officer in the French Navy. These two tried to convince Murphy that Admiral Darlan was now convinced of Hitler's ultimate defeat and was more than willing to co-operate with the Allies. Darlan, however, had been built up as such a villain in both the British and American press that neither Roosevelt nor Churchill relished the political consequences of making any kind of deal with him. Besides that, they did not trust him and thought that in General Giraud they had the right man anyway.

Thus Murphy made contact with General Charles Mast, commander of the Algiers Army division, and several others who had excellent contacts with Giraud in France. Eisenhower, with D-Day for the invasion of French Africa growing near, decided to send his own number two man, General Mark Clark, to meet with the Mast group near Algiers.

On October 22nd, the day before the Battle of El Alamein began, a British submarine brought Clark and his American aides to a meeting with Mast and his Frenchmen at a seaside villa just west of Algiers. The two groups got along well together but there was little really accomplished as the Americans were not yet willing to let the French in on the fact that D-Day was a little more than two weeks off. The French went ahead with their planning on the assumption that nothing was going to happen until the following spring.

Eisenhower's thinking was that Giraud could be brought in as the supreme political leader of all French North Africa as Governor General and possibly Darlan used as commander of French military forces. But this line of thinking was not revealed to General Mast and his group. The Frenchmen did bring up the matter of command, and what they wanted was General Giraud in command of all forces, British and American as well as French. This was a point of French honor and, as General Giraud had put it in a letter from France, "We don't want the Americans to free us; we want them to help us free ourselves, which is not quite the same." [5] Clark, appalled as he was at the thought of Eisenhower becoming junior to Giraud, just said that the question would be settled "at the appropriate time." This was all right with General Mast as he thought there were six months, not three weeks, to go.

The meeting was finally broken up by the arrival of some nosy French police. The American generals hid in the wine cellar and were not discovered. General Clark lost his pants in the heavy surf when they all had to get into their little rubber boats for the return trip out to the waiting submarine. With the help of the British commandos who were wet-nursing the group, the boarding was finally accomplished and the commandos were well rewarded when Clark personally brought them a bottle of whiskey after they were all safely back on board.

[5] Howe, *Northwest Africa: Seizing the Initiative in the West*, p. 82.

General Mast had greatly impressed the American officers and within a week of the meeting Murphy was allowed to tell him that the invasion would not be in the spring but within a week or two. Mast was horrified at the thought of all the details to be taken care of before then. Then, on November 1st, a letter came to Africa from Giraud protesting to Murphy that he couldn't possibly leave France before November 20th. As D-Day was November 8th, it looked like the whole conspiracy was falling apart.

Murphy immediately wired to President Roosevelt, "I am convinced that the invasion of North Africa without favorable French high command will be a catastrophe. The delay of two weeks, unpleasant as it may be, involving technical considerations of which I am ignorant, is insignificant compared with the result involving serious opposition of the French Army to our landing." [6]

The technical considerations of which Murphy was indeed ignorant were rather overwhelming. Six hundred and fifty ships were already at sea carrying just over 100,000 men on their way to Africa. Murphy was overruled and General Giraud decided to leave France earlier in a British submarine but with an American captain, a concession to French honor.

Three days after Murphy's message was received and overruled, Dwight Eisenhower left London for his command post in the bowels of Gibraltar. His last fling in London had been a private showing of the Bob Hope and Bing Crosby movie, "The Road to Morocco." His plane, a B-17 bomber, took off on the morning of the fifth even though the weather was typically bad for an English November. The plane, named the *Red Gremlin,* landed at the tricky Gibraltar airstrip in the afternoon, expertly handled by Major Paul Tibbets who, three years later, would handle a B-29 named *Enola Gay* when it took the first atomic bomb to Hiroshima.

The great buildup of shipping at Gibraltar had not been missed by Axis reconnaissance planes. The Italian General Staff and Mussolini himself divined that this meant an attempt,

[6] Murphy, pp. 120–121.

probably American, against French North Africa. But the Italian General Staff and the Duce were junior partners in the Axis. Hitler and his own staff thought otherwise and wired Rome on the 7th that "all defensive preparations should be made in Tripoli and Benghazi, including the erection of road blocks." [7] The Fuehrer also ordered the reinforcement of Crete and then boarded his special train for the trip from East Prussia to Munich where he would join the old-timers of the Nazi party in celebrating the 1923 Beerhall Putsch which Robert Murphy had so long ago witnessed.

On November 7th, as Hitler's train began its long trip, the submarine carrying General Henri Giraud arrived at Gibraltar and the General went into conference with Eisenhower. The conference turned out to be rather unpleasant. Henri Giraud made it quite plain that he intended to have Eisenhower's job, commander of all Allied forces, and intended to have it there and then. That seemed to be overdoing the honor of France a bit. Eisenhower argued until he was quite literally red in the face. Clark told Giraud, "We don't need you after tonight." [8] Giraud continued to argue.

The Battle of Algiers

NOVEMBER 8, 1942

While Giraud argued in Gibraltar, Robert Murphy waited in Algiers. Just before midnight his radio picked up a message from the BBC—"Allo, Robert. Franklin arrive." That meant that the invasion was on. Murphy alerted General Mast's pro-Allied French and quickly they moved in on the sleeping city. Military headquarters, police headquarters, the radio station and various key points were soon under Mast's control. They expected the American troops to arrive between three and four in the morning. They waited, but the troops did not arrive.

Murphy was getting itchy. Giraud was meant to appear and with him Murphy would call on Army Commander-in-Chief, Juin. But Giraud was arguing with Eisenhower and

[7] Warlimont, *Inside Hitler's Headquarters*, p. 271.
[8] Butcher, *My Three Years with Eisenhower*, p. 171.

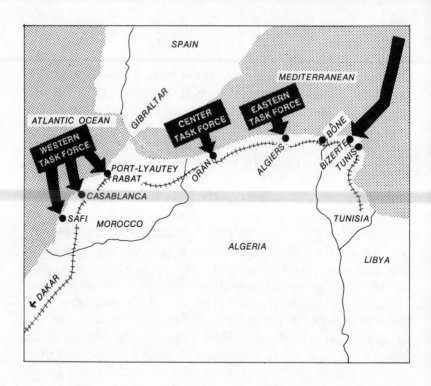

OPERATION TORCH Under the command of General Eisenhower, with his headquarters at Gibraltar, Allied landings were
made on November 8, 1942, at Algiers, Oran and Casablanca.
French resistance ceased by November 11th and Eisenhower immediately dispatched troops from Algiers westward to take Tunis,
where a scratch force of German paratroopers had been landed.

Murphy had to tackle General Juin on his own. The General
got the news dressed in his pink-striped pajamas. An invasion!
No, said Murphy, the United States forces were arriving at the
invitation of General Giraud. Where was Giraud? Not in
Algiers. But Admiral Darlan was. His son, Alain, had con-
tracted polio and the Admiral had come over from France to
be with him. Juin explained that anything he did could be
instantly overruled by the Admiral who was, after all, commander of all French forces everywhere. "Very well," said
Murphy, "let us talk with Darlan." [9]

In twenty minutes the little Admiral came over to Juin's

[9] Murphy, p. 128.

villa with Admiral Fénard, his deputy for Algeria. Darlan was thunderstruck at the news. "A massive blunder," he called it.[10] Without previous warning, there was little he could do. He paced the floor puffing his pipe and muttering. Murphy, pacing beside him, argued the American case and wondered just where the troops were. They should have been at the house by now. A horrible thought occurred to Murphy—could he have gotten things confused and started everything a day early?

Then, just as Juin had passed the buck on up to Darlan, the Admiral decided that he must pass it on up to Marshal Pétain in Vichy. He wrote a message to the'Marshal asking for a free hand in dealing with what was to him a confused situation at best. But when Darlan and Juin went out the front door to find a messenger, they found that some of Mast's irregulars had disarmed Juin's guards and were holding them all prisoners.

Murphy found a United States vice-consul outside and told him to get the Admiral's message downtown and have it sent off. The French naval officer who got the message smelled a rat. He phoned Darlan and word went out to Vichy that Darlan was a prisoner of the Americans. By the time Vichy heard this, it was no longer true. A bunch of tough *Gardes Mobiles*, alerted by Juin's headquarters, had arrived and Murphy was now a French prisoner. Darlan and Juin left to find out what was going on.

The troops that Murphy had been expecting were still, by dawn, tangled up in the extremely difficult task of getting ashore on a strange beach. The military plan had called for an American regiment to land about fifteen miles east of Algiers and for a similar British force, a brigade, to land about the same distance to the west. These two landings went relatively well but that of another American regiment only eight miles west of the city had been badly fouled up.

The British crews manning the landing craft were, like the United States infantry they were carrying, not even half-trained for their mission. There had been too little time. The landing force was scattered over miles of beach and the

[10] Murphy, p. 129.

regimental commander, "Iron Mike" O'Daniel, was put ashore seven miles off target. O'Daniel's troops were lucky. There to meet them on the beaches was General Mast, who had ordered no resistance. There his orders had been obeyed.

Mast had performed his part nobly. His men in the city, though, could not hold out too long and by the time O'Daniel's troops started for Algiers, Juin's men had taken over. French resistance began to make itself felt. Fortunately, many of the French troops were by now confused as to whether they should fight or not. One United States battalion met a company of Vietnamese whose French commander was away downtown. The second-in-command had no idea what to do and the Americans passed by the Vietnamese quite peacefully. O'Daniel, once he had enough men ashore, got them moving fast. Shortly after noon they were on the outskirts of the city.

In Algiers harbor the Allies had met with disaster. Two British destroyers, the *Broke* and *Malcolm,* with a battalion of United States troops aboard had been ordered to break into the harbor and land the troops who were then to prevent the French from sabotaging the docks. The shore batteries, under French naval control, opened fire as the two ships, blinded by searchlights, tried to find the narrow harbor entrance. The *Malcolm* was hit in the engine room and limped away. The *Broke* crashed into the boom stretched across the harbor entrance and got into the harbor itself. She got her company of troops ashore but they were soon surrounded and, low on ammunition, forced to surrender, although they had held out much longer than would have been necessary if the troops coming overland had met their schedule. The *Broke* managed to limp away, badly hit, only to sink the next day while under tow.

The time for decision was fast approaching for Darlan and Juin. Not only were O'Daniel's men now approaching the city but the other United States regiment which had landed to the east had taken the Algiers airport and the British brigade was coming up to join O'Daniel. In mid-afternoon Darlan came back to see Murphy. He said he wanted to get in touch with the American commander. Murphy, borrowing a car from

Darlan, drove to the beaches, found General Ryder, the United States commander, and by evening a cease-fire had been agreed to. The Allies had taken Algiers.

At Oran and Casablanca, where landings had been carried out at the same time, things were not going as easily.

The Battle of Oran

NOVEMBER 8–10, 1942

Oran and the French naval base of Mers-el-Kebir, just west of it, had been figured as a rough objective. At Mers-el-Kebir, in 1940, the British had attacked the French fleet, not for a minute believing Darlan's assurance that it would never be allowed to fall into German hands. French losses had been very heavy and the bitterness that resulted in the French Navy was, correctly, thought to be unabated.

Even so the plans for the Oran attack called for two former United States Coast Guard cutters, now in the Royal Navy, to sweep into the harbor as the *Broke* and *Malcolm* had done at Algiers. Aboard were some 393 men of the United States 6th Armored Infantry. The two cutters, *Walney* and *Hartland,* went crashing into the harbor almost on schedule at three in the morning of D-Day, November 8th. They carried large American flags but also the hated White Ensign of the Royal Navy. Instantly they were brought under fire by everything the French could throw at them, shore batteries, machine guns and by French submarines and destroyers in the harbor. Neither British ship had a chance although they fought with extraordinary courage, the *Walney* narrowly missing an attempt to ram a French destroyer. At Algiers the French had seemed to fire mostly to keep the men ashore pinned down. At Oran they were shooting to kill from the start. Both British ships were soon on fire and sinking with the dead in many places piled two or three deep on the decks. Only forty-seven out of the 393 American troops they carried got ashore unhurt where they were immediately taken prisoner by the French.

With a liking for military gimmicks, the Oran attack also included the use of American paratroopers who were flown

1,200 miles from England to land or parachute on the two air-fields south of the city. The operation was a mess from the beginning. The twin-engined C-47's took off from southern England after Eisenhower's headquarters had mistakenly given them the word that there would be a peaceful landing. During the night the flight formations disintegrated, the planes never picked up the homing radio beam off Oran, and none of them knew that they weren't to land but to make a combat jump.

One plane landed at Gibraltar, two in French Morocco and three in Spanish Morocco. One arrived over the Oran air-field and was fired at, thus learning that this was a combat operation. Some planes landed too near Oran and their pas-sengers were quickly captured by the French police. Some landed about twenty-five miles from their objectives. None was at all effective on D-Day.

Aside from the gimmicks, there was, fortunately, the more orthodox landing of Major General Terry Allen's 1st Division and a combat command, about half, of the 1st Armored Division. Two of Terry Allen's three infantry regi-ments and most of his tanks were to come in through the beaches and tiny port of Arzew about twenty-five miles east of Oran. The other regiment and tanks would land west of the city. The two infantry forces would converge and sur-round the city, while the armored forces captured the two airfields just to the south.

The attacks to the west, the minor ones, went well enough though there were the inevitable confusions and delays. The big guns of the French batteries near Mers-el-Kebir were greatly discouraged by the even bigger guns of the British battleship *Rodney*. Interference by French warships was smothered by the Royal Navy, which sunk three French ships.

At Arzew, where the main landings were scheduled, United States Rangers came ashore first to capture the French forts whose fire could cover the beaches. In one of the forts, by a lucky coincidence, was a Foreign Legion captain who was an American. With his help, and due to the utter lack of preparedness of the garrisons, the Rangers took the forts easily. Allen's two infantry regiments came ashore against almost no opposition and by breakfast time were moving inland while light tanks came in behind them. Tank landing craft for the bigger Sherman tanks had been improvised for the invasion by cutting away the bows from some oil tankers of very shallow draft used in peacetime on Lake Maracaibo in Venezuela. They were quite successful, and by breakfast the tanks were ashore and headed for Tafaroui airfield ten miles south of Oran. They had the field by noon and there were Spitfires on it by late afternoon.

Six miles inland on the Arzew-Oran road French resistance began to stiffen. A battalion of the United States 18th Infantry came up against the masonry and concrete houses of the small farming village of St. Cloud manned by men of a Tunisian regiment and the 1st Battalion of the Foreign Legion. The first American attack was quickly thrown back. A second battalion of the 18th Infantry came forward plus some self-propelled 105mm howitzers. The second American attack was repulsed with the Legionnaires living up to their Beau Geste reputation. A third American battalion came forward, but another attack was put off until the next morning.

But at dawn the following day, the 9th, it was the French who attacked first. They came in from the south against the Arzew beaches in an attack that seemed to threaten the rear of the United States troops advancing on the city. A flap ensued at task force headquarters. Communications were bad, messages were garbled and no one was quite clear as to just how powerful the French attack was. "Help coming: tanks, engineers, bombers, Spitfires," radioed the task force commander to the American battalion that was holding the critical area south of the beaches.[11] Even a British light cruiser was ordered up to give gunfire support. But then it turned out that all this was quite unnecessary. The single battalion there dealt with the weak French attack quickly and easily.

Another French attack was spotted coming up from the south headed for Tafaroui airfield captured the day before. The French tanks, though, turned out to be obsolete World War I models and were easily driven off. Fourteen French

[11] Howe, p. 217.

tanks were lost as against only one American. The United States forces then captured the second of Oran's airfields but, when they attacked again at St. Cloud, they were once more driven back. General Allen now decided that it was best to leave the Foreign Legionnaires in St. Cloud and simply move around it.

Indeed, there was now enough American strength ashore that the isolated pockets of French resistance could be masked, and the United States columns of tanks and infantry detoured around them. This was done and, on the following morning, an armored column drove into the middle of the city right up to French headquarters. By noon Oran had surrendered. Terry Allen had won a victory all right, but there were some of his men who wondered out loud just what would have happened if there had been a battalion or two of Germans around.

The Battle of Casablanca

NOVEMBER 8–11, 1942

While Algiers and Oran were falling, Eisenhower sat in his headquarters at Gibraltar bedevilled by lack of information. To ease the strain the Commanding General jotted down a list of things he was most eager to get word on. Topping the list was "West Coast Operations." For on the west coast of Africa it was to be an all-American operation—land, sea and air. Mounted directly from United States ports, the Western Task Force had to cross the ocean, dodge the U-boats and then tackle the beaches. The troops of Auguste Noguès, ashore, were some of the best the French had. The ships under Admiral Michelier were a very real threat. And above all there was the heavy Atlantic surf which could, at this time of the year, be bad enough to prevent any landing at all.

There was also the United States military commander, George S. Patton, Jr., a strange combination of Virginia military aristocrat, Western badman, religious mystic, professional soldier and P. T. Barnum. In 1909 his future father-in-law asked Patton to write him his reasons for wanting a military career. Patton wrote, "I have tried to give myself reasons but have never found any logical ones. I only feel it inside. It is as natural for me to be a soldier as it is to breathe and it would be as hard to give up all thought of it as it would be stop breathing." Then Patton told him exactly what he thought a soldier was. "Being a soldier and being a member of the army in time of peace are two different things. I would only accept the latter as a means to the former." [12]

Patton had proved his taste for action under Pershing in Mexico on the fruitless chase after Pancho Villa when, in 1916, he had gunned down one of Villa's bodyguards in the best Western style. He proved it again when, in 1918, he led the brand-new American Tank Corps at St. Mihiel and the Argonne and impressed not only old Pershing but a young staff officer, George Marshall.

In 1920 Congress had appropriated only $500 for tanks, and Patton had gone back to his first love, the cavalry. His career was then well summed up by one of his commanders who wrote in Patton's efficiency report, "This man would be invaluable in time of war but is a disturbing element in time of peace." [13] To the "old army" Patton was more trouble than he was worth but in Marshall's book it was the other way round.

Marshall resurrected Patton and in the fall of 1941, in the big Louisiana maneuvers, he made his mark as commander of the 2nd Armored Division. A year later he was Marshall's own choice to command the attack on Casablanca.

On October 20th Patton made out his will and with the expedition's naval commander, Admiral Kent Hewitt, went to say farewell to President Roosevelt. "Sir," said George Patton, "all I want to tell you is this—I will leave the beaches either a conqueror or a corpse." [14] The next day he knelt before an ancient General Pershing in Washington's Walter Reed Hospital, received his old commander's blessing and exchanged salutes with him. It was all a rather medieval beginning for a modern campaign.

As the opening guns of Alamein thundered out, Hewitt

---

[12] Farago, *Patton: Ordeal and Triumph*, p. 56.
[13] Farago, p. 112.
[14] Farago, p. 195.

took Patton aboard his flagship, the heavy cruiser *Augusta*, for the trip across. The Admiral, looking more like Hollywood's idea of a friendly druggist than a sea dog, was quite the antithesis of the General. Unruffled, friendly, both a fine seaman and administrator, Hewitt won the General's confidence but could never keep him from putting a "goddam" in front of the word, "Navy."

Hewitt's fleet and Patton's army were powerful forces on paper. In reality their inexperience appalled the commanders. Hewitt's four small escort-carriers, converted oil tankers, had not even finished their normal shaking-down period. The air group on his one big carrier, the *Ranger*, had only been on board three weeks. The crews of the attack transports, of the small landing craft and of many a warship were just as green. Nor was the United States Army any better off. As soon as any unit became even adequately trained, it would lose many of its most experienced men to make up cadres for new units just being formed. And an amphibious operation was just as new and mysterious to General Patton as it was to the greenest of his privates.

There was no question of a direct assault on Casablanca itself. The city was covered by powerful shore batteries, and moored in the harbor was the French battleship *Jean Bart*, immobile but with four 15-inch guns operating. Eighteen miles north of Casablanca were the inviting beaches of the small port of Fedala. Here Patton planned to attack with the three infantry regiments of the 3rd Division. Medium tanks could not be landed across beaches, and the nearest spot with docking facilities to receive them was at Safi, 140 miles to the south. Here one regiment of the United States 9th Infantry Division would come ashore to capture the port. Then the tanks of Patton's old division, the 2nd Armored, would be unloaded and readied for the 140-mile drive north to Casablanca.

About eighty miles north of Casablanca was the port and invaluable airfield at Port-Lyautey which, with its all-weather runways, would have to be the buildup point for shore-based air. Another regiment of the 9th Division was to take Port-Lyautey. All this would have to be done with considerable speed. It was a dead certainty that once the operation started, the U-boats of Admiral Karl Doenitz would start heading for the scene.

Admiral Hewitt had charted the huge convoy's path across the Atlantic with such skill that not a single U-boat sighted it, but two days before the November 8th D-day came something worse than U-boats. It was a weather report from Washington and London which predicted fifteen-foot surf on the Moroccan beaches. Hewitt's own weather officer disagreed. Hewitt decided to stick with his own man and the convoy divided into three parts for the assault.

While Hewitt's fleet headed for its objectives, the pro-Allied French under General Béthouart went into action. Unfortunately, their attempts to get Patton's men ashore peacefully were a complete flop. One of the earlier American plans for the West Coast landings had called for a landing at Rabat, the capital of Morocco, official residence of the Sultan and Resident General Noguès. Later, the plans had been changed and the Port-Lyautey landing had been substituted for the one at Rabat. No one thought to tell General Béthouart.

So, on the night before D-Day, Béthouart had waited in vain for an American landing at Rabat. His men, who had surrounded Noguès', stated that General Giraud had arrived in Africa to take command there and that Giraud's orders were for everyone to cooperate with the Americans. Noguès could see no Americans and Giraud had not arrived in Africa but was arguing with Eisenhower and Clark in Gibraltar instead.

One of Béthouart's men took a similar letter to Admiral Michelier at naval headquarters in Casablanca. Michelier simply did not believe a word of it. There were, as yet, no reports of large Allied forces anywhere around; Michelier got Noguès on the telephone and told him he thought Béthouart had been taken in by some sort of a hoax.

Later in the morning, Noguès heard of the fighting in Algiers and Casablanca, but he heard nothing of General Giraud. He ordered Béthouart to surrender and this order was obeyed. Béthouart had never wanted to be responsible for Frenchmen fighting Frenchmen and, not having any idea of what had gone wrong, gave himself up. He was sent to the interior of Morocco to await trial on charges of treason.

While Béthouart's conspiracy was falling apart, the attack transports bearing the United States 3rd Division were approaching Fedala to make the main attack. Patton's staff had hoped to put some 6,000 troops ashore before daylight which was a bit overoptimistic as the plans of inexperienced staffs usually are. Boats from one ship had to find another in the dark to pick up their load of troops and not all the transports were in their exact positions. Troops carrying as much as ninety pounds of equipment were painfully slow in climbing down cargo nets from the decks of their transports to the little landing boats bobbing around below. And three hours before H-hour the BBC had started broadcasting President Roosevelt's proclamation to the French that the invasion was a peaceful one. The broadcasts were timed to coincide with the earlier H-hour in Algeria. It didn't give anything away as no one of importance in Morocco heard the broadcasts except the German Armistice Commission.

About forty minutes before dawn the first waves of the United States troops finally hit the beach. There was silence and it looked as though there would be no opposition. But as dawn came, the French shore batteries opened up on the beaches. Four American destroyers closed in to silence them. The French batteries switched their fire to the destroyers. One of them, the *Murphy*, radioed, "This damn turkey is getting our range." [15] The *Murphy* was right and limped out of action with one engine knocked out. The cruiser *Brooklyn* came up with her 6-inch guns and poured in better than ten shots a minute for over an hour. When the 3rd Division troops arrived, the French gun crews were all sheltered in the undamaged concrete latrine. Some French guns were hidden among the tanks in the oil storage area and American gunners were told to be careful. The oil would be of great value later. Most of the tanks, though, were dry.

The ground opposition simply consisted of about 200 dispirited Senegalese troops who surrendered as soon as they

[15] Morison, *History of United States Naval Operations in World War II*, Vol. II, *Operations in North African Waters*, p. 75.

got the chance. They were unable to put a crimp in Patton's plans but the weather soon did. It was a relatively calm day, but the Atlantic surf was hard on the landing boats anyway. They got in to the beach but found it very hard to get back off. Soon the beaches were strewn with landing craft being battered into hulks by the waves. The troops were ashore but, with so many landing craft lost, the supplies that must follow them would be badly slowed up.

General Patton, on board the cruiser *Augusta,* was waiting anxiously to get ashore. He sent off an aide to get his two pistols, a Colt .45 and a Smith and Wesson .357, out of the ship's boat that was swinging in its davits, ready to be lowered to carry the General into battle. Patton strapped on the pistols just as the *Augusta's* aft turret fired and the concussion knocked the bottom out of the boat dumping all Patton's gear into the Atlantic. But he had his two pistols.

The General was not to get off the *Augusta* for a while yet as she now had urgent business. At 8:18 A.M. word was received that the French Navy was making its move. Seven destroyers followed by a light cruiser were coming out of Casablanca harbor headed straight for the transports. Admiral Michelier had decided to take on the United States Navy.

For a bit over an hour Hewitt's covering group, the brand-new battleship *Massachusetts* and the heavy cruisers *Wichita* and *Tuscaloosa* had been dueling with the anchored *Jean Bart* and the heavy coastal guns of Casablanca. The *Massachusetts,* at a range of nearly seventeen miles, fired nine salvos at the *Jean Bart* and got an incredible five hits. The last one jammed the French ship's turret and effectively put her out of action. Dive-bombers from the aircraft carrier *Ranger* had joined in the fight and had sunk three French submarines in the harbor.

While firing, the United States heavy ships had paraded up and down in front of the port. When their parade had carried them well away from the transport area, Admiral Michelier ordered Admiral Gervais de Lafond to sortie. De Lafond did so without even knowing the nationality of the ships he was attacking. With him he had two big destroyer leaders and five destroyers, carrying thirty guns of better than

5-inch and thirty-eight torpedo tubes all told. Within forty-five minutes they had been joined by eight submarines and the light cruiser *Primauguet*.

Between the transports and the French were the American destroyers *Ludlow* and *Wilkes*. The *Ludlow* got a hit on Admiral de Lafond's flagship, the destroyer *Milan*, but in return took one that set her on fire and knocked her out of action for the morning. Then, to the great relief of the men on the transports, up came the heavy cruiser *Augusta*, the light cruiser *Brooklyn* and two destroyers.

The American and French ships sparred for a while but then the heavy artillery of Admiral Hewitt's support group, including the 16-inch guns of the *Massachusetts*, joined in. De Lafond sent two of his destroyers streaking toward the Americans in a torpedo attack. The *Massachusetts* and the heavy cruiser *Tuscaloosa* blew the leading one out of the water. The French submarines went into action without any luck. A torpedo missed the *Massachusetts* by fifteen feet and another missed the *Tuscaloosa* by only a bit more.

The French ships fought with great skill, dashing in and out of smoke screens to present as little opportunity to the American gunners as possible. The odds against them were far too great. Later in the morning the rapid-firing *Brooklyn* got another destroyer. De Lafond's flagship, the destroyer *Milan*, was badly holed and the light cruiser *Primauguet* took a fearful pounding whenever she showed herself. Dive-bombers from the carrier *Ranger* added their bombs to the ships' shells. By noon the French ships were back in Casablanca harbor, two more destroyers so badly hurt they sank in the harbor. The French had only one ship, a destroyer, left undamaged.

After some totally ineffective fighting in the afternoon, with the French simply getting pounded badly without accomplishing anything, the naval fighting came to an end. How the honor of the French Navy, for which the battle had been fought, now stood, it was hard for anyone to say. Four destroyers and eight submarines had been sunk, other ships badly damaged and some four hundred French sailors were dead. The United States Navy had lost three men.

General Patton had been an unwilling spectator to the naval battle but had finally gotten off the *Augusta* and ashore at Fedala by early afternoon. His assault troops had done well against only very light opposition. The big problem was supplies. Landing craft were littering the beaches and the cargoes afloat could not be brought ashore. The 3rd Division had suffered only 148 casualties, but had to call a halt three miles short of their D-Day objective for lack of supplies.

For George Patton, aching for speed and action and getting precious little of either, it was a frustrating day. By evening, though, he had one piece of good news. One hundred and fifty miles to the south, at the small port of Safi, things were going well. It was an important piece of news, for at Safi the Sherman tanks of his old 2nd Armored Division were to land and then race north to Casablanca.

The whole Safi operation with a battleship, a small carrier, cruisers, destroyers, landing craft, assault infantry and the rest actually hung on one ship, which had been built two years before as a railroad ferry to operate between Florida and Cuba. Although called "the sea train" her cargo was now fifty-four Sherman tanks. She was the only ship which could carry them and Safi was the only port at which she could dock.

The dock area at Safi was, therefore, critical and, as at Algiers and Oran, two destroyers were assigned the suicide mission of breaking into the harbor. The two here were the twenty-four-year-old four-stackers, *Bernadou* and *Cole,* with their masts removed and their funnels cut down to stumps. Each carried an assault infantry company. At 4:28 in the morning the *Bernadou* swung into the harbor. She fired a parachute flare over the town to which was attached a huge United States flag. The French fired flares of their own, but without flags, and their shore batteries opened up.

The *Bernadou,* firing everything she had from her 3-inch guns to an army grenade launcher, came on. The ancient battleship *New York* put her 14-inchers to work and the cruiser *Philadelphia* joined in. The French defenses were smothered and the *Bernadou* grounded on a beach at the far end of the harbor. Her troops were soon storming ashore.

"*Cole. Cole.* Come on in," blared out the radio but the *Cole* was lost. She was following another destroyer thinking it was the *Bernadou*.[16] Just in time to miss ramming the harbor's jetty, the *Cole* discovered her mistake, swung out to sea and then back into the harbor. Fire greeted her too but not on the scale which it had the *Bernadou*. Untouched, she came alongside a pier. A grappling hook attached to a hawser was fired ashore and caught neatly on to a railroad track. An American soldier, thinking it some devilish French device, cut the hawser and ruined the trick. But there were other soldiers from the *Bernadou* already there and with their help the *Cole* was safely berthed and her troops ashore by dawn. It had been a vastly successful suicide mission as the total cost had been one sailor wounded.

There were only about 450 French troops around Safi and what little fighting there was ended quickly. By two in the afternoon the "sea train" eased her 465 feet into the harbor and one by one the Shermans were derricked ashore. The only real threat to the operation's success now lay in the large French garrison at Marrakech, eighty miles inland. But their commander, General Henri Martin, had been a confederate of Béthouart's and now proceeded to move too slowly to be a threat at all.

If all was well with the southern attack at Safi, things were far from it in the northern attack at Port-Lyautey. Here the main objective was the concrete, all-weather airstrip, the only one of its kind in Northwest Africa. Port-Lyautey itself was nine miles up the narrow winding Sebou River. Just beyond the river's mouth and the small town of Mehdia were two 5-inch coast defense guns and a wire boom stretched across the river. Beyond this point, the river swung in a large loop to the north and within its bend was the vital airfield. The destroyer *Dallas* had disembarked a raiding party for an upriver trip to grab the airfield but first the coastal guns had to be stormed and the boom cut.

Good landing areas were scarce and the northern forces

[16] Morison, p. 146.

commander, General Lucian Truscott, planned for two of his three infantry battalions to land both well north and south of the Sebou's mouth, with one battalion landing right at the mouth to storm the old, stone fortress-like Kasba of Mehdia, take the guns and destroy the boom across the river.

The transports arrived offshore out of formation and in the pitch black night, the whole operation began to hit innumerable snags. H-hour was postponed. Many troops were landed far from their proper beaches and second waves landed ahead of the first waves. Once ashore the troops found that the rumors of a peaceful landing, which they had so readily believed aboard ship, were quite untrue. French planes strafed the beaches, shore batteries opened up and a party sent by small boat to cut the boom across the Sebou was turned back by heavy fire.

Truscott's battalion in the center finally got an attack going on Mehdia and the Kasba where there were less than 100 French defenders. The French guns at Mehdia were, though, targets for the United States Navy who did not know that the United States Army was advancing. Thus, when the troops went forward they ran right into a barrage of Navy shells and went back in some disorder. Green cease-fire flares went up and messages went out over the radio. Communications failed and when the battalion formed up for a second attack the Army was once again defeated by the Navy.

Truscott's battalion tried to bypass the Kasba but ran into the 1st Moroccan Infantry coming up from Port-Lyautey. The battalion went back again, losing quite a few prisoners to the tough French colonials. Finally a second lieutenant firing a bazooka from behind a wall at different positions tricked the French into thinking there was a whole battery of artillery there. The French at that time, had never heard of a bazooka. By nightfall Truscott's center battalion had not only failed to take its objectives, but seemed to be in danger of being thrown back into the sea if there was a determined French attack the next day. Neither of the battalions that landed north and south of the river had been of much help, and to the south there was already pressure from French forces advancing from Rabat.

November 9th, D-Day plus one, was another frustrating day for George Patton. His 3rd Division slowly ground down the road from the Fedala beaches toward Casablanca. Fighting was light but the supply situation was frightful, just as it had been during the first hours ashore for Vandegrift on Guadalcanal. Fortunately for Patton, the French were not putting up an all-out fight and most of the Casablanca garrison stayed put within the city. General Noguès refused a German offer of aerial assistance. He disposed his troops more to block an American advance inland than for an attack against them. It was a negotiating position rather than a military position.

Things proceeded well at Safi where those precious Shermans were coming ashore. A broken derrick had slowed things down, but by evening there were enough tanks ashore so that any French advance from inland could be held while the main force drove north for Casablanca, 140 miles away.

Even at Port-Lyautey things started to pick up on the 9th. The French force advancing from Rabat northward was easily repulsed as its obsolete Renault tanks were hardly a match for the Americans' and the cruiser *Savannah* got in some devastating supporting fire. The Kasba remained untaken but the French and Moroccan troops, realizing the fight could only end one way began to show their good sense by surrendering as the opportunity offered itself.

Just before dawn on the 10th the old stripped-down destroyer *Dallas* appeared at the mouth of the Sebou determined to force her way upstream and land her army raiders at the airfield. At the wheel was René Malavergne who had left Port-Lyautey some time before under the aegis of United States secret agents. As an expert pilot of the Sebou, he was indispensable. French gunners took the *Dallas* under fire but either their aim was terrible or their hearts weren't in it for all through her passage she remained untouched. She was touched, and often, by the muddy bottom of the river but under Malavergne's expert hand and with her old engines working at full speed she oozed her way ahead. By eight in the morning she was off the airfield, her raiders paddled ashore in rubber boats and the airfield was captured.

Now the Kasba was finally taken after some beautiful precision bombing by the Navy. The Army and Navy, finally fighting together, were too much for the French. More French reserves coming up were taken under fire at 17,000 yards by the old battleship *Texas* and broken up and dispersed. By the evening of the 10th there was little resistance to Truscott's forces other than sniping. Port-Lyautey was captured.

Outside Casablanca on the 10th, George Patton was planning his big battle. Communications with Eisenhower's command post at Gibraltar had been bad but a message had come through telling Patton that Algiers had fallen and Oran was about to. "Only tough nut left to crack is in your hands. Crack it open quickly. Ike." [17] Patton would crack it open all right. Hewitt's warships would bombard the city and his planes would bomb it. The 3rd Division would move in, supported by all the artillery it could muster, and when the Sherman tanks from Safi got there they would go in, too. The show was scheduled for 7:30 A.M., November 11th. All this meant a big and bloody battle between Americans and French.

At 3:30 the next morning, November 11th, Patton was awakened to meet a French officer who had driven down from Noguès' headquarters at Rabat under a white flag. The officer was carrying a note from Noguès' ground forces commander ordering French troops to "cease hostilities with American troops." Patton smelled a rat. French troops, yes, but what of the real villains of the piece, the French Navy? The French officer assured Patton that he was known to Admiral Michelier's chief of staff and could guarantee the French Navy would go along.

The French officer, accompanied by one of Patton's staff officers, drove on into Casablanca, Patton making it quite clear to his own man that "unless the French Navy immediately signifies that it is bound by this cease-fire order, the attack jumps off as scheduled."

Patton went forward to 3rd Division headquarters. Guns, planes and ships moved into position. Patton's staff waited for the 7:30 A.M. jump-off. At 6:48 Patton talked to them by radio—"Are you in touch with Hewitt?" "Yes, sir." "Good, call it off. The French Navy has capitulated." [18]

[17] Howe, p. 174.
[18] Farago, p. 207.

But the German Navy had not. That evening U-173 showed up and hit a transport, a tanker and a destroyer. The next day U-130 fired six torpedoes and with them sank three transports. Such successes were too late to affect the outcome. The amphibious phase of Operation Torch had been a success but as a military operation it had creaked and groaned from the greenness of so many—from generals to privates—engaged upon it. Success over the poorly equipped, half-hearted French defenders blinded many to the truth of General Truscott's description of the Port-Lyautey invasion as "a hit-or-miss affair that would have spelled disaster against a well-armed enemy intent upon resistance."

On to Tunis

NOVEMBER 11–30, 1942

With Casablanca, Oran and Algiers taken, it was time for Eisenhower to get on with the main objective of the Torch expedition, the capture of Tunis. It was hoped that it could be taken in a rush, before the Germans could get reinforcements across the central Mediterranean. Once Tunis was in Allied hands, Eisenhower's forces could move to join hands with Montgomery's who were now crossing the Egyptian-Libyan frontier. Between them, the last of Rommel's army would be destroyed and the entire African shore of the Mediterranean would be in Allied hands.

If Eisenhower were to get on with the capture of Tunis, it was essential that his troops not get bogged down as an army of occupation of French Africa. Thus, in Algiers, immediate priority had to be given to the task of setting up a workable French government for North Africa. General Giraud, having given up his idea of being supreme Allied commander, arrived in Algiers the day after the fighting stopped. He was not, though, a rallying point for all Frenchmen, as the Allies had hoped. It was a point of honor to most of the senior French officers that they get their orders from a properly constituted authority, and no Frenchman had constituted Giraud anything. They could accept him as a general, but not as a political leader.

The man who could represent proper authority was Admiral Darlan, Marshal Pétain's second-in-command. When, on the night of November 10th, German troops moved into Vichy France and proceeded to occupy the whole country, it was realized that Pétain was no longer a free agent. With the Germans at his elbow, any orders he issued from Vichy were, in effect, dictated by the Germans. Exactly such a situation, Darlan now claimed, had been foreseen by the Marshal and himself as far back as 1940. Darlan claimed that the Marshal had made clear to him what should then be done, which was, of course, that Darlan would take over supreme authority outside France.

The French senior officers, although many of them were skeptical of Darlan's claim of knowing the Marshal's "secret thought," were willing to accept him, for if they didn't then, there would be no French authority at all. Giraud, too, realized that Darlan was a fact of life which had to be faced. He himself could not exercise political authority.

Thus, Mark Clark and Robert Murphy, the soldier and the diplomat, facing the same facts, put together a French government for North Africa. Darlan would be High Commissioner as well as Naval Commander, Giraud would be French Army and Air Force Commander. Noguès would be kept on as top man in Morocco. Under these men, the French would join the Allies in the fight against Germany and Italy.

It seemed a tidy package as it would keep Africa calm, while Eisenhower got on with the business of fighting Germans. But when the British and American public heard that a "deal" had been made with Darlan, they blew up. To them, de Gaulle's Free French in London were the heroes and anyone connected with Vichy was the villain. Roosevelt and Churchill could do little but plead military expediency, and Roosevelt issued a brief statement in which he assured the public that the arrangement with Darlan was "temporary"—and he used the word not once, but five times.[19] The Allied press and public smoldered but Darlan got the point, saying to Clark, "I am only a lemon which the Americans will drop after they have squeezed it dry." [20]

[19] Robert E. Sherwood, *Roosevelt and Hopkins: An Intimate Biography* (New York: Grosset & Dunlap, 1950), pp. 653–654.
[20] Sherwood, p. 654.

The Darlan "deal" did achieve its major objective as it kept the political pot in North Africa below the boiling point. It did not accomplish Churchill's great objective of bringing the French fleet, anchored at Toulon in France, over to the Allied side. Darlan did order its commander, Admiral de Laborde, to sail for African ports but was answered with the effective expletive, "Merde." De Laborde did, however, obey the standing orders that the fleet must be scuttled rather than fall into German hands.

The Germans moved fast to set up twin bridgeheads around Tunis and the port of Bizerte, 30 miles to the north. Hitler, who had for so long fatally neglected the Mediterranean theater, was stung into action by the Allied invasion. He wrote Mussolini that he intended to pour in troops until it was possible to drive Eisenhower clean off the continent.

On November 9th, the day after Eisenhower's landings, German fighters, dive-bombers and a handful of paratroopers landed at the Tunis airport. Three days later, two Italian freighters sailed into the harbor of Bizerte and put ashore 340 German troops and seventeen German tanks. On the same day, General Walther Nehring arrived in Rome. Nehring had served with Rommel, had been wounded in the desert back in August and was now on his way back to Rommel's army. Nehring was a tough, experienced African veteran and exactly the man needed to take command of the Tunis-Bizerte buildup. His orders were changed and, from Rome, he flew to Tunis. There Nehring set up headquarters with one staff officer and with communication handled through the local phone company and by a single French taxi.

He used his German paratroopers and the few tanks he had to build up his bridgeheads around Tunis and Bizerte. He sent mainly Italian troops south along the coast road which was his only link with Rommel's army in Libya. But in a week the advance elements of the first-class 10th Panzer Division were due to arrive. He had an idea that the British and Americans might be arriving at just about the same time.

The French in Tunisia were in a quandary. Admiral Estéva, the overall commander, had been told that the Allies would land in Tunisia simultaneously with their landings in Algiers. They had not done so. The Admiral had made up his mind that he would obey the orders of Marshal Pétain but he was getting orders in Pétain's name from Admiral Darlan in Algiers and was getting orders direct from Vichy at the same time. Darlan ordered him to join the Allies, while Vichy ordered him to join the Axis. Estéva sat on the fence while German strength increased daily.

The French Army troops in Tunisia, a division of about 10,000 men commanded by General Georges Barré, stood by like sullen spectators as Germans and Italians arrived. Barré did not feel that he could fight the Germans, much as he wanted to, without Allied help. His troops were very poorly equipped, not having even one single anti-tank gun. Barré equivocated when the Germans proposed that he join them. Slowly he pulled his men back into the hills surrounding Tunis and Bizerte and waited for some Allied assistance to show up. He had no idea of when the Allies might arrive or in what strength. There was little he could do but play a game of "I won't fire on you if you won't fire on me" with the Germans.

Within a week of the landings, Eisenhower's forces were already deployed along the Algerian-Tunisian frontier. To the south, United States paratroopers floated down on Youks-les-Bains. There they took the airfield while the French looked on passively. Then they fanned out into Tunisia and toward the mountains bordering the coastal plain that ran south from Tunis to the Libyan frontier. With some help from the French, their mission was to guard the southern flank of the Allied attack on Tunis itself.

On the Mediterranean coast, light British forces occupied the port and airfield at Bône. There, a brigade from the British 78th Division prepared to advance along the coastal road which led to Bizerte, some 185 miles away.

South of Bône, the British, coming up overland from Algiers by rail and road, began to establish a base of operations at Souk-Ahras. From here the main road to Tunis ran along the valley of the Medjerda River flanked on either side by rocky, deeply eroded djebels, the Tunisian mountains, which

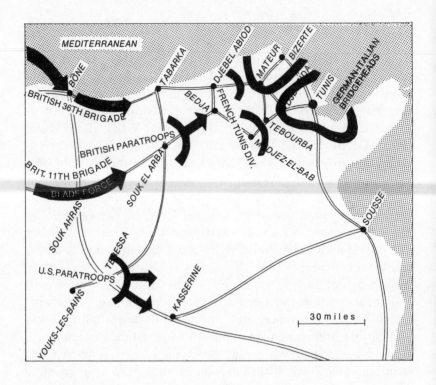

THE TUNISIAN BATTLEFIELD   Screened by American and British paratroopers, Allied forces arrived at the Tunisian border by sea at Bône and overland through Souk-Ahras. The poorly equipped French Tunis division retreated into the hills outside Tunis and Bizerte, where German and Italian forces were built up more rapidly than Eisenhower and his generals had thought possible. The Allied plan was to make a rush for Tunis with two British infantry brigades and the tanks of Blade Force.

offered the Germans many fine defensive positions. Here the main advance would be made by another infantry brigade from the 78th Division and a British tank regiment called Blade Force.

The main hope for a quick dash to Tunis lay with this British tank regiment, the 17th/21st Lancers. It had been formed by the pre-war amalgamation of two old cavalry regiments, the 17th Lancers, who had led the famous Light Brigade in its great charge at Balaclava, and the 21st Lancers with whom Winston Churchill, as a young lieutenant, had once charged along the banks of the Nile. The regiment's horses were gone and, unfortunately, had been replaced only by old, mechanically unreliable Valentine and Crusader tanks. There had been no time before the beginning of Operation Torch to re-equip the regiment with newer tanks like the Shermans.

These were pitifully weak forces for the task ahead of them. The planners of the invasion had overloaded the initial convoys with troops and equipment to take and hold Algiers. They had sacrificed the troops and equipment necessary for a powerful thrust on Tunis. There were not enough trucks to carry supplies forward. They had to rely on the ramshackle French railroad that ran from Algiers to Tunis and which could handle only 1,000 tons daily.

Nor could the troops advancing into Tunisia count on more than sketchy air support. Not only would the British and American squadrons supporting them have the same supply problems as the troops themselves, but air reconnaissance had shown that the Germans were flying a new plane into Tunis, the Focke-Wulf 190. It was superior to anything the Allies could put into the air. And even worse, the Germans had the use of the concrete, all-weather runways at Tunis and Bizerte while the Allied fliers would be using dirt fields which would become unusable swamps with the first heavy rains.

In overall command of the whole Tunisian operation was British General Kenneth Anderson, a dour Scot, who was a competent, if not brilliant, commander. Anderson's command was called the British 1st Army although, with so few troops available, it was an "Army" in name only. Under Anderson, and in direct charge of the attack, was Major General Vyvyan Evelegh, an excellent soldier who commanded the 78th Division to which the two attacking infantry brigades belonged. Evelegh's third brigade would not arrive until the end of the month.

Both Anderson and Evelegh knew that they had to make do with what they had. They knew their weaknesses and they knew that the only way they could make up for them was to move fast. On November 16th, Evelegh's 36th Brigade moved out along the coast road, the British 1st Parachute Battalion was dropped onto the airfield at Souk el Arba, fifty miles up the Medjerda valley toward Tunis.

The British paratroopers were not opposed by the French troops at the field as some had feared, but were received by the happy mayor of the town with flowers and champagne. Even happier was an Arab who managed to gallop off with one of the parachutes from which, so it was said, he could make 544 sets of silk underwear, enough to make him a rich man. Disentangling themselves from flowers, champagne and happy Arabs, the paratroopers set out to look for the Germans along the road to Tunis, now only eighty miles away.

But it was Evelegh's 36th Brigade advancing along the coast road which found the Germans first. On the night of the 16th, the leading battalion of the brigade, the Royal West Kents, had pushed ahead to seize the small village of Djebel Abiod. From here, the coast road continued on toward Bizerte and another road branched off to the south and connected with the main road through the Medjerda valley. In these tangled mountains, connecting north-south roads were scarce and thus, holding Djebel Abiod, important. The Royal West Kents dug in right away.

It was well that they did, for the importance of Djebel Abiod had not been lost on the German commander, Walther Nehring. Just as the British got themselves dug in, German paratroopers supported by fifteen tanks came charging in. There was some bloody fighting with the British anti-tank guns being knocked out, but in turn getting half of Nehring's tanks. Djebel Abiod was held and the other two battalions of the British 36th Brigade moved up along the coast road. It was no easy move, though, as the Luftwaffe dominated the skies. One trainload of British troops was jumped by two of those new Focke-Wulf 190's and suffered forty-three casualties. Advancing along the coastal road was not going to be an easy affair.

As the fighting raged at Djebel Abiod, British paratroopers clashed with the Germans along the main road from Souk-Ahras to Medjez-el-Bab. These minor actions did not worry Nehring. What was worrying the German commander was the French troops under General Barré at Medjez-el-Bab. Here, only thirty miles from Tunis, they were holding positions which were a perfect jump-off spot for an advance on Tunis itself. Nehring knew that at any moment British and American troops might join the French in force. It was time for a showdown with General Barré. Before dawn on the 19th Barré got an ultimatum from Nehring—pull back by 7:00 A.M. It was backed up by a direct order from Marshal Pétain. But since the German occupation of Vichy France, no French general could consider the old Marshal a free agent. His orders were now German orders and thus to be disregarded. Barré disregarded them.

Nehring's handful of paratroopers waited beyond the 7:00 A.M. deadline, and at 9:15 they advanced. Barré's troops opened fire on them and France was back in the war. Light German attacks were beaten back, but Barré knew he couldn't hold without Allied aid, and all he got was twelve British guns served by American artillerymen. What strength the Germans lacked on the ground they made up for in the air and the terrifying Stukas, whistling down in their steep dives, made the difference. After dark Barré pulled his troops back and gave up Medjez-el-Bab. Although orders from the high command in Rome were to push east, Nehring sensibly stayed put at Medjez and built up his Bizerte-Tunis bridgehead.

Major General Evelegh was, at the same time, trying to build up enough strength to make his dash for Tunis. It was imperative that he get going before Nehring became too strong for him. Troops, tanks and long columns of supply-laden trucks moved up along the skimpy road network and along the antiquated French railway. But Evelegh found his movements continually interrupted by the Luftwaffe's planes operating out of the all-weather fields at Tunis and Bizerte. The dominance of German air power beyond Souk el Arba was such that the British and Americans could only move at night.

General Anderson, Evelegh's boss, didn't think much of the chances of success. Building forward airfields for the British and American fighter planes was a slow business and the dirt runways were sure to be washed out at the first good rain. Evelegh had only one British infantry brigade, the 36th, to attack along the coastal road and another brigade, the 11th, reinforced by a battalion of American light tanks, and those of the 17th/21st Lancers, to hit back through Medjez-el-Bab. American units, including the Sherman tanks of Combat Command B of the 1st Armored Division, and the third brigade of his 78th Division were on the way but Evelegh could not wait.

The Allied generals now knew that they had seriously underestimated the Germans' ability to move into Tunisia. By November 24th, when Evelegh was ready to attack, Nehring had more than 15,000 German troops on hand, two paratrooper regiments, a Panzer battalion and twenty new 88's, invaluable in the rocky defiles of the Tunisian djebels. There were also 9,000 Italians available to guard his southern flank.

Before dawn on the 25th Evelegh's attack went in. In the north his 36th Brigade put on a well-planned attack. It hit nothing as the Germans were already pulling back. Against German rearguards the 36th Brigade went forward, but not, in that rugged country, at a very fast clip.

In the south Evelegh's other available brigade, the 11th, went in to retake Medjez-el-Bab. The attack was a failure. The Lancashire Fusiliers had a wide sweep of open ground to cover and tried it at night. A brilliant moon gave the German machine gunners all the light they needed. The British battalion commander was killed by the first burst of fire. The Fusiliers made it to the river. Some waded across but could get no further. On their right the Northamptons stormed the high ground overlooking the town but were thrown off it when the German paratroopers counterattacked with tanks. British casualties were heavy but the brigade commander got his third battalion, the East Surreys, ready for an attack the next morning.

In the center things went much better for Evelegh. One hundred American and British tanks, called Blade Force, advanced against very light opposition. After passing Sidi Nsir the force commander detached the 1st Battalion, United States 1st Armored Regiment with its Stuart light tanks along the Sidi Nsir–Tebourba road. Some of the tanks were held up by German paratroopers but one company, seventeen tanks, slipped past them, bypassed Tebourba and went dashing on to reconnoiter toward Djedeida. It was a daring penetration and it paid off. At Djedeida the Luftwaffe had just gotten the airfield into operation and parked off the runway were the tankers' deadly enemies, the Stuka dive-bombers.

As though they were the cavalry of Confederate General Jeb Stuart, after whom their tanks were named, the 1st Armored Regiment swept across the airfield in a mechanical cavalry charge. Guns blazing in all directions, they shot up everything in sight, including seventeen Stukas, before pulling back into the dusk. They had lost only one tank.

Next day the Stuarts took on a small German tank force with six of the long-gunned Mark IV Specials along. One company of Stuarts drew the Germans into an ambush set by a second company and got all six of the big Mark IV's, but it cost them six tanks to do it. Although losses were even, the light American tanks had fought the far bigger German ones to a standstill.

Meanwhile, the British 11th Brigade had put in its attack on Medjez-el-Bab but, as along the northern route, there were nothing but German rearguards around. Nehring was pulling in his horns to a tight defensive perimeter. By the 27th the 11th Brigade had Tebourba but during the day German infantry and tanks counterattacked. British infantry and gunners held, but at heavy cost. The next day, the 28th, more British infantry and some medium-sized American tanks came up and a try was made at taking Djedeida. It failed.

A worse failure came along the northern route where Evelegh's 36th Brigade was closing in on Mateur. A Highland battalion leading the way was caught in an ambush where the road passed between Green Hill and Bald Hill. One company was overrun and a hundred prisoners taken. Another British battalion and some commandos attacked the two hills, but the German paratroopers were barricaded among the rocks and what little artillery the 36th Brigade could bring to bear on them had little effect. The British assaults were thrown back with heavy British casualties and the northern prong of Evelegh's attack came to a dead stop.

The climax came on the 29th as the Northamptons and the American tanks made a last try at Djedeida. With strong air support, the Germans beat the attacks back with very heavy Allied losses. A British parachute battalion had been dropped near the Germans' airfield at Oudna, south of Tunis, and the

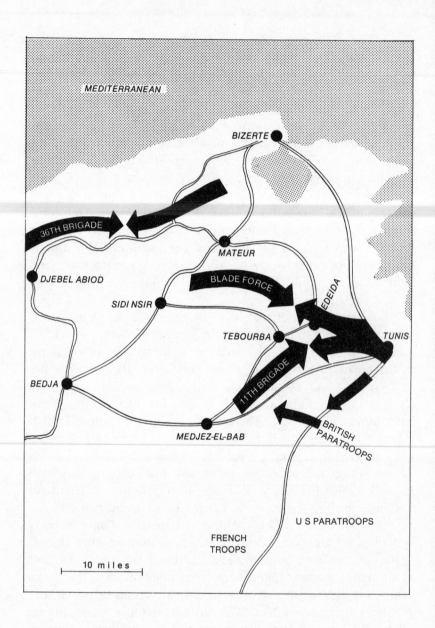

THE BATTLE FOR TUNIS   In the north, the British 36th Brigade was stopped in the narrow mountain defiles short of its objective, Mateur. In the south, a British paratrooper attack failed. In the center, though, American light tanks raided the German airfield at Djedeida and got within ten miles of Tunis. The British 11th Brigade attacked at Djedeida but was halted with heavy casualties. German planes, operating out of Tunis and Bizerte, held command of the air.

failure of the Djedeida attacks left it stranded. Less than half the paratroopers made it back to the Allied lines.

Eisenhower, getting away from the political duties of a supreme commander had, meanwhile, arrived in Tunisia in an armored Cadillac. He conferred with his overall commander in Tunisia, General Anderson. He heard some pretty ugly stories about lack of air support but, on the whole, found morale high. What Eisenhower failed to gauge was the weakness of his troops. Casualties had been heavy, and, in many battalions, physical exhaustion was setting in.

In a mood of optimism, Eisenhower cabled General Marshall in Washington, "My immediate aim is to keep pushing hard." [21] There would be some hard pushing in the days to come, but it would be done by Nehring, not by Eisenhower. The German commander had sensed the weakening of the Allied attack and was now planning to counterattack in strength on December 1st.

Rommel versus Hitler

NOVEMBER, 1942

While Nehring had been winning his desperate defensive battle for Tunis, Rommel had been waging a no less desperate one against German headquarters. He had saved what was left of his army after Alamein and had retreated 800 miles to the El Agheila position where he could make a temporary stand.

Rommel had been thrown back to El Agheila before. It was from that position that he had launched his great counterstroke that had taken Tobruk and then had petered out at Alamein. He knew, though, that no such riposte was possible for him now. Montgomery's pursuit was methodical and thus deadly. It gave Rommel no chance to counterattack with any chance of success. Sooner or later, Rommel knew, Montgomery would attack his new position. The attack would come only when Montgomery was ready, when all the necessary men, tanks, planes, guns and supplies had been brought forward over those 800 miles from Alamein to El Agheila.

[21] Howe, p. 309.

As he waited at El Agheila, Rommel had time to think, to consider his own tactical position at El Agheila and the whole strategic position of the Axis in the Mediterranean. He reached certain conclusions that he was determined his superiors should accept.

His orders, regarding the El Agheila position itself, were to hold it "to the last man." To Rommel this was nonsense. Even to hold on to El Agheila too long would mean losing half the Army. His mobile troops, mostly German, the Panzers and motorized infantry, could make a last-minute escape as they had at Alamein. His non-mobile troops, mostly Italian infantry, would simply be rounded up by the British. Nor could he expect to put up the same fight at El Agheila as he had at Alamein. His inland flank was wide open and he knew that once Montgomery had built up sufficient strength he would circle round that flank with vastly superior forces. He now judged Montgomery as a cautious commander who would only attack when completely ready. But this also meant that when the attack came, it would be unstoppable.

Rommel's weakness stemmed from insufficient reinforcements and supplies. Since the Axis emphasis was on holding Tunisia, Rommel, at El Agheila, was being sent far less than he needed. Even with Allied sea and air power redeployed for the Torch operation, a quarter of what was sent him never arrived. With Malta resupplied, this situation could only get worse.

Rommel's solution to this dilemma was to withdraw completely from Libya, all the way back to the Tunisian border. There, in front of Gabès where the great salt marshes of the Shott el Jerid approach the Mediterranean, was a position which, like Alamein, could not be flanked and where Rommel's immobile troops could be used with some safety. While Montgomery built up a set-piece attack on this line, Rommel's mobile troops could join those in Tunisia for a smash at Eisenhower.

Rommel's basic strategic premise went even beyond this thinking. In due course Allied power, backed by United States war production, would become overwhelming. As it did, all Axis forces in Africa must be evacuated to Italy where, no longer dependent on sea communications, they could await Eisenhower's future attacks with some confidence. Basically, every action in Africa must be taken with eventual withdrawal in mind.

Hitler's Commander-in-Chief, South, Kesselring, conferred with Rommel on November 24th. Kesselring's objection to any withdrawal from Libya was that it would bring the powerful and expert Allied Middle East air forces within striking range of northern Tunisia and its vital supply line across the Mediterranean narrows. To Rommel this was simply a narrow Luftwaffe point of view and the Luftwaffe was not particularly popular at Rommel's headquarters. The talk was that Hermann Goering wanted to make Africa a Luftwaffe theater of war and was politicking to get Rommel relieved of his command. His pitch was that Rommel was a fine general when things were going right but a defeatist if anything went wrong.

Rommel, a babe in the political woods of the Third Reich's high command, decided all could be set right by a personal interview with the Fuehrer. He, Rommel, was *the* authority on Africa. He had always commanded from the front and Hitler would respect firsthand knowledge. Rommel could hardly have been more wrong.

Hitler, all during the war, had kept himself totally immune from the sights, sounds and smells of the front line. He was a firm believer in command from far in the rear. A front-line general, he once told his Chief of Operations, Jodl, while talking about Rommel, "gradually loses his nerve. It's different if one's in the rear. There, of course, one keeps one's head. These people can't stand the strain on their nerves. . . . Think what it's like. He had to go on shadow-boxing out there with a few wretched units. So it's not surprising if, after two years or so, he gradually loses his nerve and gets into a situation where he says, 'I'll hold on'—then things which to us in the rear don't appear so terrible, seem frightful to him. . . . In the long run you can't command in the midst of the roar of battle." [22]

[22] Warlimont, p. 298.

On November 28th Rommel flew from Africa to the Wolfschanze in the cold, gloomy forest in East Prussia. It was evident to Rommel when ushered into the Fuehrer's presence that the chill was not only in the forest. Disregarding his cold reception, Rommel calmly described the pitiful condition of his army. Then, without diplomatic preamble, he bluntly came straight to his main point, withdrawal from Africa. The word "withdrawal" sent the Fuehrer into one of his finer rages and Rommel was treated to a ranting, shouting, table-pounding tirade including the oft-repeated story of how Hitler, alone, had saved the German Army the year before by his "no withdrawal from Moscow" orders. There was no further rational discussion.

On one point Hitler did agree, that the supply situation needed considerable bucking up. The man he picked to do it was Rommel's number one enemy, Hermann Goering. Rommel was even ordered to return to Rome aboard the personal train of the Reichsmarschall. There Rommel saw Goering bedeck himself in the gaudy uniforms he loved so well and wallow in the flattery of his courtiers. The Reichsmarschall lightly dismissed the problems of the war and instead, with relish, discussed the jewels and the works of art which were his share of Hitler's conquests.

Although Rommel was no diplomat he had an aide, a former member of the Propaganda Ministry, who was. Rommel sent this aide to Goering's private railway car to influence the Reichsmarschall. By the time the train arrived in Rome, Goering was better disposed to Rommel's plans if not toward Rommel personally. At least, in conferences with Mussolini, Goering agreed to some modification of the stand-or-die orders for El Agheila. Mussolini knew that it would be the Italian divisions which would be lost if the orders stood. Rommel flew back to Africa knowing that he must now fight two enemies, Montgomery and Hitler. Now it was the latter he most feared.

Nehring Attacks

DECEMBER 1, 1942

Walther Nehring had much the same trouble as Rommel. Kesselring, the optimist, had not approved of the withdrawal from Medjez-el-Bab. And back at the Wolfschanze Hitler and his personal staff were thinking offensively and bandying about such objectives as Algiers and Casablanca. Realism was fast vanishing from the Fuehrer's headquarters, but not from Nehring's.

General Wolfgang Fischer, commander of the 10th Panzer Division, had arrived in Tunis and Nehring gave him personal charge of the coming battle. There was no sophisticated communications net, and Fischer would have to do much of his leading in person. But he would have air superiority over the battlefield. The winter rains had now turned most of the Allied fields into mud while the German fighters and dive-bombers could still use the concrete runways at Tunis and Bizerte, only minutes flying time from the battlefield.

And a glance at the map showed Fischer that the Allies were not in position for his attack. They had not, when their November offensive had failed, pulled back to the Tebourba Gap. They were still holding on to their forward positions. Far out in front, and just short of Djedeida were the Hampshires, a freshly arrived battalion of the 1st Guards Brigade. The Brigade's two other battalions, the Grenadier and Coldstream Guards, had not yet arrived. Covering Tebourba, by holding the key observation points on Hill 186 directly in the rear of the Hampshires, were the Surreys. They were not very thick on the ground as they were also covering the bridge across the Medjerda River at El Bathan. Some six miles north of the El Bathan bridge, at a crossroads village named Chouïgui, the Allied northern flank was protected by the much battered tanks of Blade Force. It was not a very powerful protection, made up mostly of light Stuart tanks. What was left of the older tanks of the 17th/21st Lancers had been sent back to Tebourba Gap for maintenance.

On December 1st, against Blade Force at Chouïgui, Fischer made his opening move, coming down from the north and northeast with a force of about sixty tanks. It was fortunate for the Allies that his force was made up mostly of the older, smaller M-III's and not the newer M-IV Specials with their long-barreled 75's. But what Fischer had was enough to

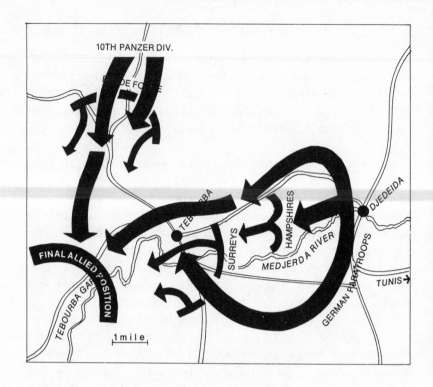

DJEDEIDA

HAMPSHIRES

SURREYS

MEDJERDA RIVER

GERMAN PARATROOPS

TUNIS→

FINAL ALLIED POSITION

TEBOURBA GAP

1mile

NEHRING'S COUNTERATTACK Allied forces, hoping to renew their attack on Tunis, had hung on to their exposed forward positions when their November attack had been stopped. German paratroopers were able to outflank two British battalions, the Surreys and the Hampshires, near Djedeida and almost wiped them out. Tanks of the German 10th Panzer Division broke through Blade Force but were stopped at the Tebourba Gap as American reinforcements arrived. A quick Allied capture of Tunis was now impossible.

give the Allies a bad jolt. He swept down through Chouïgui, knocked out most of the Allied force there and then swept on toward the Tebourba Gap. The 17th/21st Lancers, true to their Light Brigade traditions, threw some of their old Valentines and Crusaders against the German armor. Fischer knew how to combine the anti-tank gun with the tank and his gun screen cut down five tanks in rapid succession. British and American gunners poured down fire on the Germans from their positions around the Gap and the Northamptons, who had been so badly chopped up in their fruitless assaults on Djedeida, joined in. Fischer didn't get to the Gap but he had the main road under fire and thus had the Surreys and the Hampshires out on a limb.

The Hampshires were hit head-on by attacks from Djedeida. Fischer had left his armor at midday and had come around to lead them himself. The troops here were mostly German replacements and Fischer found them a dispirited lot. He relieved one company commander on the spot for "lurking under cover for hours." [23] He personally positioned platoons and even squads. It was no use. The Hampshires, inexperienced as they were and only a week off the boat from England, were far from dispirited. They fought off every German attack.

By nightfall American reinforcements were coming up the Medjerda Valley toward Tebourba. It was Combat Command B of the 1st Armored Division. CCB, as it was called, had a battalion of light tanks, a battalion of Shermans and two battalions of the 6th Armored Infantry. They would immediately come into action against Fischer's tanks to the north of the Tebourba Gap. But to the south, against the El Bathan Bridge, Nehring had now deployed ten infantry companies, five of them paratroopers. The Surreys, holding the bridge, were in for trouble. The United States artillery battalion supporting them, having failed to get an ammunition resupply during the night, had pulled away.

On December 2nd the German attacks against the Surreys and the Hampshires were intensified. The Hampshires had the unpleasant honor of being the first troops in Africa to receive the deadly attentions of the Germans monster 55-ton Tiger tanks. The Hampshires had nothing that could more than dent their massive armor and the Tigers' 88mm guns could shoot with the accuracy of a sniper rifle. Fischer poured in more infantry and pounded away with his Stukas which were barely seconds flying time away from their targets. The Hampshires were simply being ground down and the Surreys hardly any less so. There were only two companies of them to guard the El Bathan Bridge and by late in the day the German paratroopers had managed to infiltrate over the river around the Surreys' right flank.

[23] Howe, p. 316.

Far worse for the Allies was the hard time Fischer's Panzers now gave the weary British Lancers and the new CCB. The Allied tank attacks were not well coordinated and the German defense was. The Allied tankers had to attack under a sky held by the Luftwaffe. The Panzers mastered what was left of Blade Force and the tanks of CCB, but complete victory was denied them by some superb shooting by the Allied gunners, particularly the British anti-tank gunners. There was little ground won or lost that day, but the failure of his armored counterattacks had put Evelegh in a bad spot.

While Fischer's tankers had been winning their battles north of Tebourba, two companies of Panzer grenadiers had flown over from Italy. On the next day, December 3rd, they went in against the Hampshires and with good tank support. Working around the flanks, the Germans now got in behind the Hampshires and took the summit of Hill 186 which dominated the battlefield. The Hampshires and the Surreys threw in counterattacks but in ever-decreasing numbers. One of the last was made by a company commander and four men. Both battalions had put up a superb fight but now there was nothing for it but to get out.

Fischer's armor had cut the main road from Tebourba to the Gap and the only route open was a dirt track that cut along the north bank of the Medjerda. Most of the Surreys' survivors got through although the road was under constant German fire. Only a few of their guns and trucks made it.

The Hampshires alone remained. Their colonel gave the men their orders—"Walk towards them slowly and when you get close enough, charge." [24] They did just that but only a remnant of the battalion got through to Tebourba, now deserted. In a column of three's, their wounded colonel calling the step, this great battalion marched through town at attention as befits members of a Guards brigade. But on the other side of town were more Germans and the colonel told his men that it was either surrender or break up into small groups and try to get back to the Gap through the hills to the south. They chose the latter and three days later, when they reformed near Medjez, the Hampshires consisted of only six officers and 120 men.

[24] Ray, *Algiers to Austria*, p. 21.

Nehring and Fischer had won their battle but behind them, at sea, battles were being lost. The port of Bône had been turned into a naval base as well as a supply port. Just after midnight on December 1st, three British light cruisers and two destroyers from Bône pounced on an Axis convoy, three merchant ships and a German war transport, and wiped it out. On the next night four British destroyers operating out of Malta finished off a four-ship convoy already hit by Malta aircraft. On the day after that, twenty American bombers, B-24's, hit at Naples, wrecking two Italian cruisers and sinking a third. Most of the Italian Navy quickly took off for more northern ports where they were out of the war.

The Axis shifted their Tunisia-bound convoys to daylight and sailed them under heavy air escort. From Sicily to Tunis was only a 130-mile run and the Allied forces, planes, submarines and mine-layers, were just beginning their assault on this route. Even so, that December, one quarter of the cargoes shipped out for Tunisia did not arrive. On the longer shipping run to Libya, which the supplies for Rommel's army had to travel, the losses were more than half of what was shipped. It was a catastrophic supply situation. As Allied power built up it was bound to get worse.

On December 6th a new general arrived on the Allied side. Enough troops were now coming up that it was thought the operations should be handled by a corps commander. British Lieutenant General C. W. Allfrey arrived to take over. Allfrey was met with bad news. That morning Nehring's paratroopers and Panzers had hit at the thin screen of United States troops holding the high ground south of the Tebourba Gap. The forward troops were very roughly handled and thrown back. The commander of CCB put in an armored counterattack. The attack was slow in going in and when it did, Nehring's men were ready for it, especially his anti-tank guns. CCB went forward with courage, but without its tanks properly coordinated with its artillery. Nehring's veterans stopped it easily.

Allfrey was nervous and ordered a retreat. Tebourba Gap was to be abandoned and Allfrey proposed giving up Medjez-el-Bab as well. This Eisenhower would not allow as he wanted

another try at taking Tunis before the worst of the winter
rains came. In Algiers there was little realization of how weak
Allied air support was and how long it would take to get it
operating properly, as well as little realization of what a fearful beating the ground forces had taken. By this time the three
battalions of the British 11th Brigade did not even have the
strength of a single battalion among them.

If Eisenhower's headquarters was somewhat out of touch
with the realities of Tunisia, Hitler's headquarters was fan-
tastically so. The Fuehrer, who had always considered Africa
as somewhat of a sideshow, now decided that Nehring was not
aggressive enough. What should be done was to build up the
Axis forces there into a full-fledged Panzer army and then, on
to Algiers. To command this new Panzer army he picked Juer-
gen von Arnim who had been commanding a Panzer corps in
Russia. Von Arnim came down to the Wolfschanze and was
told he would go to Tunisia where his troops would be beefed
up to three Panzer divisions and three motorized divisions.
Just how that battered supply line from Sicily to Tunis would
support such an army on a 400-mile advance to Algiers was not
mentioned. Such things, as well as the brilliant performance of
Nehring, were now more and more disregarded in the Wolfschanze wonderland.

Von Arnim arrived in Tunis on December 9th and immediately took over command from Nehring. He ordered Fischer's
tanks and infantry to attack the next day. This time the Germans struck just south of the Medjerda River and CCB had a
hard time holding them. But Fischer's tanks also swept well to
the south, hoping to swing completely around the Allied flank
and take Medjez-el-Bab. If successful, they would trap CCB in
the Medjerda Valley.

Some light American tanks attacked the German out-
flanking column but they were up against German heavies and,
losing nineteen tanks, failed to halt the German advance. But
then the Germans ran into a roadblock held by some French
Zouaves backed by artillery. Here they were finally stopped.
But the threat that they might break through the next morning
and cut off CCB could not be ignored.

That night the American armored force formed up for retreat. They planned to make their way across the north bank of the Medjerda to the main road and then back to Medjez. When CCB's mass of tanks and trucks approached the bridge across the Medjerda at Bordj Toum, they found it was under sporadic German fire and sounds of a fight could be heard just north of it. The commander at the head of the column decided to give up crossing there. Instead he turned back along a dirt road running along the south bank of the river. The leading vehicles churned the wet dirt into a swamp and the entire column became completely bogged down. Vehicles had to be abandoned and by the time CCB got back to Medjez, mostly on foot, they had lost 18 tanks, 41 guns and 150 other vehicles. With CCB knocked out there was nothing to do but postpone the attack on Tunis. Eisenhower still hoped it could get going by Christmastime.

Stalemate in Africa

DECEMBER, 1942

While a temporary lull came to Tunisia, Montgomery's 8th Army made its attack on Rommel's El Agheila position. Rommel knew that it was coming and was already pulling his troops away. The British tangled with the German rearguards but Rommel made his getaway with very slight losses.

Rommel retreated to another position, 300 miles in the rear, and there prepared to repeat the performance all over again. But it was a performance which could not be repeated endlessly. Sooner or later, Rommel knew, he would run out of space.

Eisenhower was determined that there should be one more attack on Tunis. As a preliminary to the armored advance that was planned, the British and Americans had to take Longstop Hill, just east of Medjez-el-Bab. From its heights the Germans could observe any movements along the road to Tunis.

The attack started on December 22nd. Three fresh battalions, one American and two British, were thrown against the hill. By Christmas Day the Allies had lost almost 500 men and had gained only a bare foothold on the rocky slopes. The December rains had turned everything into a mud pit and no vehicle could get to within 5,000 yards of the hill. It was impossible to supply the men there and the whole thing was called off. When the Germans tried, in their turn, to advance beyond Longstop, they ran into a stone wall of Allied resistance and their attacks, too, came to nothing.

As the fighting was dying down, Eisenhower again came forward to Tunisia to confer with his commanders there. As he watched vehicles of every kind struggling in the glutinous Tunisian mud, he realized what the soldiers had known for some time—there could be no further advance on Tunis until the winter rains were over.

There were questions of command to be settled and Eisenhower tried to settle them at dinner at British headquarters. He didn't get very far. The phone rang. It was his deputy, Mark Clark, calling from Algiers. There was, Clark said, very serious trouble there. On the phone, he could only hint at what it might be.

Eisenhower left at once and, after an all-night drive, stopped for breakfast and finally learned just what the trouble was. Admiral Darlan had been shot and killed in Algiers by a fanatic belonging to a French monarchist group. The former Vichy men had no one to put in for Darlan and so General Giraud, as had been originally planned, finally became chief of state in French North Africa. Giraud, however, was no politician and already the Gaullists were moving into Algiers. They were smart politicians and, very soon, simply talked Giraud into handing over his political power to them.

For Eisenhower, a bleak, frustrating winter lay ahead but at least the New Year started well when, at a midnight bridge session, the General bid and made a grand slam in hearts. For his German opponents there were no grand slams in sight. Rommel could do little but retreat before Montgomery's superior power. Von Arnim could only dream of those massive reinforcements which Hitler had so freely promised him. What chance there had been of their ever arriving had vanished, along with much else, on the frozen steppes of southern Russia.

focus four: STALINGRAD

KALACH

STALINGRAD

ROSTOV

DON RIVER

KOTELNIKOVO

VOLGA RIVER

CASPIAN
SEA

BLACK SEA

To all the generals and admirals planning attack and defense in the Mediterranean and in the Pacific one question kept recurring—would Hitler win in Russia? German victory there could throw all their schemes into a cocked hat. By early October, Hitler's armies had driven forward hundreds of miles. They were deep into the Caucasus Mountains and only a few miles from the oil Hitler so desperately needed. But at their furthest point of advance, at Stalingrad on the Volga, the Germans had been stalled. Here the question would be answered—victory or defeat for Adolf Hitler.

On the first of the ninety decisive days of World War II, October 4, 1942, the German 6th Army of General Friedrich Paulus launched what was hoped would be the last offensive against the Russians in Stalingrad. There were over a quarter of a million men in the 6th Army and, on its roster, some of the best divisions in the German Army. The Army's task did not, at first glance, look too difficult. In September, they had squeezed the main force of the Russian defenders into a pocket which ran along the Volga for about five miles and which was only 2,000 yards deep. Since June, 1941, the Germans had advanced 800 miles, from Poland to the Volga, and now there were only 2,000 more yards to go.

Paulus' men surged into the attack through the gutted

rubble of concrete and steel which was all that was left of the city. There was no room here for the wide sweeping maneuvers of the blitzkrieg, the war of maneuver, at which the German Army was a master. Here it was a toe-to-toe slugging match, a head-on fight where the capture of a single room within a building was a significant advance. In the first days of October, Paulus could measure his gains in yards, and precious few yards at that. Toe-to-toe slugging with the Russians was a nasty, slow business.

Three days after his offensive had begun, Paulus sat down to write a letter explaining why things were not going as fast as Hitler's headquarters would have liked. He wrote to General Schmundt who was a good friend of Hitler's as well as of Army chief of staff, Kurt Zeitzler: "Things are going very slowly, but every day we make just a little progress. The whole thing is a question of time and manpower." [1]

Chief of Staff Zeitzler, who was responsible for the entire Eastern Front, could do nothing about the time factor. There were only a few weeks left before the onset of the brutal Russian winter. The German Army would be far better equipped to face the bone-numbing cold than it had been the year before. No German, though, looked forward to winter battles with the Russian Army which seemed completely at home in below-zero temperatures.

Nor was there much Chief of Staff Zeitzler could do about the manpower factor. German casualties had far exceeded replacements in the past year and every day found the German Army with fewer men than the day before. There was one manpower pool which had remained untapped, a 170,000-man excess in Hermann Goering's Luftwaffe. These men were no average conscripts. They were picked men, the cream of German youth. Zeitzler, as well as many other generals, wanted them transferred to the Army at once. Goering, however, had other ideas. The Luftwaffe was his own private empire and he was not about to lose 170,000 of his men to the Army. He pointed out to Hitler that these young men were all fine Nazis, deeply imbued with the spirit of National

[1] Goerlitz, *Paulus and Stalingrad*, p. 170.

Socialism. It would be criminal, claimed Goering, to turn them over to the Army with its "chaplains" and its "aristocratic traditions." Goering proposed that he make Luftwaffe Field divisions with these men with every man in each division, from major general to private, a Luftwaffe man. Goering ignored the fact that neither major general nor private would know the first thing about infantry fighting. So did Hitler when he agreed to the scheme that fall. Zeitzler got no men from the Luftwaffe.

Nor could Zeitzler use any of the divisions guarding Hitler's empire from the North Cape of Norway to the Mediterranean. Zeitzler, as Army chief of staff, had responsibility only for the Russian Front. All these other troops were under Hitler's direct command. The Fuehrer had no intention of moving any of them to Russia. In October he still had no idea where the British and Americans might hit.

Without sufficient manpower Zeitzler could not reinforce Paulus' 6th Army and without reinforcements the 6th Army had little chance to take Stalingrad quickly. And Zeitzler knew that unless Stalingrad were captured within a month or so, the whole German position in southern Russia would be a precarious one, to say the least.

The big maps at Army headquarters showed the situation all too clearly. Far to the south was Army Group A, commanded by Hitler himself since the firing of Field Marshal von List. The infantry of the Army Group's 17th Army and the tanks of its 1st Panzer Army were completely bogged down in the Caucasus Mountains. There they would stay, as Hitler looked upon the positions they held as jump-off points for an offensive over the Caucasus in the spring of 1943.

From the Caucasus north to Stalingrad, the German Front of some 300 miles was covered only by small patrols. There was no front in the usual meaning of the term. This meant that the northern flank of the Germans in the Caucasus and the southern flank of those at Stalingrad were essentially wide open.

Around Stalingrad itself there was a powerful grouping of German forces. Just south of the city was General Hermann Hoth's 4th Panzer Army. Paulus' 6th Army faced the city itself but only with part of its forces. Two Army corps were deployed

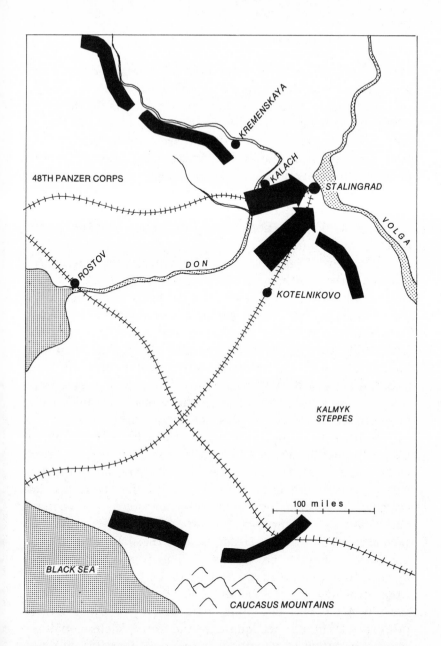

KREMENSKAYA

48TH PANZER CORPS

KALACH

STALINGRAD

VOLGA

ROSTOV

DON

KOTELNIKOVO

KALMYK
STEPPES

100 miles

BLACK SEA

CAUCASUS MOUNTAINS

HITLER'S OFFENSIVE   By October, 1942, all German offensive
effort was concentrated on taking Stalingrad, but attacks by Paulus'
6th Army and Hoth's 4th Panzer Army went ahead at a snail's
pace. Two German armies were bogged down in the Caucasus with
only small patrols covering the Kalmyk Steppes to their north.
Both flanks of the German forces at Stalingrad were covered only
by weak, poorly equipped Rumanian and Italian divisions.

facing north where the German lines bent back at right angles and ran westward from the Volga and back across the Don.

This right angle in the line, held as it was by the crack German troops of Paulus and Hoth, was no worry to Chief of Staff Zeitzler. What did worry him were its flanks. For the front lines south of Hoth's 4th Panzer Army and to the west of Paulus' 6th Army were held by Rumanian troops. To the south of Stalingrad there had been very little Russian activity, and there was a chance that the Rumanians would be an adequate flank protection there. But along the Don, to the north, it was a different story.

Westward, from a point near Kremenskaya which marked the end of the front manned by Paulus' men, the line was held by General Dumitrescu's 3rd Rumanian Army which had taken over this sector late in the summer. Beyond the Rumanians, farther to the west, lay the Italian 8th Army and then the Hungarian 3rd. All these troops plus the Germans around Stalingrad and the Rumanians south of it were under the command of General von Weichs' Army Group B. It was a large force but with its hodgepodge of nationalities, a difficult one to command. Von Weichs was not happy with it.

Neither, for that matter, was General Dumitrescu. When his 3rd Rumanian Army took over its sector of the Don Front, Dumitrescu immediately noted that the so-called Don line was not along the Don at all. South of the river, Russian bridgeheads pushed into what were now his lines. To have any chance of a successful defense, Dumitrescu told von Weichs at Army Group Headquarters, those Russian bridgeheads would have to be eliminated. This would require major German formations and von Weichs' major German formations were with the 6th Army battering at Stalingrad. Furthermore, the 6th Army was becoming more and more the exclusive property of Hitler's headquarters and von Weichs could not move a battalion of it without permission. Dumitrescu's suggestion was turned down.

His Rumanian divisions were pitifully weak. They were organized along the line of pre-war French divisions, Rumania having been a staunch ally of France, and were almost devoid of anti-tank guns. The regular Rumanian artillery had no

armor-piercing shells at all. These weak divisions were holding
fronts of better than ten miles each. The Rumanian peasant
soldiers repeated to each other an old Rumanian proverb that
he who sheds blood in Russia will not leave it alive.

Dumitrescu also reported to von Weichs concrete evidence of Russian offensive intentions. Reconnaissance noted
an increasing flow of men and materials into the Russian
bridgeheads south of the Don. There was a steadily increasing
tempo to the sharp, small-unit attacks all along the front. The
Russians were obviously probing for soft spots.

Worries of a Russian attack along the Don Front did
penetrate Hitler's headquarters. There, both Hitler and Chief
of Staff Zeitzler took comfort from the situation maps which
showed a reserve behind the Don Front, the 48th Panzer Corps.
What the map didn't show was that this corps consisted of two
very weak armored divisions. One was Rumanian and equipped
with obsolete Czech light tanks. The other, the German 22nd
Panzer Division, had been sitting for so long behind the front
that mice had chewed through the wiring on many of its tanks.
Thus it was considered, with good reason, "below standard tech-
nically." [2] The 48th Panzer Corps was a very weak reserve
to put behind such a weak front.

Zeitzler was certain that with the coming of the winter
there would be Russian attacks, although in what strength
he had no idea. The sensible course, thought Zeitzler, was to
pull back Paulus' 6th Army and Hoth's 4th Panzer Army from
the Volga to the Don. The front would thus be shortened and
some of the crack German divisions of these two armies could
be formed into a real reserve. But Zeitzler quickly discovered
that even hinting at such a policy would put Hitler into one
of his towering rages.

Zeitzler, therefore, came up with an alternative suggestion for the Fuehrer, one that was, at best, a weak compromise.
The right angle at Stalingrad would be held until the Russian
offensive began. If the Russian attack appeared to be in major
strength, the angle would be quickly abandoned. Hitler held
out to Zeitzler a vague hope that he would seriously consider

[2] von Mannstein, *Lost Victories,* p. 297.

such a solution. Zeitzler, instead of seizing on this hope, would have done better to have listened to Hitler's speech to the German people that October when the Fuehrer proclaimed that "where the German soldier sets foot, there he remains." [3] For that was Hitler's real strategy—no retreat, anywhere.

Hitler pointed out to his generals that there was one simple solution to all their problems—take Stalingrad. Orders from the Fuehrer to that purpose went to Zeitzler, then to von Weichs and finally on down to Paulus at 6th Army headquarters. Take Stalingrad before winter comes.

So the pressures on Paulus built up. Not the least of them were the pressures from within himself. Paulus had entered the Kaiser's Army in 1910 after the snobbish Imperial Navy had refused him a commission. His family was middle class, his father a civil servant with no aristocratic "von" in front of his name. In 1912 Paulus had married into the Rumanian aristocracy but that still didn't put a "von" in front of his name. Throughout his Army career Paulus cultivated the attributes of his social superiors and became noted for immaculate dress, perfect manners and a self-effacing friendliness. Militarily, he made himself into the perfect staff officer, someone's number two man. He willingly took on the drudgery and never spared himself from hard work, but the hard decisions he was content to leave to others. Said one mid-twenties report on Paulus, "This man lacks decisiveness." [4]

To such a man, that October of 1942, came General Schmundt, whose friendship for Zeitzler had not hurt that officer's progress at all. Paulus knew Schmundt from the old days in the pre-war army. He knew Schmundt was an intimate of Hitler's and had written to congratulate him on his recent promotion to chief of the Personnel Branch with its great powers over promotions and assignments. To the good Nazi Schmundt, Paulus had been careful to sign his letter, "Best wishes and Heil Hitler!" [5] The 6th Army was Paulus' first

[3] Freidin and Richardson, *The Fatal Decisions*, p. 140.
[4] Goerlitz, *Paulus and Stalingrad*, p. 12.
[5] Goerlitz, *Paulus and Stalingrad*, p. 170.

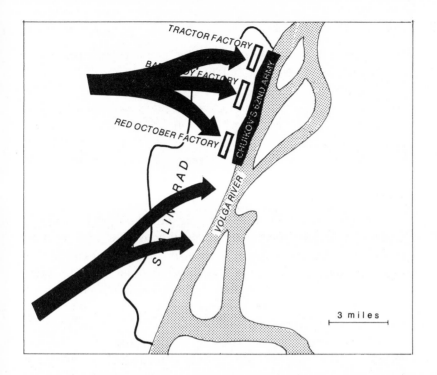

3 miles

THE BATTLE FOR STALINGRAD While Hoth's 4th Panzer Army took most of southern Stalingrad, Paulus' 6th Army concentrated its attacks on a narrow strip of the city along the Volga where Chuikov's Russians held out in the ruins of three factory complexes. In extremely bloody fighting during October and the first half of November, Chuikov's bridgehead was reduced to a few hundred square yards around the Red October Factory but Paulus' army was exhausted and could go no further.

major command and he was looking forward to going still higher.

Schmundt talked to Paulus and let him know that the capture of Stalingrad would have a very marked effect on his future career. It was well known in the Army that Hitler's current chief of operations, General Jodl, had been in the doghouse even since he had disagreed with Hitler over operations in the Caucasus. It was surely possible that Paulus, after the capture of Stalingrad, might have Jodl's job. But Paulus' wife thought that something better was in the offing, second-in-command over the Army to Hitler himself. And there was the baton of a Field Marshal to be won.

Although all these glittering possibilities were dangled before him by Schmundt, Paulus did point out the weakness of his position with nothing but second-rate Rumanian troops guarding his flanks. He did not do so quite as strongly, though, as did his two Panzer Corps commanders who were fired by Hitler as a result. What Paulus did do was to try his level best to take Stalingrad.

In September the Russian hold on Stalingrad had been loosened but not broken. The central and southern portions of the city were, by October, mostly in German hands. Paulus' opponent, General Vasili Chuikov, who was just about as tough a defensive fighter as the Red Army possessed, had concentrated some of the best troops of his 62nd Army at the northern end of the city.

There, the bomb-blasted ruins of three great factory complexes had become the last-ditch fortresses of the 62nd Army. To the north was the Tractor Factory. In the center was the Barrikady Factory and to the south, the Red October. Chuikov's command post was behind the Barrikady Factory in the center. There were shell fragments in the General's soup and conversations were held in shouts because of the incessant crash of the German bombardment. Chuikov thrived at such a headquarters and adamantly refused to move to the relative peace of the east bank of the Volga.

Paulus struck Chuikov's fortress area from the north on October 4th. The German attack came in against the Tractor Factory but Chuikov had anticipated it. He had the newly arrived 37th Guards Infantry Division ready and waiting and the German attack faltered. There was a lull on the sixth and then on the seventh the Germans tried again. The 37th Guards held again. Both sides started to regroup.

During lulls or regroupings, the fighting went right on. Always there were small raids, snipers at work and incessant bombardments. Casualties were continuous and time and again Paulus pleaded for more infantry, for this was an infantryman's fight. He got what could be scraped together:

police battalions, engineer assault battalions, anti-aircraft companies. The fresh divisions which were what he really needed were nowhere to be found. With what he had, Paulus mounted his next major assault on October 14th. It came very close to success.

Again Paulus' attack came with its main weight in the north against the Tractor Factory. This time, to pave the way, von Richthofen's 8th Air Fleet put in everything it could lay its hands on. A German corporal noted, "Everything in sight is being blotted from the face of the earth." [6]

Just before noon Chuikov got a fearful jolt. The 37th Guards Division, which had saved the Tractor Factory the week before, had been smashed by a massive assault led by 180 tanks of the 14th Panzer Division. By mid-afternoon it looked as though two divisions and part of another were cut off. The Tractor Factory could not hold out for long. Casualties at Chuikov's command post were rising, already there were thirty dead. By nightfall there were 3,500 wounded lying along the banks of the Volga waiting to be ferried across to safety.

That evening Chuikov was called to the phone. It was Nikita Khrushchev, political boss of the entire front. The conversation seemed fairly innocuous. Khrushchev wanted to know if the Tractor Factory could be held and was told by Chuikov that it would be foolish to throw the whole Army in there. Khrushchev reminded Chuikov of the military and political significance of Stalingrad. Then he threw in a loaded question, "What is your major need at the moment?" By the answer, Khrushchev, the politician, could measure Chuikov, the general. Supplies for the wounded, reinforcements, what?

Chuikov's answer was short and to the point, "More ammunition." [7] There couldn't have been a better answer.

The drive of the 14th Panzer Division had rushed past the Tractor Factory to the banks of the Volga and Chuikov's northern sector was cut in two. At the far northern end were scratch forces under Colonel Gorokhov. They hung on through the

[6] Chuikov, *The Battle for Stalingrad*, p. 252.
[7] Chuikov, p. 183.

days to come with Gorokhov proving himself a smaller version of his commander. But Paulus was swinging south against the next factory, the Barrikady, behind which were Chuikov's headquarters.

Russian headquarters was crowded with refugees from units which had simply been blown apart by the German advance. Messages streamed in asking for help and for instructions in the incredible confusion that now existed everywhere in the ruins of the factories. There was little Chuikov could do but order, "Stay put."

The Germans started to move down from the Tractor Factory. Chuikov sent his own headquarters guard unit into action. Only 300 yards separated the Germans from Russian Army Headquarters but it was that last 300 yards that the Germans could not make.

The remains of the 37th Guards and the 95th Russian Division were now defending the Barrikady and were down to one-quarter of their strength. But on the night of the 15th, one regiment of the Red Army's 138th Division came across the Volga.

This single regiment went straight from its boats to face the Germans coming from the captured Tractor Factory. They fought beside the dug-in tanks of the Russian 84th Armored Brigade; a tank well dug into the piles of rubble was a fortress in itself. Massed artillery from the far bank of the Volga enfiladed the German attack, and the Red Air Force, taking an awful beating in the process, added the weight of its bombs. The German attacks were stopped.

That night the other two regiments of the 138th Division crossed the river and so did Chuikov's immediate superior, General Yeremenko, who commanded the whole Stalingrad front. The two Generals talked well into the night. Uppermost in Chuikov's mind were his very limited ammunition supplies. He complained that he was getting far too little from the other side of the river.

The next day, Yeremenko having left, Chuikov received a message from Yeremenko's headquarters saying that instead of the month's supply of ammunition Chuikov needed, he was only going to get enough for one day's hard fighting. Chuikov blew up. He finally talked Yeremenko out of some more—but not much.

Chuikov wondered why the higher command was so chary of ammunition. The answer, he was sure, was that ammunition was being hoarded for some large-scale Russian counteroffensive. He asked no questions of his superiors for such a practice was not a healthy one in the Russian Army. He knew that his job remained the same: hold Stalingrad.

On October 17th, the Germans hit the Russian force isolated to the north of the Tractor Factory. Two brigade commanders radioed Chuikov for permission to retreat to two islands in the Volga. Chuikov radioed back that any such retreat would be considered cowardice in the face of the enemy. The brigade commanders knew the penalty for that military sin and they stayed put.

The fighting for the Barrikady and Red October factories went on. On the 18th, Paulus' men got a clean breakthrough to the river, but a Russian counterattack threw them back. The Germans came on again, slowly nibbling away at the Russian position. Bit by bit, Chuikov's men were compressed against the bank of the Volga. One more big German attack like that on the 14th and they might have been thrown into the river itself. But there was no attack on that scale. During the first two weeks of November, Paulus' 6th Army attacked again and again but never with quite the strength needed to break through. Paulus persisted in his attacks because his orders were to persist, but he had little faith in their success.

Chuikov, on the other hand, knew that he had won his battle. He could sense that the Germans had reached the point of exhaustion, that they were stretched to the extreme limit of their powers. The ground in mid-November was frozen hard, just right for mass tank operations. Chuikov reasoned that the Russian counteroffensive could not now be long in coming. He was right.

Zhukov Plans a Trap

The great series of attacks which Paulus had launched on October 4th had, all along, been playing right into the hands of General Georgi Zhukov, Deputy Supreme Commander of all Russian Forces, second in authority only to Stalin himself. Since mid-September, Zhukov had been planning an enormous counterstroke designed to do nothing less than completely wipe out Paulus' 6th Army.

On September 12th, Zhukov and his chief of staff, General Vasilievsky, had met at the Kremlin with Stalin. Until then Russian reinforcements, as they had arrived in the Stalingrad sector, had been thrown into the defense of the city or into fruitless attacks against the Germans to the north of it. The talk was about more of the same. Possibly, as more reserves came up, Paulus could be stopped and then finally pushed back away from Stalingrad. Such a limited victory was not for Zhukov and he spoke in a whisper to Vasilievsky about there being some alternative. Stalin overheard him and ordered the two of them to come back the next night with their thoughts for an alternative.

On the following evening, Zhukov and Vasilievsky came back with the bare outlines of their plan. They met alone with Stalin, for what they had to tell him was too secret for anyone else to be present. The two Generals agreed that the defense of Stalingrad must go on and the German 6th Army worn down. But this should be accomplished by the minimum possible number of troops. All the Russian reserves available should be assembled on the Southern Front, not to be thrown into the battle for the city, but to be used later for two massive attacks against the 4th Rumanian Army south of Stalingrad and against Dumitrescu's 3rd Rumanian Army along the Don. These two attacks were to penetrate deep into the enemy rear and link up on the Don behind Stalingrad, thus surrounding all of Paulus' 6th Army. Then two fronts would be formed; one around Paulus' army at Stalingrad and a second, further to the west to prevent any German forces from coming to Paulus' relief. Here was a plan, not for pushing Paulus' army away from Stalingrad, but for a classic double envelopment with the enemy's army not just defeated but annihilated. It was a plan to win a battle and to win a war as well.

Stalin ordered Zhukov and Vasilievsky to inspect the Southern Front personally and return with more details. He enjoined them to the strictest secrecy. For the time being, only the three of them should know that such a plan existed.

By the beginning of October, Zhukov was ready to present Stalin with the full details of what was now called Operation Uranus. Eleven armies would have to be moved into position, 13,500 guns brought up and over a thousand planes. Russian industry, now relocated well back from the fighting fronts, was producing ammunition in satisfactory quantities. From the United States and Great Britain, huge amounts of supplies were now arriving, including two things the Russians badly needed for any far-ranging operations—canned foods for the troops to eat and trucks for them to ride in.

Of most importance to Operation Uranus, though, was the item of 1,000 new tanks. Without them, there could be no deep penetrations and no decisive battle. They were essential to the Zhukov plan. They had to be more than just ordinary tanks and they were indeed quite out of the ordinary. Their story started on another October 4th, twelve years earlier.

On October 4, 1930, a board had been convened by the United States Army, including as a member, Major George S. Patton, United States Cavalry, to assess the performance of a new tank chassis. The vehicle was the brainchild of an irascible inventor, J. Walter Christie, and was called the M.1928. In its tests it forded a three-foot stream, ran an obstacle course, turned in its own length and climbed a thirty-five-degree slope. With its tracks removed it did 70 m.p.h. on the road and then, with tracks, managed 40 m.p.h. cross-country. For 1930 it was like something out of science fiction.

The board approved the M.1928 and the United States Army got seven of them. Three went to the infantry and four to the cavalry. The latter had to be called combat cars as "tanks" were not officially allowed in the cavalry. The United States Army quarreled with Christie and produced a later version of its own in 1936. For both economy reasons and because tactical thought in the Army was not on a par with Christie's, the whole project was then allowed to drop. Christie tried the British but here too there were quarrels, recriminations and another dropped project.

Neither the British nor the American military had grasped the new concepts of wide-ranging mechanized warfare then being preached by Liddell Hart, J. F. C. Fuller and others in England. This was not true of the Russians. In the early thirties the Red Army was being remade by a dynamic group of younger generals headed by Marshal Mikhail Tukhachevsky, and they saw tanks in a deep penetration role as well as their then conventional one of infantry support. They even tried to get Liddell Hart to come to Russia but failed. They did buy two of J. Walter Christie's M.1928's.

In 1936 Western military observers at the Red Army's autumn maneuvers were astonished to see more than a thousand tanks on display. Most impressive of these was the B.T. (Bystrokhodnii tank), a fast, light tank developed directly from Christie's M.1928. Russian progress in tank design was going full speed ahead.

Not so the development of military doctrine to go with the tanks. The young military élite of the Red Army was seen by Stalin as a possible counterrevolutionary threat. Within two years of the 1936 maneuvers, Tukhachevsky and at least 15,000 other officers were dead at the hands of Stalin's police. Stalin was a military conservative and the generals that survived agreed that tanks were better fitted to support the slow-moving infantry masses than to roam independently beyond them. Some generals, like Zhukov, who disagreed, managed to survive by keeping their mouths shut.

In 1940 the German Panzers swept across France in a convincing demonstration of what far-ranging tanks could do when not tied down to an infantry support role, and Stalin realized that he had been wrong. The Red Army tried to reorganize its tank forces in the year between the fall of France and Hitler's invasion of Russia. It could not be done in that short a time. Too many experienced officers had been liquidated by Stalin.

In the first few months of fighting in 1941, the Russian tank forces were all but wiped out. But that fall, as the German Panzers neared Moscow, they suddenly and unpleasantly found themselves faced, although on a small scale, by a new Russian tank, the latest in the B.T. series. This was the T-34. Fortunately for Russia, Stalin had not purged the tank designers. Developing Christie's ideas still further and marrying them with a beautifully designed 500-horsepower diesel engine, they were building the best tank in the world.

With the German Army overrunning the great industrial areas of Russia in 1941, there was a considerable problem of where to build tanks. The answer lay in the mass evacuation of industry ahead of the advancing Germans and a special Evacuation Soviet was formed to do the job. One of its members was Alexei Kosygin. The job was done and a vast industrial complex, called Tankograd, was established beyond the Urals in Asiatic Russia. There, in 1942, 5,000 T-34's were produced.

It was with the T-34 tanks that Georgi Zhukov meant to make his coming offensive decisive. It was their job to sweep from north and south into the rear of Paulus' army. The infantry and artillery would move up behind the armored spearheads and an iron ring would be thrown around Stalingrad.

All through October, Zhukov and Vasilievsky worked on the preparations for the offensive. Supplies and men rolled up to their designated positions, moving mostly at night. Twenty-seven thousand trucks rolled along the roads and the railways delivered 1,300 carloads of supplies a day. Over a million men were moving up.

On November 13th, Zhukov and Vasilievsky went to the Kremlin for a final conference with Stalin. They found him in a good mood, puffing at his pipe, stroking his moustache and, above all, listening to them without interruption. The offensive was now scheduled for November 19th, six days off.

Russian forces on the Southern Front had been divided into three army groups which the Russians called "Fronts." General Yeremenko commanded the Stalingrad Front and under him Chuikov's 62nd Army was still beating off Paulus' rapidly weakening attacks. South of Stalingrad, Yeremenko had three more armies. Immediately south of Chuikov, one

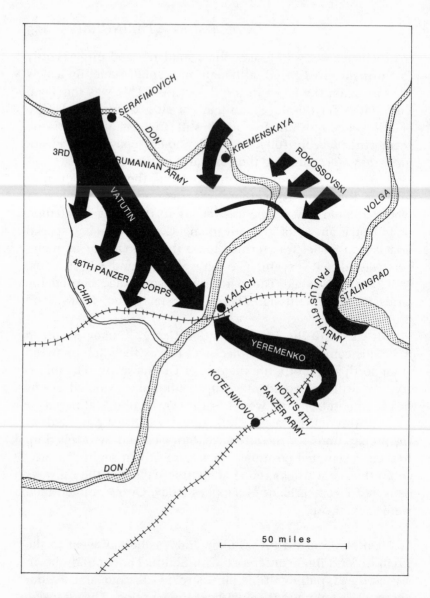

OPERATION URANUS On November 19th, the Russian offensive opened with Vatutin's tank armies breaking through the 3rd Rumanian Army and the weak German 48th Panzer Corps. On the next day, Yeremenko's tanks swept south of Stalingrad and met Vatutin's men at Kalach. Paulus' thin line running west from Stalingrad to Kremenskaya held the Russian attacks and then slowly retreated east of the Don to form a perimeter around Stalingrad. Within a week, the German 6th Army was completely surrounded. Paulus wanted to break out at once, but Hitler ordered the 6th Army to hold on to Stalingrad and await relief.

army, the 64th, would hit hard at the Germans just south of the city. Further south, the 57th, under a very able tank commander, General Tolbukhin, was to go through the Rumanians and dash for Kalach on the Don, thirty-five miles to the rear of Paulus. On Tolbukhin's left, the 51st Army was to drive southwest to Kotelnikovo to set up blocking positions against any German attempt to counterattack from the south.

North of Stalingrad, where the lines bent back at right angles to the west, General Rokossovski's Don Front, composed of three armies, faced the German troops of Paulus' 6th Army along a fifty-mile front. The Don River bisected the German Front here, and it was hoped that Rokossovski's 65th and 24th armies would be able to cut off the Germans west of the Don near Kremenskaya from their main forces closer to Stalingrad.

The main effort of the whole Russian offensive, though, was to come from General Vatutin's Southwest Front which faced the Rumanians beyond Kletskaya. On Vatutin's left, the 21st Army would sweep in right behind those Germans facing Rokossovski west of the Don. To their right, in the center of Vatutin's Southwest Front, was the 5th Tank Army under General Romanenko. With 500 of the new T-34 tanks they were to crush the Rumanian center and race down to Kalach where they would meet Yeremenko's troops coming up from the south. On Vatutin's right was the 1st Guards Army which was to sweep down to the Chir River and start setting up blocking positions against whatever German forces that might try to relieve Stalingrad from the west.

As the two big breakthroughs were to be made against the weak Rumanian divisions, Zhukov and Vasilievsky had confidence in the initial success of the operation. The crisis would come as German reserves began to arrive from other sectors. To pin down as many of these as possible, Zhukov was planning another Russian offensive against the Germans near Moscow.

All was ready. Stalin agreed to the plans. Vatutin's attack would start on November 19th; Yeremenko's, which did not have as far to go, on the 20th. Then, on the 17th, with only two days to go before the offensive started, a strange thing happened. Stalin called Zhukov and Vasilievsky back to the Kremlin. He showed them a letter from General Volsky whose corps was to spearhead the southern pincers of the drive. Volsky thought that the whole offensive was doomed to failure as there was not enough manpower or supplies available to insure success. Zhukov and Vasilievsky defended their planning. Stalin then talked to Volsky on the phone and persuaded him to proceed as planned. But Stalin, who had had many a general shot for less, spoke calmly and quietly. Was he testing Zhukov's and Vasilievsky's confidence? Was he setting them up as scapegoats in case the offensive failed? Or was General Volsky really suffering from the jitters? No one knew.

One night later, on the 18th, General Chuikov and his generals sat in his headquarters within that small piece of Stalingrad that now remained in Russian hands. They were waiting for a midnight call from Front Commander Yeremenko. The word they got was what they had been expecting. The great counteroffensive would start at dawn the following morning. The long defense of Stalingrad was over.

Exactly at five the next morning, November 19, 1942, thousands of Russian guns opened fire along Rokossovski's and Vatutin's fronts. So great was the roar that it was heard by Chuikov's soldiers in Stalingrad. "Nachalos," they said to one another, "it has come."

The Trap Is Sprung

NOVEMBER 19–23, 1942

The Russian guns of Vatutin's Southwest Front poured forth a massive barrage on the defenses of the 3rd Rumanian Army. For ninety minutes Russian shells tore at the Rumanian front line, puffs of black smoke slowly obscuring the grey snow of dawn. At 6:30 A.M. the bayonet-tipped masses of the Red infantry divisions surged forward to the charge.

There was no continuous Rumanian front line, only a series of scattered strong points. Some of these, their occupants stunned by the barrage, were overrun by the Russian infantry. From some the Rumanians fled for their lives. In others they fought hard. But then, behind the Red infantry came the masses of T-34 tanks. Absolutely defenseless against the Russian armor, the 3rd Rumanian Army began to disintegrate.

As it did, Vatutin unleashed his main armored forces for the breakthrough. On his left, near Kletskaya, the 4th Tank Corps poured through a ten-mile gap in the Rumanian line and advanced toward the rear of the Germans holding the line opposite the Kremenskaya bridgehead. This Russian attack, coupled with that of the divisions on the right of Rokossovski's Don Front, was an immediate threat to Paulus' flank and to the divisions he had to the west of the Don. It caused the first reaction of the day on the German side.

Acting on orders from the Fuehrer's headquarters, the 48th Panzer Corps, with its antiquated Czech tanks and its mouse-eaten German ones, started to the west for this sector of the front. But hardly had the Corps gotten started when its orders were changed. It was to head north to the assistance of the Rumanian 5th Corps, for this Corps was being hit by Vatutin's main force, the 5th Tank Army. By the time the 48th Panzer Corps got into action, there was no Rumanian Corps left for them to assist. By the end of the day, the 48th Panzer Corps was fighting for its existence thirty miles behind where the front lines had been that morning.

On the next day, November 20th, the armies of Yeremenko's Stalingrad Front went over to the offensive south of the city and the Rumanian 4th Army here in the south suffered the same fate as the 3rd Rumanian Army had in the north. Blasted by artillery and then attacked by infantry and tanks, it fell apart.

To the north, the Russian 13th Mechanized Corps had the mission of swinging in sharply behind the Germans who were facing the southern limits of Stalingrad. The German troops here belonged to Hermann Hoth's 4th Panzer Army and Hoth was a first-rate Panzer general. Immediately behind his front he had the full-strength 29th Motorized Division, a crack outfit which was under orders to go south to the Caucasus later in the month. Hoth quickly reacted to the Russian breakthrough. By 10:30 in the morning he had the 29th Motorized heading for the flank of the Russian's 13th Mechanized Corps. The experienced Germans stopped the Russian attack in its tracks and, for the moment, the left flank of the Stalingrad line was safe.

Further south, though, Yeremenko's 4th Mechanized Corps swept forward against very little opposition. This was the corps of General Volsky, who had had the opening-night jitters and had caused such a flap at Stalin's headquarters only three days earlier. Fighting Rumanians had been a tonic for Volsky's pessimism and by the end of the day he was almost halfway to Kalach on the Don.

On that second day of the Russian offensive the disintegration of the 3rd Rumanian Army in the north had continued at a frightening pace. In its center, more than three divisions had been surrounded but were fighting as best they could. The 48th Panzer Corps tried to attack northward toward them but with no success. The Rumanian tank division was lost and by the end of the day German tank strength had been cut in half. The 48th Panzer Corps was forced to pull back to avoid total destruction. Vatutin's tanks had a virtually clear path to Kalach and their planned link-up with Volsky's corps.

News of the Russian offensive had reached Adolf Hitler, not at his Wolfschanze headquarters in East Prussia, but at his mountain retreat at Berchtesgaden in southern Germany where the Fuehrer was contemplating the changed situation brought about by the Allied landings in French North Africa the week before. To Hitler, the situation in Russia looked serious but not critical. There was no question that the Russian attack was on a large scale, and it was dangerous, but there had been worse crises than this during the previous winter. At Demyansk, near Leningrad, 100,000 German troops had been surrounded. They had held out for three months, supplied by air, and had finally been rescued. Now, when Zeitzler came on the phone with the suggestion that Paulus' 6th Army be pulled back from Stalingrad immediately, Hitler thought there was a note of panic in such a suggestion. He turned it down, convinced that now, as during the past winter, only the iron will of the Fuehrer could save the German Army. There must be no retreat.

In addition to imposing his iron will on the Army, Hitler saw that the unwieldy command structure in southern Russia would have to be changed. Army Group A in the Caucasus, which Hitler had been commanding himself, was now put under von Kleist. Von Weichs' Army Group B was now to command the Italian, Hungarian and German troops who were west of the areas of Russian penetration. The armies in the actual area of crisis, the broken Rumanians and the Germans of Paulus and Hoth around Stalingrad, were now to be formed into the Don Army Group and to lead them Hitler chose the best of all his generals, Field Marshal Fritz Erich von Mannstein, a master of the art of war.

It had been von Mannstein who had conceived the operational plan whereby France had been crushed in 1940. He had commanded a Panzer corps in Russia in 1941 with true brilliance. In the summer of 1942, it had been his victories in the Crimea which had brought him to the rank of Field Marshal. He had received the baton to go with his new rank only the month before, in October, from Hitler's hands. The Fuehrer had then sent him to the central front opposite Moscow where a Russian attack was feared but had told him that he would soon bring him south again to take over command of a motorized army group which was to cross the Caucasus and thrust into the Middle East in the spring of 1943. Now von Mannstein was ordered south on quite a different mission. Now his orders from Hitler were to "bring the enemy attacks to a standstill and recapture the positions previously occupied by us." [8]

Bad weather made it impossible for von Mannstein to fly south and he was forced to make the long trip by train. The trip was made even longer by Russian guerrillas who laid mines under the tracks. It was a sorrowful one for von Mannstein who had just buried his son, an army lieutenant, under Russian soil. He had little information to go on but he knew he was headed for a crisis, one that could easily become a catastrophe.

By November 21st, the third day of the battle, Paulus was fully aware of the extent of the disasters which had occurred on

[8] von Mannstein, p. 294.

either flank of his 6th Army, but within the 6th Army there was no panic. The army corps on its left flank, next to the Rumanians, was folding back before the Russians, retreating, but slowly and in good order. To the south the same thing was happening. Hoth's infantry had held that sector and was now transferred to the 6th Army. With them, and the fine 29th Motorized Division, Paulus began building a southern front.

On the next day, the 22nd, both Vatutin and Yeremenko had light forces astride the railway which ran west from Stalingrad and which was Paulus' lifeline. By that night they would be in Kalach and the encirclement of Paulus' 6th Army would be complete. These Russian forces, curling around the 6th Army, were only armored spearheads backed by truck-borne infantry. Paulus knew that this was only a light net that was being thrown around him. But he also knew that behind the armored spearheads would come the slower moving masses of Russian infantry and artillery that would make the light net into an iron ring.

That afternoon, 6th Army Headquarters was set up in a railway station just outside Stalingrad and there Paulus met with his chief of staff, General Arthur Schmidt. Paulus had asked Hitler for a free hand in dealing with the situation and had been refused. He was a bit shaken but not so his Chief of Staff. Schmidt was a hard-nosed, tough character, never given to pessimism and quite at home in a crisis.

Immediate orders were issued to move the divisions of the 6th Army into a position of all-round defense. Schmidt and his staff officers were thorough professionals and the complications of such a maneuver did not bother them. The divisions west of the Don were ordered back over the river and the perimeter began to form. When it was completed, there would be twenty German and two Rumanian divisions within it. Paulus and Schmidt had plenty of troops to withstand any Russian attacks—that is, as long as their supplies held out.

With their perimeter formed, what should be their next move? Paulus and Schmidt separated and for an hour each thought out the problem. Then they met and found that they had arrived at identical solutions. The 6th Army must prepare to break out of the trap. That would take four days. Then, on the 26th, the Army would attack to the southwest where the Russian net seemed to be weakest.

The Paulus-Schmidt plan went back to the Fuehrer in Berchtesgaden and was immediately disapproved. Hitler ordered that the 6th Army stay put and "await relief from outside." [9] On no account were the positions won within Stalingrad or along the Volga north of the city to be given up. Paulus was told that large-scale countermeasures were being taken by headquarters.

This, however, was not so. Large-scale countermeasures were certainly called for. Although, at the time, Hitler did not realize it, the decisive battle for the survival of his Nazi empire was now being fought. His own planning staff suggested that five Panzer divisions and as many infantry divisions begin moving from France to Russia, but Hitler would not hear of it. He did not realize that all American and British strength was fully deployed in the Pacific and in Africa. He did not, therefore, want to strip France of German divisions. Nor did he think that it would take more than a division or two to clear up the situation in southern Russia.

It was not, therefore, an overly worried Hitler who, having given his orders to Paulus to hold on, started by train and plane for his Wolfschanze headquarters in East Prussia. From there he could better control the battle and control his generals with their incessant talk of retreat.

When Hitler arrived at the Wolfschanze on the following evening, he was met by an agitated General Zeitzler. The Fuehrer was in an affable mood and greeted the Chief of the General Staff soothingly, "Don't let yourself be upset. We must show firmness of character in misfortune. We must remember Frederick The Great." [10]

Zeitzler, like any German general, knew his Frederick the Great. He knew Frederick's epigram on defensive warfare: he who would defend everything, defends nothing. Zeitzler argued that Stalingrad was no place to defend, that the quarter

[9] Goerlitz, *Paulus and Stalingrad,* p. 222.
[10] Freidin and Richardson, p. 149.

of a million men of Paulus' 6th Army must not be locked up there.

Hitler would have none of such arguments. He explained that, on the trip to the Wolfschanze, he had worked out a plan to bring a Panzer division north from the Caucasus. Zeitzler objected that that was hardly enough. "In that case," rejoined the Fuehrer, "we shall bring up two divisions from the Caucasus." Zeitzler argued again and slowly the Fuehrer's affable mood left him. His fist slammed down on the table. "I won't go back from the Volga." [11]

Von Mannstein Takes Over

NOVEMBER 24–30, 1942

On November 24th, von Mannstein's train arrived at the headquarters of Army Group B and he received a review of the chaotic situation from von Weichs and his staff. Von Mannstein saw that he was faced with two crises. The first and immediate one was the 6th Army surrounded in Stalingrad. The second, and more vital one, was the situation of Army Group A in the Caucasus. If the Russians were now to move down along the Don to Rostov where the river empties into the Black Sea, Army Group A would then be cut off as well. With both the 6th Army and Army Group A gone, a loss of a million men, the whole southern flank of all the German armies in Russia would be exposed. There would be a 300-mile void from Kharkov to the Black Sea and through it the Russian armies could move at will. That would mean the loss of the war.

Fortunately, from von Mannstein's point of view, most of the Russian forces were now being thrown against Paulus' surrounded army in an attempt to wipe it out quickly. The Russians thought that there were less than 100,000 Germans surrounded at Stalingrad rather than the 250,000 Paulus had under his command. Both Rokossovski's and Yeremenko's troops smashed against the perimeter formed by the Germans, but to no avail. For the moment, Paulus' 6th Army was safe

[11] Freidin and Richardson, p. 150.

within what would soon become known as the "Stalingrad Cauldron."

Von Mannstein reasoned that it was now too late for Paulus to break out on his own. Orders for such a breakout should have been given immediately after the Russian offensive started but they had not. With the 6th Army under heavy Russian attack, a retreat back toward the Don would be a very bloody business. Von Mannstein was afraid that if such a retreat were now ordered, all that would be left of the 6th Army when the retreat was over would be shattered remnants. Therefore, the 6th Army should stay within the Cauldron until a relief force could be assembled and then it could be brought out in one piece.

Von Mannstein explained his thinking over the phone to Zeitzler. He emphasized one point. Paulus' 6th Army should stay within the Cauldron to await rescue at a later date only if, and the "if" was crucial, it could be properly supplied by air. If it could not be, then it must break out at once no matter what the risks.

The question of supplying the 6th Army by air was one which had to be decided at Hitler's headquarters. The Fuehrer was commander-in-chief of all the German armed forces and aerial resupply was a problem for the Luftwaffe. Thus it was that Hitler turned to the commander of the Luftwaffe, Reichsmarschall Hermann Goering.

The Luftwaffe had not been too high in the Fuehrer's favor since it had failed to bomb Britain out of the war in 1940 as Goering had promised. Now, when Goering was asked whether he could supply the 6th Army by air, his answer was not that of an airman facing realities but that of a courtier seeking to regain favor. The immediate needs of the 6th Army were 400 tons a day and Goering said that the figure could be met.

An honest answer would have been far more on the pessimistic side. Running an airlift in the midst of a Russian winter could hardly be a matter for optimism no matter how many aircraft were available, and the fact was that all too few were available. It was only ten days since Hitler had ordered the immediate and massive buildup of the German bridgehead around Tunis. Seven hundred of the invaluable, tri-motored Ju 52's were being used in Africa and there were not enough left for southern Russia. Even on its best day, Goering's airlift into Stalingrad would not hit the 400-ton minimum figure. The Luftwaffe could not supply Tunis and Stalingrad at the same time.

Hitler accepted Goering's assurances on the feasibility of the airlift. The Ju 52 pilots flew into appalling weather and into the machine guns of Russian fighters with extraordinary courage, but with little hope of succeeding in their mission. The commander of the Luftwaffe's 4th Air Fleet supporting the 6th Army, General von Richthofen, told Goering flatly that the thing couldn't be done. His expert and on-the-spot opinion was completely ignored. Von Richthofen noted in his diary— "As things are, we commanders, from the operational point of view, are now nothing more than highly paid NCOs!" [12] Only time could prove whether Goering or von Richthofen was right.

As to the immediate future, Hitler and von Mannstein were agreed on several points. Paulus' 6th Army would now stay put in the Stalingrad Cauldron. Some sort of front would be built up along the Chir River extending to the Don at Nizhne-Chirskaya where the Germans still held a small bridgehead on the east side of the Don. Another makeshift front would be built up north of Kotelnikovo on the railroad running south-west from Stalingrad. Then, with reinforcements coming in, the Germans would go over to the attack and cut a corridor through the Russian armies to Stalingrad. The German attack would come from either the bridgehead at Nizhne-Chirskaya or from Kotelnikovo or from both at once.

Where Hitler and von Mannstein were in total disagreement was on the point of what should happen after the corridor to Stalingrad had been established. Hitler wished to use such a corridor to resupply the 6th Army so that it could stay on the Volga until spring. This was not, with the Fuehrer, simply a matter of personal prestige as so many of his generals thought. He was thinking in terms of a massive offensive he intended to launch in the spring of 1943 for which German

[12] Goerlitz, *Paulus and Stalingrad*, p. 241.

factories were now producing the new tanks, the Tigers and the Panthers, which Hitler was sure could master the Russians' T-34. He had not given up his plan for crossing the Caucasus and taking the oil fields that lay south of the mountains.

Von Mannstein's eye was not on Caucasian oil; it was on the Russian Army. What von Mannstein wanted was enough troops to take on the Russians in a fluid war of maneuver, where retreat would be followed by riposte and attack by counterattack. In this kind of warfare the Germans were still far superior to the Russians. In order to wage it, von Mannstein needed those twenty divisions of the 6th Army and he was determined to use any corridor to Stalingrad to get them out.

As disastrous November drew to a close, von Mannstein could look to two bright spots on the front of his Army Group Don. The Russians had thrown very heavy attacks against Paulus' perimeter but the 6th Army had thrown them back. Within the Cauldron, the Germans were standing fast.

In addition, something resembling a front was being thrown up along the Chir. This was desperate work, for units had to be formed out of stragglers from the 3rd Rumanian Army, from rear echelon units of Paulus' 6th Army that had been working along the railroad near Kalach and from men returning from leave in Germany. At one point, movie shows were put on at a crossroads and wandering stragglers, attracted by such a rarity, were rounded up. Battle groups were formed out of anyone who could shoot a rifle—cooks, clerks, bakers, messengers. Along the Chir the line was held by these groups formed into what was called "Army Detachment Hollidt," after the general commanding it.

North of Kotelnikovo the same thing was being done by General Hoth's 4th Panzer Army. But as both these patchwork fronts were being built up, von Mannstein's intelligence noted that, having failed to wipe out Paulus quickly, the Russians were turning men away from Stalingrad and sending them toward the Chir and Kotelnikovo. German divisions, too, were on the way. These were first-class divisions, not scraped up collections of stragglers. But would they arrive before the Russians? Von Mannstein could do nothing but sweat it out.

Crisis on the Chir

With Zhukov occupied in Moscow planning an offensive on the Moscow front, operations in the south were under the general control of his chief of staff, General Vasilievsky. To Vasilievsky, the Germans along the lower Chir and around Nizhne-Chirskaya were the biggest threat to his encirclement of Stalingrad. Only twenty-five miles separated them from Paulus' troops in the Cauldron.

While the Russians prepared a major attack over the Chir, they also sent a strong probing force down the railroad to the southwest of Stalingrad toward Kotelnikovo. They attacked on December 3rd but were just too late to achieve a major success. The 6th Panzer Division had just arrived from France. Fresh off their trains, they counterattacked the Russians on the 4th and drove them back. Then the Kotelnikovo Front settled down to a short period of quiet.

Such was not the case along the Chir. Here the Russians' 5th Tank Army, which had blotted out the Rumanians with such ease at the beginning of the Russian offensive, led the attack. But just as the Russian 5th Tank Army attacked, the German 48th Panzer Corps arrived on the scene. Only in name was this the same formation which had been so ineffective in stemming the Russian November attacks with its mouse-eaten tanks. Now the 48th Panzer Corps had a new commander, General von Knobelsdorf, a first-rate corps commander. It also had two new divisions, the 336th Infantry Division under the panic-proof General Lucht and the full-strength 11th Panzer under General Herman Balck, who was a master of the art of leading a Panzer division.

On December 6th, Lucht's 336th Infantry Division took up a position from Nizhne-Chirskaya to a point about twenty miles up the Chir River. On the next day, the Russian 1st Tank Corps burst across the Chir past the left flank of Lucht's division and poured south fifteen miles to State Farm 79, directly in the rear of the German infantry. Von Knobelsdorf ordered Lucht to stand firm while Balck brought up his 11th Panzer Division to take on the Russians.

At dawn the next day, December 8th, the Russian 1st

Tank Corps was preparing to attack directly into the rear of Lucht's division. Truck-borne Russian infantry was coming up when suddenly it was hit by Balck's tanks. The Russians were massacred. Then Balck drove his tanks into the rear of the Russian armor at State Farm 79. Caught at a disadvantage, the Russian tanks took a bad beating and before the day was over more than fifty were destroyed. The rest pulled back to the Chir.

Balck had won a neat victory but he and his division were to have no rest. North of the 336th Division's sector, the German line along the Chir was like a sieve and the Russians broke through at one point after another. Balck's division raced from one emergency to another. The line of the Chir held, but only by the barest possible margin.

Defensive victories along the Chir were looked upon at von Mannstein's headquarters near Rostov as a mixed blessing. The Russian attacks were being held, but the 48th Panzer Corps was fully engaged in holding them. This meant that the Corps would not be available to attack toward Stalingrad from the Nizhne-Chirskaya bridgehead. There could not, therefore, be a two-pronged attack toward Stalingrad as von Mannstein had hoped. Hoth would have to attack from Kotelnikovo by himself which, as von Mannstein knew, would be a desperate venture.

But von Mannstein realized that time was against him. Goering's airlift into Stalingrad was proving a dismal and costly failure. Daily deliveries were averaging about 100 tons, only a quarter of the absolute minimum necessary. Supplied at this rate, Paulus' 6th Army would begin to wither away. If it was to be gotten out of Stalingrad, it would have to be done quickly, or it would never be done.

Winter Tempest and Thunderclap

DECEMBER 1–19, 1942

What hopes there were of relief for Paulus' surrounded 6th Army now lay with the attack Hoth's 4th Panzer Army was to make northward from Kotelnikovo. It was not at all an impossible attack. With the Russians deeply committed to their attacks along the Chir and to their attacks on the besieged 6th Army, they did not have very powerful forces between Kotelnikovo and Stalingrad.

Von Mannstein did his best to assemble as strong an attack force under Hoth as was possible. The main attack would be made by the 57th Panzer Corps. Its 6th Panzer Division had arrived from France and had already, on December 4th, handed the Russians a sharp setback. The under-strength 23rd Panzer Division was on the way up from the Caucasus front but it was slow in coming. A thaw had made the roads impossible for anything but tracked vehicles and so all the Division's wheeled transport had to come north by rail. It would arrive only just in time for Hoth's attack.

Von Mannstein had hoped that Hoth's attack would be made with the 57th Panzer Corps at a strength of three divisions, for the 17th Panzer Division was on its way from the Moscow front. But Hitler and Zeitzler held the division behind the Chir front for a few days. By the time von Mannstein convinced them that adding a division to Hoth's attack was more important than having a reserve behind the Chir, it was too late for the 17th Panzer to arrive in time for the beginning of Hoth's offensive.

Nor did von Mannstein have any luck in getting the two Panzer divisions of the 3rd Panzer Corps released from the Caucasus. He pointed out to Hitler's headquarters that, bogged down in the mountains, the two divisions were accomplishing nothing. Added to Hoth's forces, their effect could be decisive. But their leaving the Caucasus meant giving up some ground to the Russians and that Hitler would not hear of. The 3rd Panzer Corps remained immobile in the mountains accomplishing, as von Mannstein said, nothing.

On December 10th, two days before Hoth's attack was to begin, von Mannstein heard that Zhukov had started his massive attacks against the Germans near Moscow. There would be no more reinforcements coming south from that sector of the front. Hoth's 57th Panzer Corps would have to move with what it had, 150 tanks of the 6th Panzer Division and twenty of the 23rd Panzer. These were good, experienced troops but there were very few of them. The only division now on its way to help was the 17th Panzer.

The code name for Hoth's attack was Winter Tempest. The operation involved not only Hoth's 57th Panzer Corps and the two Rumanian Corps which were to guard its flanks as it advanced, but Paulus' 6th Army as well. According to the orders for Winter Tempest, once Hoth's Panzers neared the Stalingrad Cauldron, Paulus was to sally out with an armored force to meet Hoth. His sally was only to be a short one, a dozen miles or so. Hoth was going to have to advance eighty miles.

Von Mannstein was fully aware that Hoth, attacking with what amounted to a Panzer division and a half, had very little chance of pushing all the way to Stalingrad. But if he could get to within a short distance, say twenty to thirty miles, then the time would come to initiate a second operation, Thunderclap. This operation called for Paulus to make a full-scale attack out of the Cauldron to meet Hoth. Such an attack would mean the sector-by-sector abandonment of Stalingrad and the German front on the Volga. The abandonment of this front was, so far, strictly forbidden by Hitler. Paulus' orders from the Fuehrer were very clear on that point, and there was a liaison detachment from Hitler's headquarters within the Cauldron with the obvious mission of reporting back to the Fuehrer any weakening of Paulus' resolve to hold Stalingrad.

At 5:00 A.M., December 12th, Hoth started the 57th Panzer Corps on its attack to relieve Stalingrad. The attack started well. The ground was frozen solid, which was what the tank men wanted, and Russian resistance was on the weak side. Both the 6th and 23rd Panzer divisions were on their way north from Kotelnikovo.

Hoth's advance, although far weaker than von Mannstein had planned, was strong enough to cause immediate alarm in the Russian high command. On the 12th, Vasilievsky was visiting the headquarters of the Russian 51st Army which was facing Hoth. Vasilievsky at once realized the danger of the German advance and put in a call to the Kremlin. He couldn't get through. So he called Rokossovski and told him that he

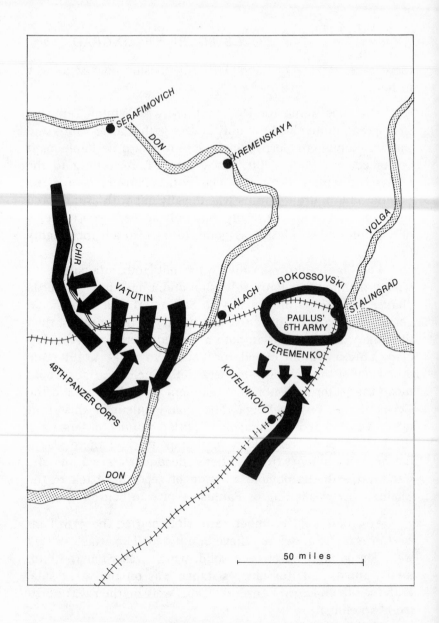

OPERATION WINTER TEMPEST The main effort by von Mannstein to relieve Paulus' trapped army was made by three Panzer
divisions of Hoth's 4th Panzer Army attacking northward from
Kotelnikovo on December 12th. Heavy Russian attacks along the
lower Chir were barely contained by the 48th Panzer Corps. As
Hoth approached to within thirty-five miles of Stalingrad, von
Mannstein wanted Paulus to break out and join up with him. This
Hitler would not allow, and Hoth's attack bogged down. By Christmas, all hope of relieving Stalingrad was gone.

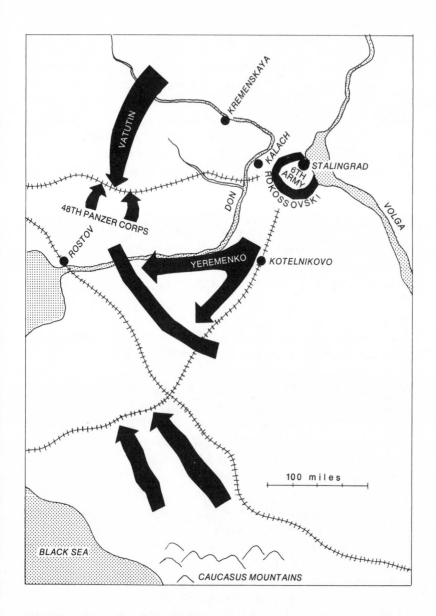

THE CRISIS IN SOUTHERN RUSSIA When Vatutin's tanks broke through the Italians far to the west of Kremenskaya in mid-December, he threatened to reach as far south as Rostov thus cutting off the two German armies in the Caucasus. Von Mannstein shifted troops from Hoth's army to the 48th Panzer Corps, and the Russian attack was held. Hitler was finally persuaded to allow a retreat from the Caucasus. Paulus' 6th Army, now in a hopeless position, continued to fight, thus keeping enough Russian divisions occupied to allow the Germans to hold open their escape route through Rostov.

wanted the 2nd Guards Army transferred immediately to the Kotelnikovo Front. Rokossovski protested. This Army was a crack outfit and he wanted to keep it for direct attacks against Paulus. Both Generals finally got their cases before Stalin by that evening. Vasilievsky sweated out a long night and not until dawn of the 13th did Stalin's answer come. The 2nd Guards Army would be switched to the Kotelnikovo Front. It wouldn't be there, though, for six days.

On the 13th and 14th, Hoth's armor continued its advance. The Russians threw in counterattacks but they were broken up by the German guns. German tanks, used with great skill, forged ahead. Mile-by-mile the 57th Panzer Corps closed the gap between themselves and Paulus. Nowhere, though, did the German Panzers achieve a decisive success. There was not enough weight to their attack. Not for three more days could the 17th Panzer Division, which had been delayed behind the Chir on Hitler's orders, get into action.

As Hoth's armor ground forward, the situation along the Chir grew steadily worse. The Russians eliminated the German bridgehead over the Don at Nizhne-Chirskaya, and, on December 15th, the Germans were forced to blow up Chirskaya Bridge. All along the Chir, the line formed by Army Detachment Hollidt buckled and bent while Balck's 11th Panzer Division plugged hole after hole.

As bad as the situation on the Chir was, there was a worse one building up along the Don beyond Army Detachment Hollidt in Army Group A's sector. There the front was held by weak, poorly-equipped divisions of the Italian 8th Army. On the 15th, Army Group A let von Mannstein know that there were signs that a Russian attack on the Italians was imminent.

On the next day, December 16th, the Russians hit. At first no one at von Mannstein's headquarters knew whether this was a major attack or not. Then word came in that a new Russian Guards Army had been identified, and von Mannstein knew that this was a major Russian effort. No one had any confidence that the Italians could hold against a large-scale Russian attack.

One hundred miles behind the Italians lay the two airfields at Tatsinskaya and Morosovsky from which supplies were flown in to Paulus at Stalingrad and there was next to nothing between the Italians and the airfields. Another hundred miles further south lay Rostov. And if the Russians reached Rostov, von Mannstein's Army Group Don, as well as Army Group B in the Caucasus, would be cut off. On December 16th, von Mannstein was no longer facing a crisis, he was facing a catastrophe.

Von Mannstein, the man of precision and logic, was also a general of considerable nerve. It would hardly have been a cautious move had he instantly halted Hoth's offensive and sent two of his Panzer divisions racing for Tatsinskaya. This, however, would have meant leaving Paulus' 6th Army stuck in Stalingrad, and von Mannstein needed Paulus' divisions if he, himself, was to go over to the attack against the Russians. He ordered Hoth's attack to go on.

On December 18th, Hoth's 57th Panzer Corps, with the 17th Panzer Division now joining the 6th and the 23rd, opened its major effort to get through to Stalingrad. It was now time for Paulus to join in the battle, to attack south out of the Cauldron as Hoth approached. The crisis of the battle was at hand.

To make sure that Paulus' operations would be coordinated precisely with those of Hoth, von Mannstein ordered his Chief Intelligence Officer, Major Eismann, to fly into the Stalingrad Cauldron. When the Major arrived, he met with Paulus and the principal staff officers of the 6th Army. Speaking for von Mannstein, he told them that, because of the increasingly bad situation along the Chir and particularly because of the debacle to the Italian 8th Army, Hoth's attack could not be kept going much longer. Nor, he explained, was there much chance that the three Panzer divisions of Hoth's 57th Panzer Corps could make it all the way through to the Cauldron. Therefore, Paulus must prepare to fight his way out. The 6th Army must begin immediately to prepare to make the short advance south called for in Winter Tempest. It must also be prepared to lay on Thunderclap—the longer advance to the south combined with the evacuation of the Army's positions within Stalingrad.

Although Paulus seemed to go along with this thinking, Eismann discovered to his horror that Paulus' chief of staff,

Schmidt, did not. Schmidt argued the obvious risks of such an attack and the difficulties of mounting it. Eismann began to get the impression that Schmidt felt that the 6th Army was far safer behind its defenses in the Cauldron than it would be out of them. Schmidt told Eismann, "The 6th Army will be in position at Easter. All you people have to do is supply it better." [13] Eismann argued, but Schmidt stood like a rock.

Then Paulus began to weaken, slowly falling into line with the thinking of his Chief of Staff. Finally Paulus pointed out the uselessness of the whole argument. There could be no real attack south from the Cauldron without the evacuation of Stalingrad, and any such evacuation was completely against the orders of the Fuehrer.

As Eismann argued with Schmidt and Paulus within the Cauldron, Hoth's Panzers lunged forward. The gap between them and Paulus narrowed to thirty miles but that was as far as Hoth's men could go. Russian resistance to their advance was now stiffening. The 2nd Guards Army, which Vasilievsky had gotten Stalin to release as the German advance had begun, was now arriving and taking up its position in that thirty-mile gap between Hoth and Paulus.

Von Mannstein saw that there was only one possibility of closing that gap, a joint attack by Paulus from the north and Hoth from the south. On the afternoon of the 19th, he proposed this to Hitler.

In a carefully composed message marked "For immediate submission to the Fuehrer," von Mannstein set out the strategic situation with impeccable logic.[14]

First, "developments in Army Group B," by which von Mannstein meant what had by now become the total rout of the Italian 8th Army, had laid bare the deep left flank of his own Army Group Don. Therefore, as all available German forces had to be rushed into this gap, Army Group Don could hardly expect any reinforcements.

Second, "an airlift is not possible for reasons of weather

[13] von Mannstein, p. 334.
[14] The entire message is in von Mannstein, pp. 560–561.

and the inadequate forces available." This fact was hardly in dispute as Goering's airlift had been running for a month now and its record had been dismal.

Third, the "57th Panzer Corps by itself obviously cannot make contact with 6th Army on the ground, let alone keep a corridor open."

Therefore, von Mannstein concluded, "I now consider a breakout to the southwest to be the last possible means of preserving at least the bulk of the troops and the still mobile elements of 6th Army." This breakout, von Mannstein pointed out, meant "giving up ground sector by sector in the north of the fortress area."

That was it—precise and logical, but precision and logic meant nothing in the Wolfschanze. There, Adolf Hitler, commander-in-chief of the German Armed Forces, procrastinated. Was there not a chance that Hoth could go on a bit farther? Wasn't Goering now assuring him that the airlift to Stalingrad was only just getting into its stride? "We must wait and see," said the Fuehrer.[15]

Von Mannstein continued the argument over the phone but he had to do so without any backing from Paulus and Schmidt. From inside the Cauldron came demands for large quantities of supplies which Paulus and Schmidt said were necessary before any attack could be made. The quantities they demanded could not be delivered by Goering's faltering airlift. But, above all else, Paulus and Schmidt harped on the fuel situation. There was, they said, not enough available for the 6th Army to cover the thirty miles that separated it from Hoth. Paulus and Schmidt were quoting the official figures and von Mannstein like any practical soldier knew that all mobile units always had a little more fuel on hand than their official reports showed. But, on the issue of fuel, Hitler had an argument with which he could and did turn back all of von Mannstein's pleas.

---

[15] Freidin and Richardson, p. 167.

The Retreat from Russia Begins
DECEMBER 20, 1942–JANUARY 1, 1943

The time for procrastination and argument was just about over. Hoth's 57th Panzer Corps, after its advance on the 19th, had been brought to a halt. Now its divisions were fighting hard just to hold on to their positions.

Von Mannstein knew he could not ignore much longer the danger to his far left flank in what had been the Italian sector. On December 23rd, the Russians captured Tatsinskaya airfield. They could be allowed to go no further. Von Mannstein ordered Balck's 11th Panzer Division to leave the lower Chir and head for Tatsinskaya. He also ordered Hoth to give up the 6th Panzer Division, his biggest, so that it could join Balck's in a counterattack on the Russians.

The two German divisions moved fast and hit hard. At this kind of wide-open, mobile warfare, the Germans were still superior to the Russians. By December 28th, Tatsinskaya had been recaptured and the Russian threat to Rostov had been, at least temporarily, removed.

But Hoth, without the big 6th Panzer Division, could not hold his position near Stalingrad. He had only the 23rd Panzers which had started the campaign far below strength and the 17th Panzers which was now almost a skeleton division. All of its battalion commanders were casualties and there were only eight tanks and a single anti-tank gun left in the division.

On the day after Christmas, the Russians attacked in force and Hoth's two small divisions were forced to give ground. Slowly the gap between them and Paulus widened. The thirty miles became forty and then fifty and finally, by New Year's, Hoth's battered divisions were back at Kotelnikovo where they had started their drive to relieve Paulus.

Inside the Stalingrad Cauldron a quarter of a million men were now completely trapped, without hope of rescue. "Ahead of us," noted one of Paulus' privates in his diary, "is either death or captivity." [16] In Russia, in 1942, death and captivity usually meant the same thing.

[16] Chuikov, p. 254.

As Hoth retreated back to Kotelnikovo during the last week of 1942, Chief of Staff Zeitzler was arguing incessantly with Hitler that it was past time to order the withdrawal of Army Group A from the Caucasus. He used every argument he could think of and every one that von Mannstein could feed him. Zeitzler put it to Hitler as bluntly as he could—"Unless you order a withdrawal from the Caucasus now, we shall soon have a second Stalingrad on our hands." [17]

Finally, on the 29th, Zeitzler got the Fuehrer alone. The argument went on and slowly Hitler weakened. Finally he gave Zeitzler his grudging approval for the withdrawal. Zeitzler left the Fuehrer and, from the anteroom, telephoned the orders directly to Army Group A. Then Zeitzler left for his own headquarters, about a half-hour's drive away.

During that half-hour, as Zeitzler thought he might, Hitler wavered. Could not the Caucasus still be held? When Zeitzler got to his headquarters, an aide brought him an urgent message. He must telephone the Fuehrer immediately. Hitler spoke: "Don't do anything just yet about the withdrawal from the Caucasus. We'll discuss it again tomorrow."

Zeitzler was ready with his answer. "My Fuehrer, it is too late. I dispatched the order from your headquarters. It has already reached the front-line troops and the withdrawal has begun. If the order is cancelled now, the confusion will be terrible. I must ask you to avoid that."

"Very well, then," said a defeated Hitler, "we'll leave it at that."

On January 1, 1942, the last of the ninety days, Paulus received a message from Hitler. It read: "Every man of the 6th Army can start the New Year with the absolute conviction that the Fuehrer will not leave his heroic soldiers on the Volga in the lurch." [18]

Paulus knew it was a lie and so did all his heroic soldiers. Their task now was to keep as many Russians as possible fighting around Stalingrad so that Army Group A could make

[17] Freidin and Richardson, pp. 172–173; the entire conversation is related on these pages.
[18] Goerlitz, *Paulus and Stalingrad*, p. 260.

good its escape from the Caucasus. Once that had happened, von Mannstein would have a chance to build up some sort of defensive line far to the west. But the 6th Army would not be part of that line. Its job was to fight and die, as slowly as possible, to give von Mannstein time.

Actually, Hitler's only plan to relieve Stalingrad was to bring three SS Panzer Divisions from France, assemble them in mid-February near Kharkov and then drive the 350 miles to Stalingrad. Such a plan was, of course, pure fantasy. By mid-February Paulus' 6th Army would have ceased to exist.

Hitler's retreat from Russia had begun and, once begun, it would not stop short of Berlin. The loss of the 6th Army's twenty divisions was one from which the German Army would not recover. From now on it could fight, like the Japanese, only to delay the inevitable moment of complete and total defeat. For Hitler, there was little left but fantasies.

focus five: BARENTS SEA

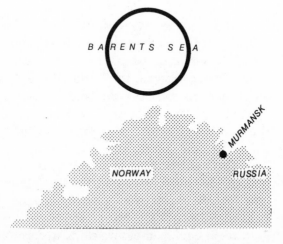

ARCTIC OCEAN

B A R E N T S   S E A

ATLANTIC OCEAN

NORWAY

MURMANSK

RUSSIA

The Allied victories at Guadalcanal, in Africa and in Russia had turned the tide of war. To exploit those victories, though, one more was necessary—victory at sea. With command of the seas, the products of American industry could be shipped to battlefields around the world and the defeat of the Axis would be certain. But on the last day of 1942, Hitler's warships sailed through the ice cold waters of the Barents Sea to what seemed like certain victory over Britain's Royal Navy.

In 1942 the naval war in the Atlantic had been very different from that waged in the Pacific. There had been no great carrier, battleship or cruiser duels like those around Guadalcanal. Instead, the Battle of the Atlantic had been one long duel between U-boats and planes on the German side against the small destroyers, sloops and corvettes that escorted the convoys of British and American merchant ships in both the North and South Atlantic.

Throughout most of the year, the battle had been touch and go. As the year neared its close, however, the American and British navies were nearing readiness for a showdown fight with Doenitz's U-boats. At last they were getting enough fast, radar-equipped escort ships to form battle groups which could join in the fight around a convoy battling one of the

German Wolf Packs. These were coming and so were the escort carriers which could provide air cover when the convoys were too far from shore for land-based planes to protect them.

Any showdown with the U-boats, though, was out of the question when Operation Torch was laid on for early November. For the protection of the massive convoys involved in the African invasion, ships of all types were necessary and escort vessels were taken off the Atlantic routes, including all the United States and British escort carriers then available. The convoys, lightly escorted, were roughly handled by the Wolf Packs. From one convoy fifteen ships were sunk; from another, eight and from yet another, thirteen. Other convoys were not sailed at all, as the protection which could have been given them was so feeble as to invite a massacre of the merchant ships.

When the Americans and British landed in French North Africa, Hitler ordered Doenitz to concentrate his U-boats against the follow-up convoys headed for Casablanca, Oran and Algiers. But the Allies were ready for the U-boats, and although the Germans scored some successes, they paid in heavy U-boat losses. By the end of December, the concentration of U-boats off Africa was broken up and they sailed, once again, for the North Atlantic. Winter storms would prevent the big U-boat versus escort battles from taking place until the spring. By then the Allies would be ready.

There was, though, one other factor in this battle of the convoys and one which could give nightmares to any Allied convoy commander. This factor was the German surface fleet headed by the 50,000-ton battleship *Tirpitz*, the most powerful single ship in the Atlantic.

Besides the *Tirpitz*, Grand Admiral Erich Raeder's battle fleet had two battle cruisers of 30,000 tons, the *Scharnhorst* and *Gneisenau*. With a speed of thirty-two knots, they could outrun whatever battleships the British might send against them and each, with its nine 11-inch guns, could smash any British cruiser which might be able to catch it.

Less powerful than the battle cruisers, but still very dangerous, were two 12,000-ton pocket-battleships, the *Lützow* and *Scheer*. With a speed of twenty-six knots, they could be caught by both British battleships and cruisers but their main armament of six 11-inch guns each made them more than a match for a cruiser. The British had only five ships in the Atlantic capable of taking on one of these pocket-battleships in a ship-to-ship action.

Finally Raeder had two heavy cruisers, the *Prinz Eugen* and *Hipper,* which carried the same 8-inch gun armament as the British heavy cruisers but which were almost half again as big, as well as faster and more heavily armored.

The thought of any of these big German ships loose in the Atlantic gave nightmares to the British admirals in London. Ordinary convoy escorts, small ships like destroyers, sloops or corvettes, were helpless against such big ships. It was not possible to put a British battleship with each convoy as an escort. There weren't enough battleships for that kind of service and a battleship, plowing slowly along in the midst of a slow convoy would only be a sitting duck for the torpedoes of a German U-boat.

In December, 1942, this nightmare of a slow, weakly defended convoy under attack by powerful, heavily-gunned German surface forces was about to become a reality. The British Admiralty had ordered the resumption of convoys to northern Russia, which had been suspended because of the need to deploy all available ships for Operation Torch. Once more British and American merchant ships would be sailing through the gray waters of the Barents Sea between the Arctic ice pack and the northern tip of Norway where Convoy PQ-17 had lost twenty-three of its thirty-four merchant ships in July. The German High Command was planning something worse for December.

Raeder Gets His Chance

DECEMBER 1–30, 1942

Grand Admiral Raeder had fought his sea war against the British under many restrictions. He had not been able to build up a naval air force because of the jealousy of Goering and the Luftwaffe. He found that a land-minded Hitler would never give the Navy its fair share of critical materials needed for ship building. And there was always a fuel shortage, not bad enough to preclude combat operations but bad enough to curtail the training cruises so necessary to keep a warship's crew at peak efficiency.

Perhaps the most irksome of all, and the most frustrating to Raeder, was Hitler's great fear of losing ships. The sinking of the pocket-battleship *Graf Spee* in 1939 had had a considerable psychological effect on Hitler. The sinking of the battleship *Bismarck* in 1941 had been worse. Hitler had gone so far as to have the name of the pocket-battleship *Deutschland* changed to *Lützow* as, to him, the sinking of a ship bearing the name of the fatherland itself was unthinkable. Hitler had even admitted to the naval liaison officer at the Wolfschanze that when any of the big ships were at sea, he could hardly sleep a wink.

There was, however, more than psychology and prestige involved in Hitler's wish to conserve his big ships. The Fuehrer foresaw not only a Swedish-Russian attack on Norway from the east but a seaborne invasion by the Western Allies as well. He wanted his big ships ready to repel such an invasion.

This fear of invasion in the far north had one good result as far as Raeder was concerned. It meant that in the fall of 1942 there were powerful German surface units stationed in the fjords of northern Norway. While waiting for the Allied invasion the Fuehrer feared, they could attack the British convoys sailing to Russia. Raeder was sure these convoys would be resumed after Operation Torch was over and when the long Arctic nights would give them cover against German aerial attack. All Raeder was waiting for was a convoy with an escort weak enough so that he could attack without the "undue risk" to the German ships which the Fuehrer had forbidden.

To the Royal Navy, the war at sea had been a series of undue risks right from the beginning. The evacuations of the British Army from Dunkirk in 1940 and then from Greece and Crete in 1941 had been enormous risks and so had been the bloody Malta convoys. But to the Naval Staff in London there was no greater risk than running convoys through the Barents Sea to Russia. The staff had expressed itself most strongly to Churchill. The admirals had told him that if they were in the position of the German admirals in northern Norway, they would guarantee that no convoy would get through to Russia. Churchill was no amateur at naval matters and appreciated the force of their arguments. But he had promised Stalin that supplies would be sent through to Murmansk that winter and he meant to keep that promise. He remembered Stalin's abuse of the British war effort that past August when the two had met in Moscow. Churchill remembered Stalin's question— "Has the British Navy no sense of glory?" So he ordered twenty-nine merchant ships to be sent through to Murmansk that December.

The British admirals' original thinking was to send all the ships in one huge convoy with an escort of two dozen destroyers. This plan was ruled out because of the winter gales which infested the Barents Sea. They could scatter a large convoy like so many matchsticks and once a convoy was scattered it was an easy matter for the German U-boats to pick off ship after ship.

It was decided, therefore, to split the coming convoy into two sections. The first section, called Convoy JW.51A, left Britain on December 15th. Its fifteen merchant ships made the passage safely. In the prevailing bad weather, they were not sighted by the Germans. Such good luck did not hold for the next section, JW.51B.

Just past noon on December 30th, U-boat 354 was in her patrol position about 200 miles north of Altafiord, the main German fleet base near the North Cape of Norway. Her commander, Lieutenant Herschleb, heard the sound of propellers and brought his boat up to periscope depth for a look around. He got a look at Convoy JW.51B. Then, at a safe distance, he surfaced for a better look before sending off his sighting message—"Convoy 6–10 steamers." Herschleb gave its position and course and then flashed out the three words that Grand Admiral Erich Raeder had been waiting for— "Convoy weakly escorted." [1]

Raeder immediately got off a wire to his liaison officer at the Wolfschanze, Vice Admiral Krancke, who was attending

[1] Pope, 73 North, p. 92.

a situation conference in the Fuehrer's own bunker. Krancke listened as the disasters taking place on the Russian Front were gone over in great detail. He then entered into a debate with Raeder's enemy, Reichsmarschall Goering, over control of sea transport in the Mediterranean. Hitler joined in with some biting comments on the Navy which he said was just sitting around the Norwegian fjords doing nothing.

When Hitler calmed down, Krancke brought up Raeder's message. The Grand Admiral reported the discovery of the weakly escorted British convoy and proposed that a force sail from Altafiord to intercept it. This force was to be composed of the pocket-battleship *Lützow,* the heavy cruiser *Hipper* and six big fleet destroyers. Even though such a force would be overwhelmingly superior to the British, Raeder's wire was careful to point out that the convoy would be attacked only if its escort was as weak as reported.

There had been news of nothing but defeat on the Russian Front for weeks and Hitler could, at that moment, use a victory. "Can the force get there in time and locate the convoy?" he asked Admiral Krancke.[2] The Admiral carefully explained that the situation was nearly perfect. The German ships could sail that evening and be in a position to attack the convoy early the following morning, December 31st. Hitler approved.

In anticipation of Hitler's approval, the *Lützow, Hipper* and the destroyers Z-29, Z-30, Z-31, *Richard Beitzen, Theodor Riedel* and *Friedrich Eckholdt* were already preparing to go to sea. In command was Vice Admiral Oskar Kummetz aboard the *Hipper.*

Kummetz's sailing orders were given him by Admiral Rolf Carls, commanding all German naval forces in the North. Carls included a few words which would have brought a smile of approval from the Fuehrer: "There is to be no time wasted in rescuing enemy crews. It would be of value to take prisoner only a few captains and others with a view to interrogation. The rescue of enemy survivors by enemy forces is not desirable."[3]

[2] Pope, p. 99.
[3] Pope, p. 103.

Thus, as Kummetz's ships sailed north on the night of December 30th, they were looking forward not only to a naval victory but, in the best Nazi tradition, to a slaughter of the defenseless as well.

Convoy JW.51B

DECEMBER 22–30, 1942

The fourteen masters, four British and ten American, of the merchant ships of the convoy had met for final instructions in a hut on the bleak northwest coast of Scotland. It was the morning of December 22nd and they were to sail that afternoon. In the holds and lashed to the decks of their ships were more than 2,000 trucks, 200 tanks, 120 war planes and 87,000 tons of assorted cargo, including highly inflammable aviation gasoline and highly explosive artillery shells. They knew they were bound for the Barents Sea.

First they met the convoy commodore, their immediate superior, Captain Melhuish, a retired officer of the Royal Indian Navy who had had his ship bombed and sunk under him during Operation Torch. Melhuish gave them the usual instructions—keep in formation, which was to be four columns, and don't make smoke that could give their position away to the enemy.

Then they met the man on whom, if the Germans were to appear, they knew that their lives would depend, the escort commander, Royal Navy Captain Robert St. Vincent Sherbrooke. What they saw was a tall, slender man, not old, but white-haired—certainly not the picture of a fighting destroyer commander. Sherbrooke spoke to them in his usual softspoken manner. The winter weather was excellent protection against German bombers and would make it difficult for U-boats to locate them. If a German surface raider attacked, the ships of the convoy would turn away and drop smoke floats. Sherbrooke would lead his destroyers into position between the raider and the convoy. Destroyers were all Sherbrooke would have, seven of them, and all the assembled ships' masters knew the Germans could attack with far bigger ships than that. When the conference ended with the traditional

"I hope we have a good trip, gentlemen," it must have seemed a very pious hope indeed.

Sherbrooke's troubles started almost immediately. As the merchant ship of the convoy headed northeast for the passage around Norway, Sherbrooke sailed for Iceland where his destroyers would fill up with fuel and catch up with the convoy before it entered the danger zone of the Barents Sea. On the passage to Iceland Sherbrooke ran through hurricane force winds and one of his two smaller destroyers, the *Bulldog*, was so badly damaged that she had to return to England for repairs.

On Christmas Day, Sherbrooke, one destroyer short, joined the convoy. To form a close, anti-submarine screen around the fourteen merchant ships, Sherbrooke had five small, lightly armed ships; two corvettes, the *Hyderabad* and *Rhododendron;* two trawlers, the *Northern Gem* and *Vizalma,* whose small size, 600 tons, and maneuverability made them good rescue ships; and a minesweeper, the *Bramble,* whose greatest value was in her new search radar.

To beef up this close screen, Sherbrooke had the old destroyer *Achates*. For serious action, should it come, he had five 1500-ton "O" class fleet destroyers: the flagship *Onslow* and the *Obedient, Obdurate, Oribi* and *Orwell*. These ships were neither as big nor as powerfully gunned as the German destroyers. All but the *Onslow* had only World War I 4-inch guns, all that was available when they had been commissioned. The ships were all veterans of the Arctic run. Sherbrooke had not made the trip before.

Two days after Sherbrooke and his destroyers joined the merchant ships, another storm struck. Gale force winds drove eighteen-foot waves at the convoy and blinding snowstorms reduced visibility to zero. The great waves sent showers of spray over the forward sections of the ships and the freezing winds instantly turned it to ice. This accumulation of ice topside made the ships top-heavy and hard to manage.

For two days, the great storm raged and not until midday of the 29th did it begin to abate. As the visibility improved, Sherbrooke saw that the storm had caused a disaster. Five of the merchant ships, one of his trawlers and the big destroyer *Oribi* were nowhere to be seen. The rest of Sherbrooke's ships were scattered from horizon to horizon and time now had to be spent in gathering them back into their proper four-column cruising formation. Already the convoy was behind schedule and off course. Sherbrooke sent the minesweeper *Bramble* with her excellent search radar off to hunt for the missing ships.

On the morning of the 30th, things began to look a bit better for Convoy JW.51B. Three of the missing merchant ships rejoined the convoy. The *Bramble* continued her hunt for the other two but without any luck. One was completely separated from the convoy and, unseen by anyone, was making her way to Murmansk by herself. The other, the American *Chester Valley*, in company with the British trawler *Vizalma*, was trying to catch up to the convoy. Actually the two ships were about forty-five miles north of the convoy proceeding eastward parallel to the convoy.

The destroyer *Oribi* had suffered from a gyrocompass failure and, unable to find any trace of the convoy at all, was proceeding on her lone way to Murmansk. Her loss to the convoy was a very serious one. Sherbrooke knew that the convoy would face its greatest danger of German surface attack on the next day, the 31st, and now he had only four of his bigger destroyers to face such an attack. He did not know that Lieutenant Herschleb, in U-354, had sighted the convoy at noon on the 30th and that an attack the following morning was a sure thing.

However, Sherbrooke's destroyers were not the only British warships whose duty it was to defend Convoy JW.51B. To provide distant cover the Admiralty had dispatched Force R, the two light cruisers, *Sheffield* and *Jamaica,* under an Arctic veteran, Rear Admiral Robert Burnett. These two ships were each of about 9,000 tons and each mounted twelve 6-inch guns. This was not much to match the 8-inch guns of the *Hipper* or the big 11-inchers of the *Lützow*. Burnett, though, was one of the better junior admirals of the Royal Navy and a fine tactician.

Force R had escorted the first convoy, JW.51A, to Murmansk and, on December 27th, had left there to run westward through the Barents Sea to meet the oncoming JW.51B. Burnett's two light cruisers were not to sail in company with the convoy where a concentration of U-boats was likely to be found. Rather than risk his cruisers to U-boat attack, Burnett would keep some forty miles away and close in only if needed. The only trouble was that Burnett did not know just where Sherbrooke's convoy was as the ships of both Force R and the convoy were maintaining strict radio silence. Burnett knew the planned route of the convoy but did not know that the big two-day gale of the 27th–29th had blown Sherbrooke's ships off course and had put them behind schedule.

On December 30th, the day that U-354 had sighted the convoy, Burnett was steaming back to the east through the Barents Sea and well south of the convoy's track. Burnett, like Sherbrooke, thought that the next day, the 31st, would be the day of maximum danger. He also thought that, if the Germans came out from Altafiord, they would try to get onto the convoy's track in a position behind the convoy and then sweep along the track until they found it. Therefore, Burnett, on the evening of the 30th, turned the *Sheffield* and *Jamaica* to the north. He planned to sail across the rear of the convoy and take up a position to the north of it. Actually he passed ahead of it, as the convoy had lost time due to the storms.

Burnett, though, was to the north of where the action might develop. This was the best tactical position for his ships. The dull grayness that passed for daylight in the Arctic was brightest in the south and any enemy ships to the south of him would be silhouetted against this light while his own remained hard to spot. With only light cruisers, Burnett was going to need every advantage he could get.

Thus, on the evening of December 30th Convoy JW.51B was steaming east at about eight knots and passing within 200 miles of Altafiord. North of the convoy, its position unknown to Sherbrooke, was the minesweeper *Bramble,* still searching for the ships which had been scattered during the great gale. Further north were the trawler *Vizalma* and the American merchant ship *Chester Valley.*

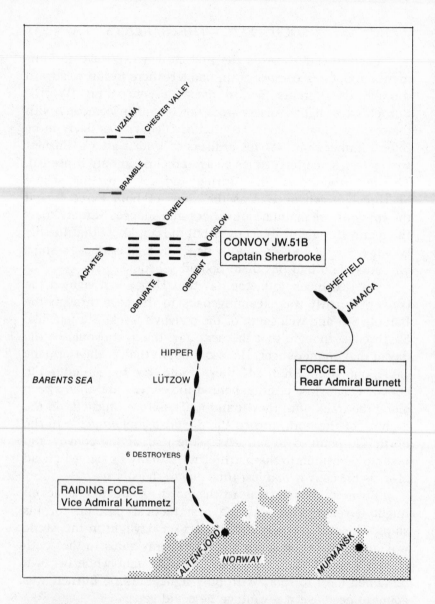

VIZALMA
CHESTER VALLEY

BRAMBLE

ORWELL

ONSLOW

CONVOY JW.51B
Captain Sherbrooke

ACHATES

OBEDIENT

OBDURATE

SHEFFIELD
JAMAICA

FORCE R
Rear Admiral Burnett

HIPPER

BARENTS SEA

LÜTZOW

6 DESTROYERS

RAIDING FORCE
Vice Admiral Kummetz

ALTENFJORD

NORWAY

MURMANSK

APPROACH TO BATTLE   On December 30th, the British Convoy
JW.51B headed around Norway for Murmansk escorted by five
British destroyers. North of the convoy, the small minesweeper
Bramble and the trawler *Vizalma* in company with the American
merchant ship *Chester Valley* sailed separately, having lost contact with the convoy during violent storms. British Admiral Burnett's covering force, the light cruisers *Sheffield* and *Jamaica*,
maneuvered to north of the convoy, but did not know the convoy's
exact position. The convoy had been spotted by a German U-boat
at noon, and by evening a German raiding force, consisting of the
heavy cruiser *Hipper*, the pocket battleship *Lützow* and six destroyers, was headed north to wipe it out.

Ahead of the convoy, Burnett's Force R was moving northward. From behind the convoy, Vice Admiral Oskar Kummetz was also headed north. In a few hours, it would be New Year's Eve.

"Use caution . . ."   6:40 P.M. DECEMBER 30–
7:25 A.M. DECEMBER 31, 1942

By the early evening hours of the 30th, pitch dark in the Arctic winter, Kummetz was away from land and headed into action. His ships sailed northward in a long column, the flagship *Hipper* leading, followed by the pocket-battleship *Lützow* and then his six big destroyers.

He had been warned before his departure that two British cruisers had sailed from Murmansk on the 27th and were probably with the convoy he was seeking. His orders though, were quite specific—"The task: to destroy JW.51B. . . . Procedure on meeting the enemy: avoid a superior force, otherwise destroy according to tactical situation." [4] His immediate superior, Admiral Klueber, had cautioned him of the danger from British torpedoes. To Kummetz it was a superfluous caution. In 1940 he had led the German Navy's attack on Oslo, the capital of Norway. In Oslofiord his flagship, the *Blücher*, sister ship of his current flagship, the *Hipper*, had been sunk by two torpedo hits and Kummetz had had to swim ashore. Torpedoes were hardly a thing that Kummetz would treat lightly.

At 6:40 P.M. a message from Admiral Klueber was received aboard the flagship and given to Kummetz. It read, "Contrary to the operation order regarding contact against the enemy: use caution even against enemy of equal strength." [5] It was hardly an inspiring message to send a fleet on the eve of battle.

Kummetz's battle plan called for no hell-for-leather attack on JW.51B. At 2:40 on the morning of the 31st, he divided his force. The *Hipper* and the destroyers *Friedrich Eckholdt*,

---

[4] Pope, p. 104.
[5] Schofield, *The Russian Convoys*, p. 134.

Richard Beitzen and Z-29 pulled away to the left. They were headed for a position behind the convoy, still being shadowed and reported on by Herschleb's U-boat. When the convoy was found, and as soon as there was light enough, Kummetz would attack. In the meantime, the pocket-battleship *Lützow* with the destroyers Z-30 and Z-31 and *Theodor Riedel,* all under command of Captain Stänge of the *Lützow,* would take up a position somewhat to the south of the convoy. Kummetz was sure that his attack would draw off the convoy's escorts and that the convoy would turn southward and run from him. If it did, it would run right into the 11-inch guns of the *Lützow* It was an excellent plan.

Later at 7:15 A.M., Kummetz started to put it into operation. The *Hipper,* to the rear and slightly to the north of the convoy, had spotted the silhouettes of two ships. Kummetz presumed it was Convoy JW.51B, which it was, and ordered the destroyer *Friedrich Eckholdt* to investigate. If it was the convoy, Kummetz wanted it shadowed, not attacked. There was still not quite enough light and he wanted a bit more time for the *Lützow* to get into position. The sea was calm. Water temperature was 41° and air temperature 25°. Visibility, except in the scattered snow squalls which bedeviled the area, should, in an hour or so, vary from seven to nine miles.

"EMERGENCY: One cruiser bearing 340."

7:25 A.M–10:08 A.M.
DECEMBER 31, 1942

As the three German destroyers, led by the *Eckholdt,* steamed warily on their shadowing mission and Kummetz on the *Hipper* held back even further, Convoy JW.51B sailed along in ignorance of what was taking place. The twelve merchant ships were in four columns with the two small corvettes, the *Rhododendron* and *Hyderabad,* and the trawler *Northern Gem* sailing close alongside. On the north, or left-hand side was the big destroyer *Orwell,* followed by the older, and smaller destroyer *Achates.* Two destroyers led the convoy, the *Onslow,* Sherbrooke's flagship, to the left and the *Obedient* to the right. On the southern or right-hand flank of the convoy was the

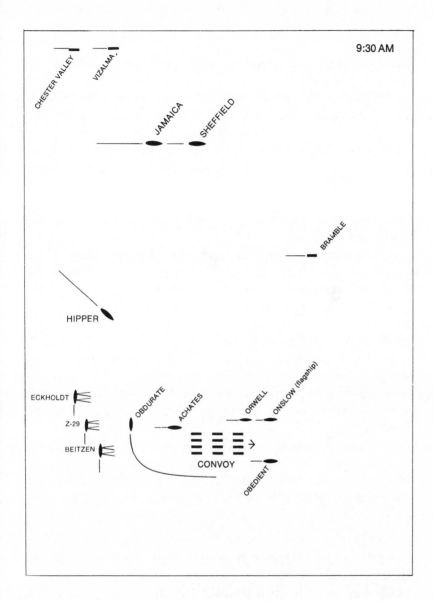

9:30 AM

CHESTER VALLEY

VIZALMA

JAMAICA

SHEFFIELD

BRAMBLE

HIPPER

ECKHOLDT

Z-29

BEITZEN

OBDURATE

ACHATES

ORWELL

ONSLOW (flagship)

CONVOY

OBEDIENT

FIRST CONTACT In the dim light of the Arctic morning, the British destroyer *Obdurate,* investigating ships to the rear of the convoy, ran into three German destroyers. German Admiral Kummetz on the heavy cruiser *Hipper* edged closer to the convoy. The British commander, Captain Sherbrooke, on the *Onslow,* ordered the *Achates* to cover the convoy with a smoke screen and the other destroyers to concentrate against the Germans. Admiral Burnett on the *Sheffield* saw the gun flashes but thought the convoy was under German air attack.

destroyer *Obdurate*. It had been a calm night but Sherbrooke was not expecting the 31st to be a calm day. At 8.00 A.M. he ordered the *Onslow*'s crew to get a hot breakfast and to change into clean underwear. Dirty underwear could infect a wound.

At 8:20 the corvette *Hyderabad* caught a glimpse of two destroyers to the south. She had had a message previously that some Russian destroyers might join the convoy. Russian ship movements were usually kept almost as secret from the British as from the Germans. As the destroyers were not behaving aggressively, the *Hyderabad* presumed that they were Russian and made no report.

Ten minutes later, the destroyer *Obdurate* also sighted two destroyers to the southwest. She made her report by signal lamp to Sherbrooke on the *Onslow*, the message being picked up and relayed by the *Obedient*. It was fifteen minutes before Sherbrooke got the sighting report and when he did he ordered the *Obdurate* to investigate.

The *Obdurate* swung out and away from the convoy and steamed back to the west. She was wary of the strangers, not knowing whether they might be Russian or German or even some of the ships which the gale had separated from the convoy. Visibility was still poor and the *Obdurate*, finally spotting three instead of two destroyers, could not accurately identify them. The *Obdurate* signaled them by lamp but there was no answer. Then, suddenly, one of the three destroyers opened fire, and the *Obdurate* knew who they were. It was now 9:30 A.M.

Less than ten miles to the north of the German destroyers, Kummetz in the *Hipper* had ships in sight, both on radar and visually. But it was all very confusing. Kummetz did not know which were British ships and which were his own destroyers. He saw ships open fire and presumed that they were his destroyers. He waited a minute or two and then slowly began to edge in closer.

Forty miles to the north Admiral Burnett's Force R, the cruisers *Sheffield* and *Jamaica*, had just made radar contact with two ships to the north of them. At first they were reported as making twenty-five knots, much faster than any merchant ship could travel. Burnett steered to investigate. Then gun flashes were seen in the south. They were from light guns, possibly some ship shooting at a shadowing German aircraft, Burnett thought. He kept tracking his radar contact which was, in fact, the British trawler *Vizalma* and the American merchant ship *Chester Valley*. He had no idea that Convoy JW.51B was forty miles to the south of him.

Sherbrooke's reaction to the flashes of gunfire behind the convoy was immediate. Action Stations was ordered and the *Onslow*, putting on speed, swung around toward the sound of the guns. The *Orwell* followed hard behind her. The *Obedient* swung around and headed back along the south edge of the convoy. The old destroyer *Achates*, in accordance with Sherbrooke's standing orders for such an emergency, began to put on speed and to lay a smoke screen across the rear of the convoy.

The *Obdurate*, after being fired on by the three German destroyers, turned away and set course to join Sherbrooke. The Germans continued northward, disappearing into the intermittent snow squalls and headed for the vicinity of the *Hipper*, which was now bearing down on the convoy.

Kummetz, for all his confusion, could clearly make out the small *Achates* laying down her smoke screen across the rear of the convoy. He ordered the *Hipper*'s 8-inch guns to open fire. With her fourth salvo, the *Hipper* drew first blood. A shell burst in the water alongside of the *Achates*, just forward of her bridge. Shell splinters by the hundreds ripped into the destroyer. Men were killed below decks and on the bridge. Water began to pour in through dozens of holes. The *Achates* slowed down and started to settle by the bow, but her captain, Lieutenant Commander Johns, continued on his course. It was vital to get that smoke laid down behind the convoy before the *Hipper*'s guns could rip apart the merchant ships.

Kummetz, though, was not to have the opportunity to polish off the *Achates*. Steering toward him were Sherbrooke's *Onslow* with the *Orwell* following. At first, the *Hipper*'s bulk was an indistinct blur to the British destroyers but as the *Hipper* turned broadside to bring all her guns to bear on the

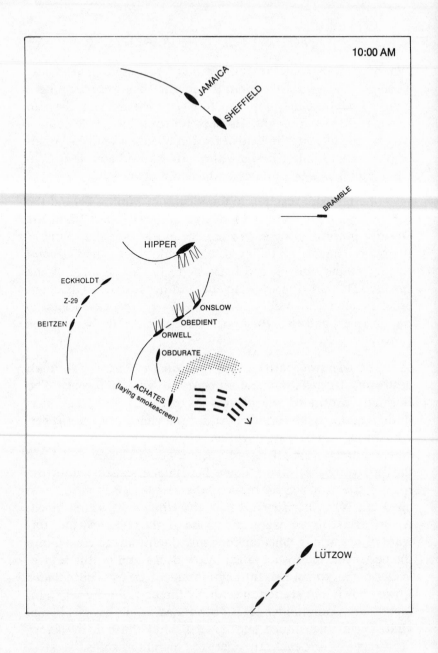

THE *HIPPER* COMES INTO ACTION   While the *Achates* laid a smoke screen to hide the convoy, the British destroyers led by Sherbrooke on the *Onslow* took on the *Hipper*. Afraid of British torpedo attacks and knowing that the *Lützow* and three destroyers were coming up from the south, Admiral Kummetz moved cautiously. Twenty miles to the north Admiral Burnett headed his two cruisers south toward the sound of the guns.

Achates, Sherbrooke could make her out more clearly. At full power, the *Onslow* radioed, "Emergency. One cruiser bearing 340." [6] The message went out to the Admiralty in London and to Admiral Burnett's Force R.

Two minutes after the *Hipper* had opened fire on the *Achates*, Sherbrooke's two fast-moving destroyers were within gun range of the *Hipper* and their little guns opened up. But it wasn't with guns that Sherbrooke could frighten the huge German cruiser whose armor was impervious to destroyer shells at such a range. It was with torpedoes.

As the *Onslow* and *Orwell* opened fire on the *Hipper*, they turned onto a more or less parallel course to the German cruiser. Kummetz was certain that the British destroyers were launching torpedoes at him and turned away. Sherbrooke, though, had only been bluffing. He knew that once his torpedoes were fired, the German cruiser would have nothing to fear from him. But how long could Sherbrooke play a game of bluff? He had just gotten a message from Admiral Burnett's Force R—"Am approaching you on a course of 170." [7] That meant that the two British cruisers were on the way, headed down from the north, but what Sherbrooke had no means of knowing was how long it would take them to arrive.

Kummetz, after having turned away from the British destroyers, had sighted no torpedo tracks coming at him. He turned back and once again engaged Sherbrooke's little ships with his 8-inch guns. Sherbrooke had now been joined by the *Obedient*, and the *Hipper* had three destroyers to contend with. The German gunnery, so fine against the *Achates*, was now erratic. Kummetz turned away again.

It now seemed to Sherbrooke that Kummetz might just be playing games with him. The German cruiser, with the odds all in her favor, was drawing away from the convoy instead of toward it. Sherbrooke decided that there was a good chance that the *Hipper* was pulling all the British escorts away from the convoy so that other German ships could get at the merchant ships from another direction. He ordered the *Obedient*

[6] Pope, p. 129.
[7] Pope, p. 136.

and the nearby *Obdurate* to go back to the convoy. He would try to hold off the *Hipper* with only the *Onslow* and *Orwell*.

Things were getting a bit tight. At 10:13 the *Hipper* turned back to the attack and this time she acted as though she really meant it.

The *Lützow Fumbles*

10:13 A.M.–11:15 A.M.
DECEMBER 31, 1942

The *Hipper*'s gunners had now settled down. They had the advantage of the northern position and they had excellent equipment. Their salvos, each more than a ton of 8-inch shells, fell tightly bunched around the *Onslow*. The *Hipper*'s fifth and sixth salvos were close enough to put shell splinters through the *Onslow*'s thin skin. One shell of her seventh salvo smashed into *Onslow*'s funnel and ripped it open from top to bottom. And one splinter from this shell hit Sherbrooke full in the face.

In rapid succession the *Hipper* put two more shells into the *Onslow* forward of the bridge. Another hit and the *Onslow* would be done for. From the bloody mess that was Sherbrooke's face, one eye hanging down from its socket, came the necessary order, "Come hard to starboard. Make smoke and come down to fifteen knots." [8] Sherbrooke was still in command.

As the *Onslow*, burning and with forty men dead or wounded, turned away, the *Orwell* pulled into position between her and the *Hipper*. She could hardly expect anything but the same treatment but, on board the *Hipper*, Admiral Kummetz, due to poor visibility, did not realize the success he had gained. Still afraid of a torpedo attack, he directed the *Hipper* into a snow squall and disappeared.

Sherbrooke ordered Commander Kinloch to take command and cover the rear of the convoy with destroyers *Obedient*, *Obdurate*, and *Orwell*, while his own badly damaged *Onslow* took up a position ahead of it. With the change in command

[8] Pope, p. 149.

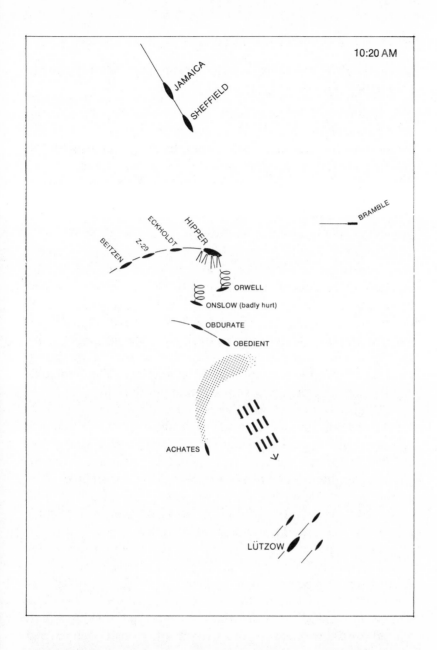

10:20 AM

JAMAICA

SHEFFIELD

BRAMBLE

ECKHOLDT   HIPPER

BEITZEN   Z-29

ORWELL

ONSLOW (badly hurt)

OBDURATE

OBEDIENT

ACHATES

LÜTZOW

THE CONVOY TRAPPED   The *Hipper*'s heavy guns severely damaged the *Onslow*, and Sherbrooke was badly wounded. The *Lützow*
and the three destroyers crossed directly in front of the convoy.
Admiral Kummetz on the *Hipper* was still wary of British torpedoes
and kept on eastward toward the British minesweeper *Bramble*.
Due to the poor visibility, the *Lützow* failed to attack the convoy
and passed to the north of it.

made, Sherbrooke finally went to his cabin and got his already hemorrhaging wounds treated. It was 10:35 A.M.

Kummetz had now been fairly successful against the British warships, damaging both the *Achates* and *Onslow*. Tactically, though, he had been completely successful. All the big British destroyers were now to the north of the convoy. Around the merchant ships were only the damaged *Achates*, two corvettes and a trawler. None of these ships could offer effective opposition even to a single German destroyer. To the south, the convoy was wide open to attack.

To make such an attack, the German southern force was now in perfect position, about to cross the path of the convoy at point-blank range. Captain Stänge of the pocket-battleship *Lützow* was in command of his own ship and its three accompanying destroyers. Ready for action, the German captain had the *Lützow's* six 11-inch guns and her eight 5.9's, the destroyers' fourteen 5-inch guns and a total of thirty-two torpedo tubes. This was strength in abundance. The weakness of this German force was Captain Stänge himself.

Where Kummetz had been cautious, Stänge now proceeded to be timid almost to the point of absurdity. His was a valuable ship. It had been the *Deutschland* before Hitler had ordered her name changed to *Lützow*. Stänge was taking no chances. As he crossed ahead of the convoy, he sighted ships in the poor visibility but wasn't sure he could identify them. He kept his destroyers with him as he didn't want to lose their protection when darkness set in about noon.

Stänge passed ahead of the convoy, about three miles from the nearest British ship, but not a single German gun opened fire nor was a single torpedo fired. The visibility was not good enough for the German captain. Once north of the convoy he turned eastward onto a course parallel to it and waited for the weather to get better. Timidity had been carried to the nth degree—or even beyond.

While Stänge missed his chance, Kummetz in the *Hipper*, with his three big destroyers, found a target and attacked with no regard for caution against superior or equal forces. Kummetz's target was the unfortunate British minesweeper,

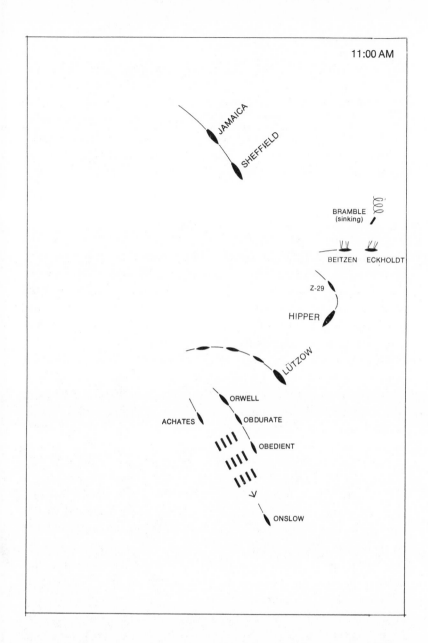

11:00 AM

JAMAICA
SHEFFIELD

BRAMBLE
(sinking)

BEITZEN   ECKHOLDT

Z-29

HIPPER

LÜTZOW

ORWELL

ACHATES   OBDURATE

OBEDIENT

ONSLOW

THE *BRAMBLE* IS SUNK   The *Hipper* ran into the minesweeper *Bramble* and overwhelmed her with her big guns. Leaving the destroyers *Eckholdt* and *Beitzen* to finish her off, the *Hipper* headed back toward the convoy. The British destroyers were now in position between the convoy and the *Lützow*, while the British cruisers *Sheffield* and *Jamaica* prepared to join the action.

Bramble, which had been searching for stragglers from the convoy for days. The *Bramble* had no armament which could hurt the Germans.

At 10:36 the *Hipper*'s 8-inch guns smashed the little *Bramble* into rubble. Kummetz then turned the *Hipper* southward once again in the direction of the convoy. The destroyers *Eckholdt* and *Beitzen* stayed behind to make sure the *Bramble* was properly finished off. They did their job well as not one of the *Bramble*'s crew of eighty survived.

Back at the convoy itself, the actual objective of all this German maneuvering, Captain Stänge was getting his *Lützow* and her three destroyers ranged along the northern edge of the merchant ships. He had been so slow that he had allowed time for Commander Kinloch, now the convoy's escort commander, to get the *Obedient, Obdurate* and *Orwell* between the *Lützow* and the convoy. The wounded *Onslow* was out in front of the convoy and the wounded *Achates* behind. But the *Hipper*, finished with the *Bramble*, was headed south. Very shortly the entire German battle force would be assembled north of the convoy and, at last, the massacre of JW.51B could begin.

However, Admiral Burnett's Force R, the light cruisers *Sheffield* and *Jamaica,* were now about to arrive. At 10:30 A.M. Burnett had been very close to the scene of the action, steering south at thirty-one knots. Then he had veered off to the eastward. He had two large blips on his radar screen which were actually the *Lützow* and *Hipper,* but Burnett was still uncertain as to the exact positions of the convoy and the British destroyers. He was about to enter an action with two German ships, each larger and more powerful than his small cruisers. To make his arrival decisive, Burnett had to come in at the right time and without having to hesitate in identifying a target as friendly or hostile.

It was the *Hipper*'s opening fire on the *Bramble* which clarified things for Burnett. The gun flashes which could be seen from the bridge of the *Sheffield* were clearly those of heavy guns, therefore German. Burnett ordered Force R to steer for them. Thus, as the *Hipper* headed south after sinking the

Bramble, she was followed by Force R. Aboard the *Sheffield* Captain "Nobby" Clarke ordered the ship's big silk battle flag, a gift from the city after which she had been named, to be run up.

"Ram the blighter, Nobby!"

11:15 A.M.–1:30 P.M.
DECEMBER 31, 1942

The *Achates,* having finished laying smoke across the rear of the convoy, was ordered by Kinloch to take station ahead of the convoy along with the *Onslow.* The *Achates* moved out of her own smoke to obey the order and as she did the *Hipper,* bearing down from the north, spotted her through a patch of clear air.

Kummetz ordered fire opened immediately and the *Hipper's* big 8-inch guns again showed what they could do to a small ship. A German shell pulverized the *Achates'* bridge and those on it. More hits holed her badly and within a few minutes the *Achates* was listing to port in a near-sinking condition. She was also continuing to lay smoke to give the convoy what protection she could.

Again, Kummetz did not get a chance to finish off the *Achates* as he was suddenly confronted with Commander Kinloch's three destroyers, the *Obedient, Obdurate* and *Orwell,* which were now between him and the convoy.

Kummetz swung to his right toward the west, in order to bring his 8-inchers broadside to bear on Kinloch's destroyers. The *Hipper* opened fire and soon had shot away Kinloch's wireless antennae. But that was all the damage she did because Force R now came into action.

As the *Hipper* had swung right in order to fire on Kinloch's destroyers, she had silhouetted herself against the southern horizon for the gunners of the oncoming *Sheffield* and *Jamaica.* Burnett ordered his two cruisers to turn to starboard as the *Hipper* had, thus bringing to bear all his twenty-four 6-inch guns. The range was eight miles, close enough for his smaller guns to be effective. At 11:31 the two British cruisers opened rapid fire.

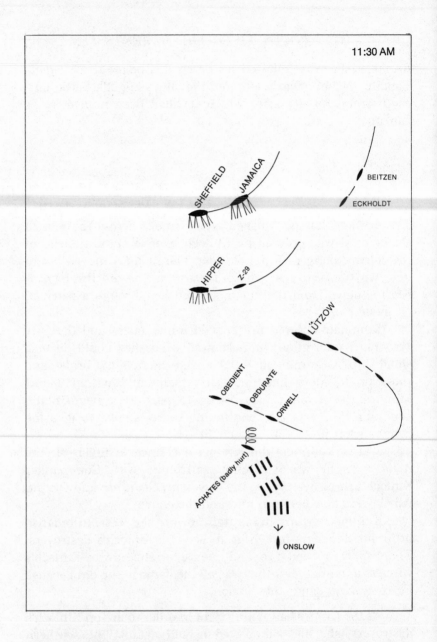

THE BRITISH CRUISERS ATTACK The *Hipper*, swinging back to the east, opened fire on the *Achates* and hit her badly, but as she did so, she was suddenly fired upon by the *Sheffield* and *Jamaica*. Kummetz was taken completely by surprise and, with the *Hipper* hit three times and her engine room damaged, he ordered a retreat.

Sheffield hit with her fifth salvo, *Jamaica* with her fourth. A British shell tore a hole in the *Hipper* next to one of her boiler rooms and it began to flood. The *Hipper's* speed went down from thirty to twenty-three knots. Two more hits produced a fire in the hangar of *Hipper's* scout plane. Kummetz was staggered. He got off only one salvo at the British cruisers, which missed, and then he and the *Hipper* disappeared into the snow and into the smoke laid down by a German destroyer. He came out once, was fired upon again by Burnett's cruisers and got quickly back under cover. Kummetz had had enough. At 11:37 he signalled all his ships, "Break off action and retire to the west." [9]

Captain Stänge in the *Lützow*, who had done nothing so far, was already proceeding westward. Suddenly he spotted the convoy and opened fire. One of his shells glanced off a a merchant ship, causing only superficial damage. It was the *Lützow's* only contribution to the planned destruction of the convoy but then it was the only hit the Germans got on the convoy during the entire battle.

Kummetz's 11:37 A.M. retirement order, though, did not end the fighting. The two destroyers, *Eckholdt* and *Beitzen*, which he had detached to deliver the coup de grâce to the *Bramble*, now ran right into Force R. The destroyer *Eckholdt* spotted the *Sheffield* coming straight at her and thought it was the *Hipper*.

The *Sheffield's* captain, "Nobby" Clarke, his two forward turrets with their six 6-inch guns pointed directly toward *Eckholdt*, ordered: "Make the battle challenge." *Eckholdt* answered with three white lights, which wasn't the right answer. "Open fire," ordered Captain Clarke.[10] The range was two miles, point-blank.

As the *Sheffield's* forward guns roared, her first shots missed. Burnett turned to Clarke. "Ram the blighter, Nobby!" It was one way of frustrating an enemy torpedo attack.

But ramming wasn't necessary. The *Sheffield's* third

[9] Schofield, p. 145.
[10] Pope, p. 188.

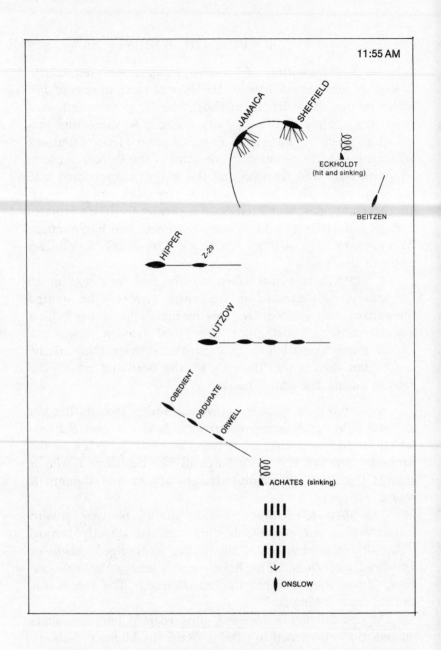

BATTLE'S END As the *Hipper* and the *Lützow* retreated east-ward, the German destroyer *Eckholdt*, which had been left behind to polish off the *Bramble*, was caught by the British cruiser *Sheffield* and sunk with all hands. Although the *Achates* sank from the pounding she received from the *Hipper* earlier, the merchant ships of the convoy were undamaged and now able to proceed to Murmansk where all arrived safely.

salvo was right on target, and the *Eckholdt* began to disintegrate in a mass of flames and explosions.

The other German destroyer, *Beitzen,* swung away at top speed and escaped. No one on the *Eckholdt* did. Her entire crew went down with the ship just as the *Bramble*'s crew had. When Kummetz, hearing the gunfire, called the *Eckholdt* on the radio to find out what was happening, there was no answer. Kummetz then repeated his earlier signal for all German ships to retire. The Battle of the Barents Sea was over.

The German battle force retired at its best speed, closely shadowed by Burnett's two cruisers. A few shots were exchanged but no one was hit. Shortly after noon, full darkness set in and Burnett shadowed until he was sure there was no longer any German threat to the convoy.

Although the battle was over, the blood-letting was not. The small destroyer *Achates* was sinking. At 1:15 P.M. it was clear that she could no longer survive. She flashed a signal to the trawler *Northern Gem,* "Not under control. Please stand by me." [11] Before *Northern Gem* could arrive, *Achates* rolled over and went down, carrying 100 of her crew with her. Only 83 men were picked up.

The remainder of Convoy JW.51B's voyage to Murmansk was uneventful.

The Commander-in-Chief, Home Fleet, Admiral Sir John Tovey, who had overall responsibility for the Murmansk convoys, noted of the defense of Convoy JW.51B, "that an enemy force of one pocket-battleship, one heavy cruiser and six destroyers, with all the advantage of surprise and concentration, should be held off for four hours by five destroyers, and driven from the area by two 6-inch gun cruisers is most creditable and satisfactory." [12]

In a service not given to flamboyance of language, Sherbrooke and Burnett could be pleased with such praise. They could be even more pleased that the battle had ensured "the

[11] Pope, p. 188.
[12] Roskill, *The War at Sea. 1939–1945,* Vol. II, *The Period of Balance,* p. 298.

safe arrival of the convoy." For the safe arrival of convoys was what the war in the Atlantic was all about.

The 90th Day

That midnight, which marked the end of 1942 and the beginning of 1943, found the Fuehrer at the Wolfschanze receiving best wishes from the high and the mighty of Nazi Germany —from Foreign Minister Ribbentrop, who had helped him blunder into the war; from Propaganda Minister Goebbels, who was helping him deceive the German people as to its course; and from Reichsmarschall Hermann Goering, who was helping him lose it.

Hitler did not go to bed until after four in the morning. He had been hoping for some message of success from the Navy but none had come in. Admiral Krancke, the Navy's liaison officer at the Wolfschanze, thought that the Fuehrer was uneasy and Krancke had been burning up the telephone lines to naval headquarters in Berlin trying to find out something. He had been unsuccessful.

On New Year's morning, the Fuehrer was up just after nine in the morning, an extraordinarily early hour for him and a sign that possibly he was a bit more than just uneasy. When Krancke saw Hitler at the noon conference, he found that the Fuehrer was in a rage. The impudence of the Navy in not having a full report for him had infuriated him and he already suspected that the hoped-for massacre of the convoy had not taken place.

By that evening Hitler was raving. He proclaimed his "irrevocable decision" that the German battle fleet be scrapped.[13] Its guns would be better used for shore fortifications. From now on the only surface ships the Navy would have were those necessary for training U-boat crews.

This was the end of any hopes Raeder and his admirals had for a joint campaign by the German battle fleet and the U-boats against Allied shipping. The U-boats would have to

---

[13] Martienssen, *Hitler and His Admirals,* p. 153.

fight alone and, fighting alone they would lose. The coming battles around the Atlantic convoys would be desperate ones but the commanders of the convoy escorts would be spared the awful specter of a German cruiser or battleship bearing down on the slow, defenseless merchant ships in whose holds were the cargoes that meant the end of Nazi Germany.

EPILOGUE

On January 1, 1943, the decisive ninety days of World War II were over. Gone were the dreams of conquest of the Germans and the Japanese. The great victories which they had so confidently foreseen for the end of 1942 had eluded them. Instead they were now faced with retreat and final catastrophe.

Their defeats were decisive, because it had been their two principal instruments of power which had been beaten— the German Army and the Japanese Navy. Both had been strategically misused and both had paid the penalty.

The war in the Pacific was primarily a naval war. Japan was an island and far from self-sufficient. To live she had to bring the products of her southeast Asian conquests back to Japan. To do that she had to control the seas. And at Guadalcanal it had been the Japanese Navy which had been beaten.

The key to the battle for Guadalcanal had been Henderson Field. The planes which flew from it had denied the Japanese control of the waters around the island in the daytime. Without daytime use of those waters the Japanese simply could not bring in enough supplies for their troops on shore and, therefore, could not build up enough strength to overwhelm the United States Marines who held the perimeter around Henderson Field.

The Japanese had come close to winning the battle for Guadalcanal in the early morning hours of October 14th when the battleships *Kongo* and *Haruna* had all but obliterated Henderson Field with their big guns. Had that bombardment been continued by the battleships on the next night and the next, there would have been no Henderson Field. Then the Japanese Navy could have moved in force against the island both by day and by night. The American Navy would have had the choice of abandoning Vandegrift's Marines to their fate or of fighting the Japanese at a terrible disadvantage in strength. And the only way of building up United States naval strength in the Pacific would have been by canceling Operation Torch.

The Japanese admirals never sent their full strength to Guadalcanal at any one time. They fed in their ships a few at a time and were beaten. They committed the cardinal military sin of not concentrating all possible force at the decisive point.

Nor, for the Japanese, was the chance to come again. By the end of 1942, American shipyards were turning out a fleet of a size and strength the like of which the world had never seen. It was a fleet which the Japanese could not hope to match, and it was a fleet which would crush the Japanese Navy into rubble. It was a fleet which after victory at Guadalcanal would make the United States an Asian power.

Germany's survival, as a continental rather than an insular power, depended on her Army. So important was the Army that Hitler had made himself its commander-in-chief and it was he who directed its strategy. As a strategist, though, Hitler did not appreciate either the strengths or weaknesses of the army he directed.

The strength of the German Army was in its Panzer and motorized divisions. These were the mobile troops who were the masters of the new warfare, the blitzkrieg. No army in the world had anything to match them. The victories which they had won in France in 1940 and in Russia in 1941 could be compared only to the greatest campaigns of Napoleon.

Yet, in October, 1942, Hitler had bogged down the German Army in a static battle at Stalingrad. In the ruined city the fighting was very like that of World War I with gains measured in yards and casualties in the thousands. In this kind of fighting the German Army revealed its main weakness, manpower. There were simply not enough German soldiers

316 THE NINETY DAYS

for such fighting and second-rate divisions from Hitler's satellites, Rumania, Hungary and Italy, had to be used to hold
important parts of the front.

Even when Zhukov, crushing the satellite divisions, had
surrounded Paulus' 6th Army in the Stalingrad Cauldron,
there was still a chance for Hitler to revert to the mobile
warfare at which the Germans were masters. In von Mannstein
he had the general for such warfare. Had Hitler given von
Mannstein every available Panzer division, those bogged down
in the Caucasus and those cooling their heels in France,
the results of the battle of southern Russia could have been
different.

Like the Japanese admirals, Hitler had failed to concentrate everything at the decisive point—Stalingrad. It was into
Africa, which he had always considered a sideshow, that Hitler
poured his valuable reserves instead of abandoning the southern shore of the Mediterranean which was an untenable
position once Montgomery had pierced the Alamein line and
Eisenhower had gotten ashore from Casablanca to Algiers.

The results of Hitler's strategy were that von Mannstein,
with insufficient troops, could only fight a battle of retreat
which finished at the end of winter along the same line from
which the Germans had launched their 1942 offensive. In
Stalingrad and in Tunisia, the German Army was to lose some
400,000 men and it was a loss from which they could never
fully recover.

These victories, plus the command of the Atlantic which
the Western Allies had firmly established by the spring of
1943, put the initiative into the hands of the Russians, British
and Americans. No longer would they be reacting to the thrusts
of the Germans and Japanese. Now it was they who would
decide where the great battles would be fought.

However, the great decisions on Allied strategy, which
were to determine the future course of the war, were not to
be made in concert. The common objective of the Allies before
the end of 1942 had been survival. Now that survival had been
assured, their objectives were no longer the same. The British
and Americans wanted to reestablish something resembling
the world as it had existed before Hitler. Stalin had other ideas.

The Red Army, not the German Army, was now the dominant power on the European continent. Its power was growing while that of the Germans was waning. The old objective of the Tsars now became that of Stalin, Russian control of all Eastern Europe. In the Far East, Stalin's eye was on Manchuria, the northern gateway to China. Victory at Stalingrad was a turning point for Russian communism. After twenty-five years of virtual quarantine by the rest of the world, it was now ready for its own march of conquest.

The realization that the victories of the ninety days had changed the course of World War II dawned very slowly upon the British and American public. Churchill soon grasped the fact that the Western Allies were no longer at war only with Germany and Japan. By 1944 he was once more sending British troops to Greece. Unlike 1941, the British went there not to fight Germans but to fight Communists. His action was taken only over heated American objections. The American confrontation with Russia would come a little later.

For after the battles of the ninety days, the power centers of the world shifted rapidly away from the old capitals of Western Europe, away from Paris and London and Berlin. Power was now passing to Moscow and Washington.

The new power struggle would not be fought as had the old. No longer would great nations deploy huge masses of men and ships for decisive battle. There would be no more Stalingrads or Alameins and no more would campaigns be decided by the guns of battleships.

For on the sixty-first of the ninety days, December 2, 1942, a small group of scientists, working in an unused squash court at the University of Chicago, had successfully completed an experiment in physics. There they had created man's first self-perpetuating chain reaction. They had made possible the building of an atomic bomb.

Within ninety times ninety days, it became possible for man to wipe himself off the face of the earth. Another world war, another life and death struggle of great nations became unthinkable for anyone—except, of course, for another man of evil, a man such as Hitler who could see glory in destruction.

a note on military terminology

For the sake of clarity as little military jargon as possible has been used in this book. There is no reference to the United States Army's CRS DRB TAGO (Captured Records Section, Departmental Records Branch, The Adjutant General's Office) nor to the German Army's Wehrmachtfuehrungsstab (Armed Forces Operations Staff).

The only terminology used that may need a word of explanation is that covering military units—division, regiment, corps, etc. The basic unit for all World War II armies was the infantry division. Its full strength was from 11,000 to 15,000 men—Russian divisions usually being the smallest and American divisions the largest, with British, German and Japanese falling in between. Exact figures mean nothing, because it is highly doubtful that any division ever fought on any given day with its complete quota from generals to privates. A few days' fighting in a malaria-infested jungle or against the enemy could bring a division well down below its proper strength. On the other hand, auxiliary units, artillery, tanks or combat engineers, would at times be added to a division and would bring it slightly overstrength. Thus it is best to let the approximations stand.

A division was divided into three regiments of infantry. In the British and British Empire divisions they were called "brigades." These regiments, or brigades, were divided into three battalions. An infantry battalion would run about 400 to 800 men depending on how much combat the division had recently been through. It could, of course, be less if things had been particularly bad.

The armored division is another matter as its composition varied greatly. The German Panzer division usually had one Panzer or tank regiment and one infantry. These infantrymen were called Panzer grenadiers and were specially trained to fight in close coordination with their own tanks or against enemy tanks on their own. The division also included a complement of mobile artillery, experts in anti-tank tactics. By late 1942 the German Panzer divisions varied greatly in their tank strength due to high casualties and the difficulties of getting replacement tanks. Some had over 100 tanks and some only a dozen.

The British armored division was not a set organization. One had two armored regiments, or brigades, and had no infantry. Another had its own infantry but only one tank brigade.

The Russians had a mechanized corps which was more or less equivalent to a full-strength German Panzer division. The United States did not have any complete armored divisions in action in 1942, only parts of divisions.

German satellite units, such as Italian or Rumanian divisions, were usually of small size and always underequipped as well.

When divisions were grouped together, they became a corps. A corps could, therefore, be formed of any number of divisions but two to six was about normal.

An army was formed of two or more corps and an army group of two or more armies. The one major exception to these rules was the Japanese army command in the Solomons. There, the Japanese campaigns against New Guinea and Guadalcanal were both managed by the Japanese 17th Army with divisions operating directly under the army headquarters without any corps headquarters.

In the text, the generals' habit of attaching units from one division to another and generally messing up good military organization has been overlooked. What General Patton put ashore at Casablanca has simply been called the "United States 3rd Infantry Division." The fact is that it included such attached organizations as one and one-half platoons (53 men) of the 443rd Coast Artillery (Anti-Aircraft) Battalion and eleven officers and nineteen enlisted men of the 1st Broadcasting Station Operation Detachment has been omitted.

a note on sources

As everyone who writes history, I am a debtor. I owe more than I can possibly acknowledge to all those whose works I have read and used in preparing this book. In fairness to them, however, I would like to make it very clear that they are in no way responsible for the opinions, judgments or prejudices which appear in this book. Those are all mine.

The bibliography which follows contains a list of the books upon which I have most relied. Any reader who wishes to probe further into the history of this period will make no mistake in reading any of them. However, I should like to note here those books which were of special help to me and which, I think, would be of the most interest to the reader.

A great deal has been written on the political leaders of the Western nations. Unfortunately, most of it is of little value in looking at them as military leaders. Winston Churchill has looked at himself in his five-volume, *The Second World War*. He has done it with a brilliance that can easily blind the reader to the fact that he is a bit prejudiced in favor of Winston Churchill. A full-dress study of Winston Churchill as general, admiral and air marshal has yet to be done.

Franklin D. Roosevelt left no record of his own, and only a glimpse of Roosevelt as commander-in-chief is available in Robert Sherwood's, *Roosevelt and Hopkins*. As far as it goes, the view is a fascinating one—but it doesn't go far enough. As Kent Roberts Greenfield points out in a fine, short essay in his *American Strategy in World War II*, Roosevelt was a true military leader and did not, as is the generally accepted view, simply leave things to the military.

Stalin, who made himself a marshal and who believed himself a military man of no little prowess, has been very carefully researched as a military leader by Erickson in his *Soviet High Command*. Although not an easy book to read, this is the best study yet done on the Russian military and is a work of impeccable scholarship.

On the Axis side, Mussolini has been well done by Christopher Hibbert in his *Il Duce*, a book which is more a fascinating personality study than a conventional biography. Alan Bullock, in his *Hitler, A Study in Tyranny*, has written a biography as a biography should be written.

In Japan, there was no single, all-powerful leader. The intricacies of the Japanese power structure and how it functioned, or often failed to function, are brought out in Robert J. Butow's *Tojo and the Coming of the War*. There is also an excellent, short study of just how the Pacific war came about in *The Road to Pearl Harbor* by Herbert Feis.

The best single account of the Guadalcanal campaign is General Samuel Griffith's *The Battle for Guadalcanal*. Although he is mostly concerned with the ground fighting of the Marines on the island, he deals with the United States Army and Navy there as well and, most interestingly, with the Japanese high command.

Griffith's account, though, should be supplemented by Samuel Eliot Morison's *The Struggle for Guadalcanal* (Volume 5 of his *History of United States Naval Operations in World War II*) for the role of the Navy and by Robert Sherrod's *History of Marine Corps Aviation in World War II* for some fine reporting on Henderson Field and its fliers. And there is an excellent account of a single action in Charles Cook's *Battle of Cape Esperance*.

The most valuable account of MacArthur's battles in New Guinea is in the United States Army's official history, *Victory in Papua* by Samuel Milner, who is equally at home in the realms of grand strategy and in the details of a small unit action.

Alamein has been the source of many books and articles. One of the best accounts is that of C. E. Lucas Phillips who was a member of the British 8th Army. He is very much pro-Montgomery; the opposite view is well presented by Corelli Bernett in his *The Desert Generals*. For the hard facts, the British official history, I. S. O. Playfair and C. J. C. Molney's *The Mediterranean and Middle East*, Volume IV, is the best account. For the overall strategic picture there is the very readable and extremely well thought out *The Battle for the Mediterranean* by Donald Macintyre.

For the German side, there are *The Rommel Papers,* which give an intimate look at a man who was often a brilliant general but who was undone by his political naïveté.

Operation Torch is the subject of one of the best volumes of the United States Army's official history, George Howe's *Northwest Africa: Seizing the Initiative in the West.* Howe treats British and German operations, as well as American, in detail and with scrupulous fairness.

Morison treats American naval participation with great verve in *Operations in North African Waters* (Volume 2 of his *History*). Robert Murphy does the same for the plots and counter-plots which preceded the invasion in his *Diplomat Among Warriors.*

Stalingrad, one of the classic battles of history, will always remain a bit of a mystery. Russian accounts vary according to the politics of the current leadership in the Kremlin. General Chuikov's account manages to avoid any mention of Marshal Zhukov, and Zhukov writes of the battle with only one solitary reference to Chuikov. It is possible that the Russian archives will be opened one day, but it is doubtful that that day will come in this century.

On the German side, von Mannstein tells his side of the story in *Lost Victories,* a book which delineates the logical working of a mind trained by the German General Staff but reveals little of the man himself. Paulus' notes for a book which he did not live long enough to write are used by Walter Goerlitz in his *Paulus and Stalingrad* but they are tantalizingly incomplete.

The Battle of the Barents Sea is recounted in detail by Dudley Pope in his *73 North*, a book which is just as exciting as any of C. S. Forester's stories of Horatio Hornblower.

The full story of the British Navy in the war is comprehensively told in the official history, Captain Stephen W. Roskill's *The War at Sea*, while the anti-U-boat campaign is dealt with in Donald Macintyre's first-rate *Battle of the Atlantic*, as are the Arctic Sea battles in B. B. Schofield's *The Russian Convoys*.

And indispensable to any student of the war is the magnificent *West Point Atlas of American Wars*. Its text is brief, accurate and to the point. Its maps are, to paraphrase the old Chinese saying, often worth 10,000 words.

bibliography

Arnold, Henry H. *Global Mission*. New York: Harper & Brothers, 1949.

Baldwin, Hanson. *Battles Lost and Won: Great Campaigns of World War II*. New York: Harper & Row, 1966.

Barnett, Corelli. *The Desert Generals*. New York: The Viking Press, 1961.

Bialer, Seweryn, ed. *Stalin and His Generals: Soviet Military Memoirs of World War II*. New York: Pegasus, 1969.

Bryant, Arthur. *The Turn of the Tide: A History of the War Years Based on the Diaries of Field Marshal Lord Alanbrooke, Chief of the Imperial General Staff*. New York: Doubleday & Co., 1957.

Bullock, Alan. *Hitler, A Study in Tyranny*. New York: Harper & Row, 1964.

Busch, Harald. *U-Boats at War*. New York: Ballantine Books, 1965.

Butcher, Harry C. *My Three Years with Eisenhower*. New York: Simon & Schuster, 1946.

Butow, Robert J. C. *Tojo and the Coming of the War*. Princeton: Princeton University Press, 1961.

Caccia-Dominiconi, Paolo. *Alamein, 1933–1962: An Italian Story*. London: George Allen & Unwin Ltd., 1966.

Carell, Paul. *The Foxes of the Desert*. New York: E. P. Dutton & Co., 1961.

Carell, Paul. *Hitler Moves East, 1941–1943*. Boston: Little, Brown & Co., 1965.

Chuikov, Vasili I. *The Battle for Stalingrad*. New York: Holt, Rinehart & Winston, Inc., 1964.

Churchill, Winston. *The Second World War*. 6 vols. Boston: Houghton, Mifflin Co., 1948–1953.

Clark, Alan. *Barbarossa: The Russian-German Conflict, 1941–1945.* New York: William Morrow & Co., 1964.

Cook, Charles. *The Battle of Cape Esperance: Encounter at Guadalcanal.* New York: Thomas Y. Crowell, 1968.

Crankshaw, Edward. *Gestapo.* New York: Pyramid Books, 1961.

Craven, Wesley F. and James L. Cate, eds. *The Army Air Forces in World War II.* 7 vols. Chicago: University of Chicago Press, 1949.

Eichelberger, Robert L. with Milton MacKaye. *Our Jungle Road to Tokyo.* New York: The Viking Press, 1950.

Eisenhower, Dwight David. *Crusade in Europe.* New York: Doubleday & Co., 1948.

Erickson, John. *The Soviet High Command: A Military Political History, 1918–1941.* New York: St. Martin's Press, 1962.

Esposito, Vincent J., ed. *The West Point Atlas of American Wars.* 2 vols. New York: Frederick A. Praeger, 1959.

Farago, Ladislas. *Patton: Ordeal and Triumph.* New York: Ivan Obolensky Inc., 1964.

Feis, Herbert. *Churchill, Roosevelt, Stalin: The War They Waged and the Peace They Sought.* Princeton: Princeton University Press, 1957.

Feis, Herbert. *The Road to Pearl Harbor: The Coming of the War Between the United States and Japan.* New York: Atheneum, 1964.

Fergusson, Bernard, ed. *The Business of War: The War Narrative of Major General Sir John Kennedy.* New York: William Morrow & Co., 1958.

Freidin, Seymour and Richardson, William, eds. *The Fatal Decisions.* New York: Berkley Publishing Co., 1966.

Fuller, J. F. C. *The Second World War: 1939–1945.* New York: Duell, Sloane & Pearce, 1962.

Garthoff, Raymond L. *How Russia Makes War: Soviet Military Doctrine.* London: George Allen & Unwin Ltd., 1954.

Gibson, Hugh, ed. *The Ciano Diaries, 1939–1943.* New York: Doubleday & Co., 1946.

Goerlitz, Walter. *The German General Staff, 1657–1945.* New York: Frederick A. Praeger, 1965.

Goerlitz, Walter. *Paulus and Stalingrad.* New York: The Citadel Press, 1963.

Greenfield, Kent Roberts. *American Strategy in World War II: A Reconsideration.* Baltimore: The Johns Hopkins Press, 1963.

Griffith, Samuel B., II. *The Battle for Guadalcanal.* Philadelphia: J. B. Lippincott, 1963.

Halder, Franz. *Hitler as Warlord.* London: Putnam, 1950.

Halsey, William F. and Bryan, J. *Admiral Halsey's Story.* New York: McGraw-Hill Book Co., 1947.

Hara, Tameichi; Saito, Fred; and Pineau, Roger. *Japanese Destroyer Captain.* New York: Ballantine Books, 1965.

Hart, B. H. Liddell. *The Liddell Hart Memoirs.* New York: G. P. Putnam's Sons, 1966.

Hart, B. H. Liddell. *The Other Side of the Hill.* London: Cassell & Co. Ltd., 1951.

Hart, B. H. Liddell, ed. *The Rommel Papers.* New York: Harcourt, Brace & Co., 1953.

Hart, B. H. Liddell. *The Tanks: The History of the Royal Tank Regiment.* New York: Frederick A. Praeger, 1959.

Hibbert, Christopher. *Il Duce: The Life of Benito Mussolini.* Boston: Little, Brown & Co., 1962.

Higgins, Trumbull. *Winston Churchill and the Second Front, 1940–1943.* New York: Oxford University Press, 1957.

Horrocks, Sir Brian. *A Full Life.* London: Collins, 1961.

Howe, George F. *Northwest Africa: Seizing the Initiative in the West.* Washington, D.C.: U.S. Government Printing Office, 1957.

Jacobsen, H. A. and Rohwer, J., eds. *Decisive Battles of World War II: The German View.* New York: G. P. Putnam's Sons, 1964.

Jones, Ken. *Destroyer Squadron 23: Combat Exploits of Arleigh Burke's Gallant Force.* Philadelphia: Chilton Co., 1959.

Kippenberger, Sir Howard. *Infantry Brigadier.* London: Oxford University Press, 1961.

Laurence, William L. *Dawn Over Zero: The Story of the Atomic Bomb.* New York: Alfred A. Knopf, 1946.

Lee, Asher. *The German Air Force.* New York: Harper & Brothers, 1946.

Lee, Asher. *The Soviet Air Force.* New York: The John Day Co., 1962.

Lenton, H. T. and Colledge, J. J. *Warships of World War II.* London: Ian Allen, 1964.

Macintyre, Donald. *The Battle of the Atlantic.* London: B. T. Batsford Ltd., 1961.

Macintyre, Donald. *The Battle for the Mediterranean.* New York: W. W. Norton & Co., 1965.

Majdalany, Fred. *The Battle of El Alamein: Fortress in the Sand.* Philadelphia: J. B. Lippincott, 1965.

Martienssen, Anthony. *Hitler and His Admirals.* London: Secker & Warburg, 1948.

Miller, John, Jr. *Guadalcanal: The First Offensive.* Washington, D.C.: U.S. Government Printing Office, 1949.

Milner, Samuel. *Victory in Papua.* Washington, D.C.: U.S. Government Printing Office, 1957.

Moorehead, Alan. *The End in Africa.* London: Hamish Hamilton, 1943.

Moorehead, Alan. *Montgomery, A Biography.* New York: Coward-McCann, 1946.

Morison, Samuel Eliot. *History of United States Naval Operations in World War II.* 15 vols. Boston: Little, Brown & Co., 1947–1949.

Morison, Samuel Eliot. *Strategy and Compromise.* Boston: Little, Brown & Co., 1958.

Morison, Samuel Eliot. *The Two-Ocean War: A Short History of the United States Navy in the Second World War.* Boston: Little, Brown & Co., 1963.

Murphy, Robert. *Diplomat Among Warriors.* New York: Doubleday & Co., 1964.

North, John, ed. *The Alexander Memoirs, 1940–1945.* London: Cassell, 1962.

Phillips, C. E. Lucas. *Alamein.* Boston: Little, Brown & Co., 1963.

Playfair, I. S. O. and Molney, C. J. C. *The Mediterranean and Middle East.* 6 vols. London: Her Majesty's Stationery Office, 1966.

Pogue, Forrest C. *George C. Marshall: Ordeal and Hope, 1939–1942.* New York: The Viking Press, 1966.

Pope, Dudley. *73 North: The Defeat of Hitler's Navy.* New York: Berkley Publishing Co., 1959.

Potter, John Deane. *Yamamoto: The Man Who Menaced America.* New York: The Viking Press, 1965.

Pugh, Stevenson, ed. *Armour in Profile.* Nos. 1–24. Leatherhead, Surrey, England: Profile Publications Ltd., 1968.

Ray, Cyril. *Algiers to Austria: A History of the 78th Division in the Second World War.* London: Eyre & Spottiswoode, 1952.

Reitlinger, Gerald. *The Final Solution: The Attempt to Exterminate the Jews of Europe, 1939–1945.* New York: A. S. Barnes & Co., 1961.

Roscoe, Theodore. *United States Destroyer Operations in World War II.* Annapolis, Md.: United States Naval Institute, 1953.

Roskill, S. W. *The War at Sea: 1939–1945.* 3 vols. London: Her Majesty's Stationery Office, 1956.

Rudel, Hans Ulrich. *Stuka Pilot.* New York: Ballantine Books, 1965.

Ruge, Friedrich. *Der Seekrieg: The German Navy's Story, 1939–1945.* Annapolis Md.: United States Naval Institute, 1957.

Salisbury, Harrison, ed. *Marshal Zhukov's Greatest Battles.* New York: Harper & Row, 1969.

Saunders, Hilary St. George. *The Green Beret: The Story of the Commandos, 1940–1945.* London: Landsborough Publications Ltd., 1959.

Saunders, Hilary St. George. *The Red Beret: The Story of the Parachute Regiment at War, 1940–1945.* London: Michael Joseph, 1952.

Schofield, B. B. *The Russian Convoys.* London: B. T. Batsford, 1964.

Sherrod, Robert. *History of Marine Corps Aviation in World War II.* Washington, D.C.: Combat Forces Press, 1952.

Sherwood, Robert E. *Roosevelt and Hopkins: An Intimate History.* New York: Harper & Row, 1950.

Shirer, William L. *The Rise and Fall of the Third Reich: A History of Nazi Germany.* New York: Simon & Schuster, 1960.

Silverstone, Paul H. *U.S. Warships of World War II.* London: Ian Allen, 1965.

Stein, George H. *The Waffen SS: Hitler's Elite Guard at War, 1939–1945.* Ithaca, N.Y.: Cornell University Press, 1966.

Tamplin, R. L. C. *Death or Glory: A Short History of the 17th/21st Lancers.* London: Combined Service Publications Ltd., 1958.

Taylor, Telford. *The March of Conquest: The German Victories in Western Europe, 1940.* New York: Simon & Schuster, 1958.

Trevor-Roper, H. R. *Blitzkrieg to Defeat: Hitler's War Directives 1939–1945.* New York: Holt, Rinehart & Winston, 1964.

von Mannstein, Erich. *Lost Victories.* Chicago: Henry Regnery Co., 1958.

von Mellenthin, F. W. *Panzer Battles.* Norman, Okla.: University of Oklahoma Press, 1956.

von Senger und Etterlin, Frido. *Neither Fear Nor Hope.* New York: E. P. Dutton & Co., 1964.

Warlimont, Walter. *Inside Hitler's Headquarters, 1939–1945.* New York: Frederick A. Praeger, 1965.

Watts, Anthony J. *Japanese Warships of World War II.* New York: Doubleday & Co., 1967.

Werth, Alexander. *Russia at War, 1941–1945.* New York: E. P. Dutton & Co., 1964.

Wilmot, Chester. *The Struggle for Europe.* New York: Harper & Row, 1963.

Periodicals

McCandless, Bruce. *The San Francisco Story.* United States Naval Institute Proceedings. November, 1958.

Tanaka, Raizo, with the assistance of Roger Pineau. *Japan's Losing Struggle for Guadalcanal.* United States Naval Institute Proceedings. July and August, 1956.

index

332

334

335

North Africa, 7–8. *See also* El Alamein; Operation Torch.
Northampton, 123, 127
Northern Gem, 289, 294, 309
Norway, 9, 57, 284ff., 289, 292

O'Bannon, 96, 100, 103, 104, 107
Obdurate, 289, 295ff., 299, 304, 305
Obedient, 289, 294, 296, 297, 299, 300, 304, 305
O'Connor, Richard, 22–23, 24
O'Daniel, "Iron Mike," 200
Oka, Colonel, 87, 88, 90, 92
Onslow, 289, 294–305 *passim*
Operation Bertram, 150
Operation Roundup (invasion of France), 32–33ff.
Operation Supercharge, 176–80
Operation Thunderclap, 275
Operation Torch, 7–8, 31–38, 145, 188–238, 283, 315
Operation Uranus, 253–62
Operation Winter Tempest, 271–77
Oran, 37, 38, 190, 194, 198, 283
Oribi, 289, 290
Orwell, 289, 294, 297, 299, 300, 304, 305
Oudna, 225–27
Owen Stanley Mountains, 20ff., 128

P-400's, 64
Patch, Alexander, 119
Patton, George S., 204–6ff., 213ff., 253, 321
Paulus, Friedrich, 44ff., 50, 240–41ff., 252, 255ff., 259, 260, 261–64ff., 269–77ff., 316
Pearl Harbor, 11–12, 13–14, 120, 121
Pensacola, 123ff.
Perkins, 123
Pershing, John, 205
Pétain, Henri Philippe, 189–90, 192, 217, 219, 223
Philadelphia, 211
Philippines, 14
Pienaar, Dan, 151, 170
Point 29, 166–67, 168, 174
Poland, 2–3, 6
Port-Lyautey, 206, 207, 212ff.
Port Moresby, 15, 16, 20, 128
Portland, 95, 97, 104ff.
Preston, 111, 112
Primauguet, 210
Prince of Wales, 14
Prinz Eugen, 284
Puller, "Chesty," 90, 91

Qattara Depression, 28, 146, 147

Rabat, 214, 215
Rabaul, 18, 19, 21–22, 67

Raeder, Erich, 53–54, 55, 283–85ff., 311
Rahman track, 176, 178, 182, 184
Ramcke, Bernhard, 147, 184
Ranger, 206, 209, 210
Red October Factory, 247, 248, 251
"Regiments," 319–20
Reidel, 287, 294
Repulse, 14
Rhododendron, 289, 294
Ribbentrop, Joachim von, 310
Richard Beitzen, 287, 294, 303, 304, 307, 309
Richtofen, General Wolfram Freiherr von, 266
Rintelen, E. von, 165
Rodney, 202
Rokossovski, Konstantin K., 257, 258, 259, 264, 271–74
Romanenko, General, 257
Romans, Reg, 156, 157
Rommel, Erwin, 7, 23–30 *passim*, 144, 145, 147ff., 155, 157, 160, 165–85 *passim*, 216, 235, 237; vs. Hitler, 227–30
Roosevelt, Franklin D., 9, 11, 31ff., 35, 208; and convoys, 57; and Darlan, 194, 217; and Giraud, 193; and lend-lease, 51–53; and MacArthur presidential possibilities, 131; and Murphy, 188ff., 196; and Patton, 205; and Tobruk defeat; Sherman tanks, 26–27
Rostov, 264, 269, 273, 275, 278
Rumanians, 25, 43, 243ff., 248, 252, 256ff., 271, 316, 320
Russia, 6, 8, 38–50, 240–80, 315–17; convoys to (*see* Barents Sea); military terminology, 319, 320
UNITS:
   Armies. 1st Guards, 257; 2nd Guards, 274, 276; 5th Tank, 257, 259, 268; 21st, 257; 24th, 257; 51st, 257, 271; 57th, 257; 62nd (Chuikov), 46, 50, 248–51, 255, 258; 64th, 257; 65th, 257
   Brigades: 84th Armored, 250
   Corps: 1st Tank, 268–69; 4th Mechanized, 260; 4th Tank, 259; 13th Mechanized, 259
   Divisions: 37th Guards Infantry, 248ff.; 95th, 250; 138th, 250
Ryder, General, 201

Safi, 206, 211–12, 214, 215
St. Cloud, Algeria, 203, 204
Salt Lake City, 66, 69, 73, 75, 81
Samoa, 15, 17
San Francisco, 66, 67, 69, 71ff., 75, 76, 78, 82
Sananda Point and Trail, 130, 132, 139

202, 233; 1st Marine, *see* Guadalcanal; 2nd Armored, 206, 211; 3rd Infantry, 206, 208, 211, 213–14, 215, 321; 9th Infantry, 206; 18th Infantry, 203; 32nd, 129, 130, 132–34, 136–40; 41st, 137

Regiments: 1st Armored, 224; 8th Marine, 119; 127th Infantry, 138, 139; 128th Infantry, 134; 164th Infantry, 65, 83, 118; 182nd Infantry, 95, 118

Uranami, 111

Vandergrift, Alexander Archer, 62, 94, 118, 119, 315

Vasey, George, 128, 130, 132, 135

Vasilievsky, Alexander, 252, 253, 255, 257, 258, 268, 274, 276

Vatutin, Nikolai F., 256ff., 262, 272, 273

Vichy, 9, 189, 190, 192, 199, 217, 219, 223

Vinnitsa, 47

Vizalma, 289ff., 297

Volga River, 39, 43, 45, 46, 50, 240, 250, 251, 263, 271

Volsky, General, 258, 260

Walke, 111, 112

Walney, 201

Washington, D. C., 11

Washington, 96, 108, 109, 111, 113ff.

Wasp, 21

Weichs, Maximilian von, 45, 244ff., 261, 264

Wheeler, Burton K., 53

Wichita, 209

Wilkes, 210

Willoughby, General, 129

Wimberley, Douglas, 152, 182

Wishka Ridge, 161, 163

Wolfschanze, 41–42, 43, 182, 230, 231, 236, 263, 264, 277, 287, 310; move from, 47

World War I, 34–35

Wright, Carleton Herbert, 121, 123ff.

Yamamoto, Isoroku, 12, 14ff., 61, 87, 108ff., 141

Yasuda, Captain, 130

Yeremenko, A. I., 250–51, 255–57ff., 262, 264

Yokoyama, Colonel, 130

Yorktown, 16–17

Youks-les-Bains, 219

Young, Cassin, 96, 105

Yudachi, 99, 100, 101, 106

Yugoslavia and Yugoslavs, 10, 23, 24

Z–29, 287, 294

Z–30, 287, 294

Z–31, 287, 294

Zeitzler, Kurt, 48–49, 241–42, 245–46, 260, 263–64, 265, 270, 279

Zero fighters, 64, 65

Zhukov, Georgi, 10, 49–50, 252–58, 270, 316

Zuiho, 92

Zuikaku, 61